GESTALT THERAPY PRIMER

Edited by

F. DOUGLAS STEPHENSON, A.M., A.C.S.W.

Consultation and Guidance Services and
Gestalt Institute of North Florida
Gainesville, Florida

NEW YORK • JASON ARONSON • LONDON

© "Second Edition Preface" 1978 Jason Aronson, Inc.

© 1975 by Charles C Thomas

Library of Congress Cataloging in Publication Data

Stephenson, F. Douglas, comp.
  Gestalt therapy primer.

1. Gestalt therapy. I. Title [DNLM: 1. Psychological theory. 2. Psychotherapy. WM420 S836g]
RC489.G4S74   616.8'914

ISBN 0-87668-358-8

Library of Congress Catalog Card Number: 78-74056

Printed in the United States of America

To the
FACULTY, STUDENTS and FRIENDS
of the
GESTALT INSTITUTE OF CLEVELAND

Sources

I. An Introduction to Gestalt Therapy—James Simkin: Gestalt Therapy Institute of Los Angeles Mimeograph, 1965.

II.An Introduction to Gestalt Therapy—John B. Enright, Langley Porter Neuropsychiatric Institute Mimeograph, 1966.

III. I and Thou, Here and Now: Contributions of Gestalt Therapy—Claudio Naranjo; Esalen Institute Paper, 1967.

IV. On Loving Encounters: A Phenomenological View—Joseph Zinker; Gestalt Institute of Cleveland Monograph, 1969.

V. Gestalt Therapy and Human Potentialities—Frederick S. Perls; H. Otto, Explorations in Human Potentialities, 1964.

VI. Fragments of Gestalt Theory—Rainette Fantz; Gestalt Institute of Cleveland Monograph, 1971.

VII. Polarities: Differentiation and Integration—Rainette Fantz; Gestalt Institute of Cleveland Monograph, 1973.

VIII. Jackie: An Experience in Self Applied Gestalt Therapy—J. Snyder and F.D. Stephenson; Tape transcript, 1974.

IX. The Ground Rules in Gestalt Therapy—Jerry A. Greenwald; Greenwald mimeograph, 1971.

X. The Art of Emotional Nourishment: Self-Induced Nourishment and Toxicity—Jerry A. Greenwald; Greenwald mimeograph, 1969.

XI. Gestalt Therapy in Interactive Groups—John Enright; Explorations Institute Monograph, 1971.

XII. Chicken Soup is Poison—Robert W. Resnick; Resnick mimeograph, c. 1966.

XIII. Techniques and Experience in Gestalt Therapy—Erving Polster; Gestalt Institute of Cleveland Monograph (paper presented to Ohio Psychological Association), 1957.

XIV. Trends in Gestalt Therapy—Erving Polster; Gestalt Institute of Cleveland Monograph, 1967.

XV. A Review of the Practice of Gestalt Therapy—Gary M. Yontef; Trident Shop Mimeograph, 1969.

Contributors

JOHN B. ENRIGHT, PH.D. is in private practice as a clinical psychologist in Corte Madera, California. He is a member of the Board of Directors of the Gestalt Institute of San Francisco.

RAINETTE E. FANTZ, PH.D. is a Gestalt therapist in private practice in Cleveland, Ohio, and is on the Post-Graduate Teaching Faculty of the Gestalt Institute of Cleveland.

JERRY A. GREENWALD, PH.D. is a clinical psychologist in full-time private practice in Santa Monica, California.

CLAUDIO NARANJO, M.D. is a psychiatrist and Gestalt therapist. He is on the staff of the Gestalt Institute of San Francisco.

FREDERICK S. PERLS, M.D., PH. D. was a psychiatrist and the originator of Gestalt therapy. Prior to his death in 1970, he resided at the Gestalt Institute of Canada, Vancouver, B.C.

ERVING POLSTER, PH.D. is in private practice in San Diego, California. Formerly Chairman of the Post-Graduate Training Program of the Gestalt Institute of Cleveland, he is now on the Faculties of the California School of Professional Psychology, the Western Institute for Group and Family Therapy and The Gestalt Training Center, San Diego.

ROBERT W. RESNICK, PH.D. is in private practice in Beverly Hills, California and is a Training Therapist at the Gestalt Therapy Institute of Los Angeles. He is a Consultant to the California School of Professional Psychology.

JAMES S. SIMKIN, PH.D. is a clinical psychologist and Gestalt therapist in private practice at Big Sur, California. He is a Consultant with the California School of Professional Psychology.

JACQUELINE SNYDER, M.H.T. is a mental health technician working in Gainesville, Florida.

GARY M. YONTEF, M.S.W., PH.D. is trained as a clinical psychologist and as a clinical social worker. He is in private practice in

Beverly Hills, California, and is on the Training Faculty of the Gestalt Therapy Institute of Los Angeles.

JOSEPH C. ZINKER, PH.D. is Associate Professor of Psychology at Lake Erie College. He is also in private practice as a Gestalt therapist and consultant, and is a member of the Board and Post-Graduate Teaching Faculty of the Gestalt Institute of Cleveland.

Foreword

THIS BOOK of papers on Gestalt Therapy is worth reading. Most of the basic principles of Gestalt Therapy are discussed here, and the authors discuss their chosen topics with variety and individuality so that you will be made aware of the complexities of Gestalt Therapy even as you are learning its basic philosophic principles.

Few books are so well thought out that the author or authors can finally set down and make those economical statements which are the mark of true communication. Poets reach that kind of economy occasionally, and so do prose writers . . . but then we speak of literature. This book is literature only occasionally, for these are professional Gestalt therapists speaking, rather than writers. Yet for all that, they do manage to convey their involvement with the Gestalt Therapy approach and, more important, they discuss specifically and clearly the kinds of questions which are of interest to the beginner. This in itself is no small accomplishment, and that is why I can recommend the book to you.

Among other things, Gestalt Therapy attempts to teach the end of suffering, that this can be possible. Once we are willing to give up those robot-like behaviors which keep us fixated in the past, there is an immense fund of creative energy available to all of us which enables us to explore new possibilities in living and the self. These kinds of understandings happen to us always in the present moment, not in the past or the future. And so you will find a continuing emphasis on the Here and Now in this book. I ask you now not to become bored with that repetition nor to take it for granted, for it is one of the primary considerations in Gestalt Therapy and in all growth and change in yourself. You are always *here* whether you are aware of this place or not; and the time is always *now*, even when you are unable to fill this moment and be it in its fullness. Filling this moment, meeting it and knowing it in its fullness, is where our suffering begins to end, and then the joy and lovingness of our marvelous world can come in yet again.

It is a marvelous experience to be a beginner in a *beginning* world. Then, so to say, we stand with empty hands, without preconceptions and the kind of conditioned experience which dulls the growing edge of the self and the world. I was a beginner once in Gestalt Therapy, and I remember that moment even now with fondness and gratitude and thanks. Gestalt Therapy changed my life: how I perceived myself, who I was and who I wanted to become. I have not come to the end of that journey yet, but as one beginner to another, I wish you well for your own journey and boundless joy in discovering for yourself what these authors have to say about Gestalt Therapy. It may be the beginning of some basic changes in your life.

VINCENT O'CONNELL
Gainesville, Florida

Preface to the Second Edition

It is good to know that there is demand for another edition of this primer. The purpose of this introductory book is to present the first principles and basic foundations of Gestalt psychotherapy to students, beginners, and professionals. These readings bring us the thought and work of gestalt practitioners as their individual experience and awareness of therapeutic process evolved. Together these chapters present a gestalt of basic interests and viewpoints giving the reader a strong configuration and foundation.

Gestalt philosophy is permeated with confidence, positivism, and optimism about the possibilities for human development and creativity. To understand and live up to the difficult yet rewarding tasks of discipline and responsibility, to fully participate, be involved, and live one's life in the present moment: these are the keys to successful psychotherapy and to complete and satisfying life experience. We must always recognize, as Carl Jung emphasized, the high value of "individual self-reflection, return of the individual to the ground of human nature, to his own deepest being with its individual and social destiny—here is the beginning of a cure for the blindness that reigns." These are the aims of Gestalt psychotherapy and the purposes to which this book is dedicated.

F. Douglas Stephenson
Gainesville, Florida
1978

About the Editor

F. Douglas Stephenson received his A.B. degree from the University of Michigan in 1961, and completed professional graduate work in clinical social work in the School of Social Service Administration of the University of Chicago, obtaining his A.M. degree in 1965. He received a Diploma in Gestalt Methods of psychotherapy from the Gestalt Institute of Cleveland in 1972.

For the past five years he has been in full-time private practice at Consulation and Guidance Services, Gainesville, Florida, working with individuals, couples, families, and groups. He has served as psychiatric social worker at Chicago State Hospital and Tinley Park (Illinois) State Hospital. He was Instructor of Social Work and Psychiatry at the University of Florida, and is currently Clinical Instructor of Social Work in the College of Medicine at the University of Florida.

Mr. Stephenson is a Fellow in the Florida Society for Clinical Social Work and the National Federation of Societies for Clinical Social Work, Diplomate member of I-CAPP, is a clinical member of the American Association of Marriage and Family Counselors, and is a member of the Otto Rank Association and the Gestalt Institute of Cleveland.

Preface

GESTALT THERAPY is now over three decades old. In recent years, sharp increases in interest and use of Gestalt methods in psychotherapy have occurred. With this lively and burgeoning interest has emerged a need for literature focused on basic orientations in Gestalt approaches to psychotherapy and personal growth.

These introductory readings are intended for those who have little or no familiarity with the philosophy, methods and practice of Gestalt Therapy. Each author brings to this primer the richness of their years of personal experience and work in Gestalt. Awareness, figure-ground formation, polarities, contact and many other key areas are covered so that the beginner, student and others can get an overview and sample of the practice and field of Gestalt Therapy.

Hopefully this collection of readings can serve several functions. One is to be a reader for those training in any of the mental health, human service professions. Students and teachers of psychology, social work, psychiatry and others will find this book useful in their education and professional training. For more experienced and veteran psychotherapists, these readings may add to their knowledge of and approach to therapy. Most literature in Gestalt Therapy has not been channeled through conventional sources until quite recently. Few books exist and the relatively small number of articles have been widely scattered in journals; some materials have remained unpublished manuscripts. This collection is an effort to bring basic, introductory material under one cover. Finally, I hope that these readings will stimulate readers to seek out a real experience in Gestalt. As always, and most especially in Gestalt Therapy, the best introduction is an actual experience through personal participation and involvement.

Acknowledgments

I ESPECIALLY want to express my warm appreciation to all of the members of the 1971-1972 Intensive Post-Graduate Training Group at the Gestalt Institute of Cleveland: Vernon Averch, Robert Birch, Ruth Cheney, Elizabeth Cole, Frederick Grosse, Terry Hunt, Robert Phillips, Patricia Rathbone, Peter Stone and Patrick White.

Our group stimulated me in several directions, one of which resulted in this collection of readings.

F.D.S.

Contents

GESTALT THERAPY
PRIMER

CHAPTER I

AN INTRODUCTION TO GESTALT THERAPY

JAMES S. SIMKIN

GESTALT IS A GERMAN WORD meaning whole or configuration. As one psychological dictionary puts it: ". . . an *integration* of members as contrasted with a summation of parts" (Warren). The term also implies a unique kind of patterning. Gestalt Therapy is a term applied to a unique kind of psychotherapy as formulated by Frederick S. Perls and his followers.

Dr. Perls began, as did many of his colleagues in those days, as a psychoanalyst, having first been trained as a physician in post-World War I Germany. In 1926 he worked under Professor Kurt Goldstein at the Frankfurt Neurological Institute where he was first exposed to the tenets of Gestalt psychology but, as he puts it, ". . . was still too preoccupied with the orthodox psychoanalytical approach to assimilate more than a fraction of what was offered [to me]." (Perls, 1969(a), p. 5). Later Dr. Perls was exposed to the theories and practice of Wilhelm Reich and incorporated some of the concepts and techniques of Character Analysis into his work.

During 1941-1943, while serving as a Captain in the South African Medical Corps, Perls wrote his first manuscript outlining his emerging theory and technique of personality integration which later appeared as a book, *Ego, Hunger and Aggression—A Revision of Freud's Theory and Method*. The term Gestalt Therapy was first used as the title of a book on Perls' methods written by him with two coauthors, Professor Ralph Hefferline of Columbia University and Dr. Paul Goodman of New York City.

A thumbnail sketch of the aim of psychoanalysis has sometimes been given as Freud's dictum, "Where Id was shall Ego be," or to replace the instinctual striving with self-control as mediated by the ego. A capsule comment describing Gestalt Therapy might be Perls', "I and Thou; Here and Now," (with a bow to the late Professor Buber). In Gestalt Therapy the emphasis is on the present, ongoing situation—which, of course, involves the interaction of at least two people (in individual therapy), the patient and the therapist.

According to the theory underlying Gestalt Therapy, man is a total organism functioning as a whole, rather than an entity split in dichotomies such as mind and body. With the philosophical backing of humanism à la Otto Rank, the organism is born with the capacity to cope with life, rather than (what I call) the original sin theory of human development, that the organism must learn to repress or suppress its instinctual strivings in order to become *civilized*. Recently the emergence of existential philosophy appears to be so compatible with the development of Gestalt Therapy that Dr. Wilson Van Dusen (1960) in an article on "Existential Analytic Psychotherapy," makes the claim that there is only one psychotherapeutic approach which unites the phenomenological approach with existential theory and that is Gestalt Therapy.

Before examining some of the main concepts of Gestalt Therapy and describing actual situations which will give the experiential flavor necessary to an understanding of the approach, I need to do a little more *talking about* (which is really a taboo approach to Gestalt Therapy) to supply an adequate context or background.

The theoretical model of the psychodynamic schools of personality—chiefly the Freudian school—envisions the personality like an onion consisting of layers. Each time a layer is peeled away, there is still another layer until you finally come to the core. (Incidentally, in the process of *analysis* of the onion, you may have very little or nothing left by the time you come to the core!) I envision the personality more like a large rubber ball which has only a thick outer layer and is empty inside. The ball floats or swims in an environment so that at any given moment, only a certain portion is exposed to the outside while the rest is submerged in the water. Thus, rather than inventing an unconscious or preconscious to account for behavior that we are unaware of, I would suggest that the unaware behavior is a result of the organism not being in touch with—not sensing—what is out there because of being submerged in its own background (environment), or in contact (preoccupied, usually) with fantasies.

In his recent paper, "A Review of the Practice of Gestalt Therapy," Yontef (1969, p. 3) summarizes the theory of Gestalt Therapy. Organismic needs lead to sensory motor behavior. Once a configuration is formed which has the qualities of a good gestalt, the organismic need which has become foreground is met and a balance of state of satiation or no-need is achieved. "When a need is met, the gestalt it organized becomes complete, and it no longer exerts an influence—the organism is free to form new gestalten. When this gestalt formation and destruction are blocked or rigidified at any stage, when needs are not recognized and expressed, the flexible harmony and flow of the organism/environment field is disturbed. Unmet needs form incomplete gestalten that clamor for attention and, therefore, interfere with the formation of new gestalten. . . . The most important fact about the figure-background formation is that if a need is genuinely satisfied, the situation changes" (Perls, 1948, p. 571).

Thus, in order to bring about change, patients are taught to focus their *awareness* which is the primary tool for effecting change in gestalt therapy. Frequently, undirected awareness alone is sufficient to insure change. At other times, a person needs to experiment with *directing* awareness as in some of the exercises in Perls, Hefferline and Goodman (1951, pp. 116 ff).

Gestalt Therapy emphasizes organismic self-regulation. The organism, in order to survive, needs to mobilize itself and/or its environment for support. The means whereby the organism contacts its environment is through the mobilization of aggression. If we successfully survive the attempts of others to civilize or enslave us, we pick and choose what we need from our environment to support ourselves. Picking and choosing, however, is not enough; we need also to chew up and swallow those parts of what is out there that we find edible and to our liking and thus make it (food or idea or whatever) part of ourselves—in here. What we do not need, we discard either as waste products or garbage, etc. Thus, if we are able to mobilize sufficient aggression, not only to pick and choose, but to chew up and swallow, we are able to get the support necessary for our survival. It is important to note that it is the organism itself which picks and chooses, chews and swallows, etc. and *not* the significant other out there who determines for us what is palatable, nourishing, etc.

In Gestalt Therapy the therapist is frequently active in attempting to have the patient once again learn to use his sensory-motor equipment. At one time Dr. Perls described the process as a sort of "losing your mind to come to your senses" activity. This means that the patient is taught how to direct his awareness via the resensitization of his primary sensory modalities. To look rather than stare, to listen rather than overhear, or to play deaf and dumb. Directed awareness experiments help the patient get off what I call the *Why merry-go-round*. Many patients trust only their capacity to intellectualize, to think, to have fantasies. Thus, when they become aware of a bit of their own behavior which is incongruous, that doesn't fit their ideal self-image or role, they jump on the Why merry-go-round only to repeat the same unacceptable behavior and then again go chasing after reasons and explanations. Frequently, learning *how* by directing his awareness, the patient is able to *undo* the unacceptable behavior. At least, the patient does not remain an intellectual cripple!

In working with my patients in the Here and Now, using the techniques of directed awareness, "Where are you now?" or "What are you aware of now?" etc., I have discovered that verbal communication may indeed be misleading or misdirecting and that body language is not. Thus both the patient and I take his symptoms seriously, in that these symptoms (I call them truth buttons or truth signals) communicate *how* a patient really feels. If he is in conflict (experimenting with first taking one side of the conflict in fantasy and then the other), he will usually bring on the body language (the truth signals) when he takes sides with that aspect of the conflict which is anti-self.

Recently a patient was describing a conflict between continuing a project on his own which he had begun with a partner or dropping the project. His *truth button* was a hard, rock-like feeling in the pit of his stomach. He worked through his conflict by imagining first that he would continue the project without his partner and would see it through to the acquisition of property, erecting a building and manufacturing the article in the new plant. As he fantasied these various steps, he experienced increasing discomfort in his stomach; his rock was getting more and more unbearable. He then proceeded to fantasize dropping the project, abandoning the plans which had already been made plus his investment of time and money and reported feeling more and more relaxed and comfortable, especially in the pit of his stomach. Experimenting several times (reversing, so that at times he fantasied giving up the project first and at other times continuing the project first) brought the same results. The patient became convinced that he knew via his truth button which was the appropriate decision for him.

Being able to self-validate what the correct solution is through one's own body language is a tremendous help in the economy of psychotherapy. Many of the transference, counter-transference difficulties can be avoided, as well as the pitfalls of interpretation, through teaching oneself and one's patients how to use their symptoms and how to listen to their own body language.

One of man's most basic experiences is excitement. If you become aware of your excitement and attempt to suppress its overt expression, inevitably you will wind up squeezing or tensing yourself. In addition, you will stop breathing. Perls formulated that excitement minus sufficient support of oxygen equals anxiety, and, as we know, anxiety is the experience least tolerated by the human organism.

In all cases that I have seen thus far, people seeking psychotherapy show an imbalance among their three primary modes of experiencing. Most patients that I see, and this seems to be also true of the bulk of the patients seen by my colleagues, are very dependent on and have overly stressed their development of the intellectual or the *thinking-about* mode of experience. Most of the time, these people are in touch with their thought processes and their experience is with a fantasy (memory) of the past or a fantasy (wish; prediction) of the future. Infrequently are they able to make contact with their *feelings;* many are also *sensory* cripples, not seeing or hearing or tasting, etc.

In the organismically balanced person, there is the capacity to experience intellectually *and* emotionally *and* sensorially. So the therapeutic task is to help the patient regain the use of his own equipment which has been desensitized at some earlier time and which now desensitized is no longer appropriately at his disposal.

Contrary to the approaches of some schools which stress insight or learning "why we behave the way we do," Gestalt Therapy stresses learning how and what we do. Gestalt therapists are convinced that the only possibility for changing behavior is through an awareness of what we are doing—using our sensory and motor equipment as well as our intellectual equipment—and how we are doing whatever it is we are engaged in.

In Gestalt Therapy, we begin with the obvious, with what is ongoing at the moment, recognizing that patients can and do quickly learn to tell us dreams if we stress dreams as the *royal road to unconscious!* Or, that they will spend session after session dredging the past (telling us stories about their previous experiences) if we are convinced that cures are dependent on the recall of genetic material. Thus, my question to the patient "Where are you now?" or "What are you experiencing now?" may lead to the past or a dream, but the patient may just as easily not be in fantasy. He may be experiencing in the Here and Now feelings of expectancy or joy or anger. He may be concentrating his awareness on sensory experiences, such as seeing the room we are in or listening to sounds or experiencing his body against the chair he is sitting in.

Many patients are quite startled to discover that they filter every experience through their *thinking machine.* That it is almost impossible for them to trust their feelings or senses without first getting approval, so to speak, from their intellect. Frequently, when a patient becomes aware that he is overly-dependent on his intellectual equipment, he will try to manipulate me into telling him that he should not be so dependent. He is very fearful of exploring other modes of experience without some support (approval from me) if he cannot experience support within himself. All people need support from within and from without. Each person finds a suitable balance of self and environment. Many patients have very little or very inadequate self-supports and tend to lean heavily on environmental supports. Then they become very hurt or disappointed or shattered when the other to whom they gave this power, by the shifting of self-support to someone out there, fails to live up to their expectations.

During Freud's time, repression appeared to be the most frequently used defense. My own clinical experience leads me to conjecture that projection is now by far the most commonly encountered defense. We project onto another person those attributes or traits which we find unacceptable in ourselves. Then, we point our finger at him and castigate him for being whatever it is we don't like in ourselves. This permits us to maintain a fantasy or fiction of how we imagine we are rather than being in touch with and accepting how we are. The problem here is the problem of the introject. Swallowing something whole without first adequately chewing up and *then* swallowing the idea (or food) *if* it is nourishing, or spitting it out if it is toxic.

My primary psychotherapeutic task, as I see it, is to help the person I am working with accept himself. My patients say to me in effect, "I want to change how I am." "I don't like myself when I act this way." "I'm so stupid." Yet, they expect to change how they are, not by fully experiencing their behavior and thus their discomfort, embarrassment, joy, humiliation, excitement, pleasure, shame (feeling); but by judging their behavior as "bad," "stupid," "unacceptable" (intellectual judgments) and thus talking about, rather than fully coming in contact with, *what* and how they do it. Paradoxically, these people will be the first to claim the organismic truism that "we learn from experience." They confuse thinking about with experiencing.

I trust that if I fully experience what I do and how I behave, I will successfully finish (complete) a particular bit of behavior and learn from this experience. The crux is *how* I learn. Do I learn by fully experiencing organismically (sensing *and* feeling as well as judging), or must I restrict my experience to thinking about? Thus, when my patient says, "I did it again. I got angry at my wife and beat her," my patient is telling me a story (a memory of an event which has already taken place). I may ask, "What are you aware of now?" If his response is, "See how stupid I am? I never learn. I repeat the same idiotic behavior!", I may ask, "In telling me stories?" Once he understands what he is doing now—telling me a story and thus keeping two situations unfinished, the beating of his wife by recalling the memory of the event *and* the using of this memory with me now, playing the good patient perhaps, in telling me how bad or stupid he is—he has the possibility of learning how he remains stupid. He can only learn by being fully aware of what he is experiencing. The other way he is split into the two (sometimes more) aspects of himself

Dr. Perls referred to these two selves as the Top Dog and Under Dog who are constantly carrying on an internal (*infernal*, might be a better term!) dialogue. "You stupid idiot, why did you beat her again?" "Gee, I'm sorry, I promise I won't do it again." Or, "How many times do I have to tell you not to repeat that silly mistake?" "I'm going to do better next time, I promise." Perls claimed that the Under Dog self, the promiser, usually defeats the Top Dog through unkept promises and sabotage. I believe that the Under Dog always wins.

The integration of these selves, the full acceptance of how one is, rather than how one should be, leads to the possibility of change. As long as people persist in remaining split and not fully acknowledging (taking sides with and experiencing) what and how they are, real change, I believe, is not possible.

There has been a sharp increase in interest and the practice of Gestalt Therapy during the past decade (1960-1970). At the time this article is being written (early 1971), there are several Gestalt Therapy Institutes throughout the United States with at least three offering systematic training (Cleveland, San Francisco and Los Angeles).

Several books have appeared in the last three years, ranging from a collection of ten older articles collected by Pursglove (1968) and twelve original articles in Fritz Perls' Festschrift (Simkin, 1968a) to the excellent collection of twenty-five articles in their book on theory, technique and application by Fagan and Shepherd (1970).

Kogan (1970), unhappy with the (then) absence of a systematic bibliography of source material in Gestalt Therapy, collected and published a pamphlet which lists books, articles, papers, films, tapes, institutes and the gestalt therapist directory. He has some ninety references. Fagan & Shepherd list over sixty. Yontef cites forty-five in his paper.

Perls' autobiographical book, *In and Out of the Garbage Pail*, (1969c) and Simkin's interview of him in 1966 give much of the historical background of the development of Gestalt Therapy. Also of historical interest are the two excellent papers written by F. Perls' widow, Laura Perls (1953, 1956).

Practically none of the Gestalt Therapy literature has been channeled through conventional sources during the three decades of its existence. Major exceptions are Fritz Perls' article in the *American Journal of Psychotherapy* (1948) and Polster's more recent article in *Psychotherapy* (1966).

Until 1969 the only films depicting Gestalt Therapy were all of F. Perls. His are still the primary source (over thirty varied films) with one exception: Simkin's training film (1969). An excerpt from Simkin's film follows:

Jim: What do you experience at this moment?

Colman: A feeling of sadness . . . I don't know why. Because I said that they were in, I said I wanted them in.

Jim: Yeah. Colman, would you be willing to say now that you are sad.

Colman: I am sad.

Jim: Again.

Colman: I'm sad. I'm sad. And I'm angry.

Jim: Yeah.

Colman: Crazy.

Jim: Okay, add that. "I'm sad, I'm angry, I'm crazy."

Colman: I'm sad, I'm angry, I'm crazy.

Jim: And now?

Colman: Now I feel good again.

Jim: Yeah. Now I think you're beginning to catch on. Any time that you acknowledge, really go with how you are, you finish . . . let go. You *are* sad, you *are* angry, you *are* crazy, you *are* happy, and so on. If you stay with . . . all of your me's.

Colman: My sad, angry, crazy me.

Jim: Yeah. Okay, I'd like to stop at this point.

The above excerpt illustrates how, by being aware (responsible), Colman's sadness changes first to anger and then his anger changes to perplexity and then he experiences the humor of his situation and then feels "good again." Much of the impact of this transaction, however, is not conveyed through the arid medium of the printed word. The best way to fully experience Gestalt Therapy is obviously through the experiential mode.

As Fagan and Shepherd say in their preface:

   ... in Gestalt therapy, much importance is attached to tone of voice, posture, gestures, facial expression, etc., with much of the import and excitement coming from work with changes in these nonverbal com- munications. . . . Fortunately, the increasing availability of Gestalt films and tapes helps in making the nonverbal communications more accessible. (1970, p. VIII)

Or, in the words of the late Fritz Perls, "To suffer one's own death and to be reborn is not easy" (1969b).

REFERENCES

Fagan, J. and Shepherd, I.L.: Gestalt therapy now. *Sci & Behavior*, 1970.

Kogan, J.: *Gestalt Therapy Resources*, San Francisco, Lode Star Pr, 1970.

Lederman, J.: *Anger and the Rocking Chair: Gestalt awareness with chil- dren*. New York, McGraw, 1969.

Perls, F.S.: *Ego, hunger and aggression*. London, Allen & Unwin, 1947; New York, Random House, 1969a.

Perls, F.S.: *Gestalt Therapy Verbatim*. Lafayette, Real People Pr, 1969b.

Perls, F.S.: *In and Out of the Garbage Pail*. Lafayette, Real People Pr, 1969c.

Perls, F.S.: Theory and technique of personality integration. *Am J Psycho- ther*, 2:565-586, 1948.

Perls, F.S., Hefferline, R.F., and Goodman, P.: *Gestalt therapy*. New York, Julian Pr, 1951. (Republished: New York, Dell, 1965.)

Perls, Laura: Notes on the psychology of give and take. *Complex*, 9:24-30, 1953.

Perls, Laura: Two instances of Gestalt therapy. *Case Reports in Clinical Psy- chology*, Brooklyn, Kings County Hospital, 1956.

Polster, E.: A contemporary psychotherapy. *Psychotherapy: Theory, Re- search & Practice*, 3:1-6, 1966.

Pursglove, P.D.: *Recognitions in Gestalt Therapy*. New York, Funk & Wag- nalls, 1968.

Simkin, J.S. (Ed.): *Festschrift for Fritz Perls*. Los Angeles, Author, 1968a.

Simkin, J.S.: *Individual Gestalt Therapy: Interview with Dr. Frederick Perls*. Audio-tape recording. A.A.P. Tape Library, No. 31. Philadelphia,

Simkin, J.S.: Innovations in Gestalt Theory techniques. Unpublished, 1968b.

Simkin, J.S.: *In The Now*. A training film. Beverly Hills, 1969.

Simkin, J.S.: An introduction to the theory of Gestalt therapy. No. 6, Cleve- land, Gestalt Institute of Cleveland.

Van Dusen, W.: Existential analytic psychotherapy. *Am J Psychoanal*, 1960.

Warren, Howard C.: *Dictionary of Psychology*. New York, Houghton Mifflin.

Yontef, G.M.: *A Review of the Practice of Gestalt Therapy*. Los Angeles, Trident Shop, California State College, 1969.

CHAPTER II

AN INTRODUCTION TO GESTALT THERAPY

JOHN B. ENRIGHT

Preface

GESTALT THERAPY is a body of theory and technique espousing a point of view about personality development and structure and mode of change which makes a great deal of sense to me and has helped me clarify my past experience and see my present experience more clearly. There are many views of *reality*; this one happened to suit me very well though it probably will not suit everyone. I am writing this introduction because there is no widely available source on Gestalt Therapy and there may be others who will find these concepts sympathetic and helpful. I have had the good fortune to work with the man who has developed this point of view. This no doubt accounts for some of its impact on me, but unlike some theories which are nothing more than one man's personality and technique, I feel that Gestalt Therapy is teachable and usefully modifiable by others.

Most of what I know of Gestalt Therapy has been learned from James Simkin, Walter Kempler, and above all, F. S. Perls. They are, of course, not responsible for what appears in these pages. This introduction represents my interpretations and extensions of what they have done and said. While writing this introduction, I found myself shifting spontaneously from abstract sentence construction to *we* and *I* construction. I realized on reading over the paper that these shifts indicate quite sensitively where I am making statements with which I feel most gestalt therapists would concur, and where my statements might represent my idiosyncratic view of Gestalt Therapy. Therefore, despite the resulting awkwardness of style, I have left these different sections as written.

Gestalt Therapy is being developed by Frederick S. Perls, M.D.,

Ph.D., out of three quite distinct sources and influences which are psychoanalysis, particularly as modified by the early Wilhelm Reich, European Phenomenology-Existentialism and Gestalt psychology. Gestalt Therapy (Perls, Hefferline and Goodman, 1965) presents the theory of personality structure and growth from which the therapy can be derived and a series of experiments in self-awareness to be used by the reader directly. This source, however, gives no notion of the range, variety and power of the techniques of therapy that have been developed by Perls and some of his associates, nor does there seem to be any other easily available source that fills this need. The purpose of this paper is simply to indicate the existence of this body of theory and technique and to introduce some of the concepts. Since underlying theory is available in Perls (1969) and in Perls, Hefferline and Goodman (1965), this paper will concentrate primarily on therapeutic goals and strategy, with occasional brief discussion of specific tactics and techniques.

In the Gestalt point of view, the healthy organism-in-its-environment is constantly attending to matters of importance to its maintenance or survival. These matters of importance are organism-environment transactions that keep or restore equilibrium or smooth functioning. *Attending* here does not refer to a conscious state, but to a behavioral focusing of parts of the organism toward relevant parts of the environment, with muscular tonus, sensory tracking, etc. Most of this directed behavior takes place at the shifting boundary of organism and environment, where that which is novel and alien in the environment is contacted and made part of the organism (food is ingested and assimilated; words are heard and understood, etc.)

In humans, in those regions in which novelty and complexity of transactions are greatest, and the most possibilities (for good or ill) exist, awareness develops. Awareness seems to facilitate maximum efficiency in concentrating all the organism's abilities on the most complex, possibility-loaded situations. The organism's behavioral attention described above is more total and effective with this awareness.

In this over-simplified account, awareness is a state of consciousness which develops spontaneously when organismic attention becomes focused on some particular region of the organism-environment contact boundary at which some especially important and complex transaction is occurring. If this view is accepted, a disarmingly simple definition of psychological malfunctioning becomes possible. Something is going wrong when awareness does *not* develop at this region of complex interaction, and the organism continues to struggle along in its task without awareness. And, a correspondingly simple theory of therapy follows from this, as a first approximation to a statement of the goal of Gestalt Therapy. Therapy consists of the *reintegration of attention and awareness*.

The task of the therapist is to help the patient overcome the barriers that block awareness, and let nature take its course, i.e. developing awareness and allowing the individual to make the best transaction he can, with all his abilities functioning. Note that the therapist in this view does not help directly with the transaction—does not help solve the problem—but helps re-establish the conditions under which the patient can best use his own problem-solving abilities.

From this simple formulation follows a considerable amount of what the Gestalt therapist does in practice. We watch for splits in attention and awareness and for evidence that focused organismic attention is developing outside of awareness. Though the patient is typically talking about some problem, he is also from moment to moment sensorily registering and motorically doing much else. Generally, but not always, his awareness is concentrated on the verbal content; he also may be gazing off at something, fiddling with his hands, shifting around, smiling—at times perhaps in seeming congruence with verbal content and at times not. His voice is varying in many dimensions of quality—again, often matching the shifts in verbal content, often not. Even within his verbal productions there is, in addition to the intended content of his words, a rich and subtle texture of imagery and metaphor, selectivity of verb, voice, mode and tense, pronounal shifts, etc. These serve as the linguistic ground which modify and enrich the lexical meaning of his words. All of this and much more might be going on in the patient's behavior and all of it bears relationship to his difficulties in living an organismically satisfying life. He is showing us from moment to moment, in detail, just how he avoids being in full contact with his current actuality and avoids awareness of ongoing matters of organismic importance to him.

As long as the patient is communicating well verbally, and the other ongoing activities are minimal or congruent, I listen. At those times, I assume, his awareness is integrated with his organismic attention, and he is doing nothing that I, as a psychotherapist, can help him with; his problems are his, and he is working on them effectively at this moment. In a family or group, at these times, they are in good contact with each other, communicating well and dealing with their interpersonal problems effectively. My task begins when these other unconscious activities begin to stand out in the total gestalt, and begin to vie with the verbal content to saliency and importance. I then encourage the patient(s) to devote some attention to these other activities, asking him to describe what he is doing, seeing, feeling, etc. I make no interpretations but simply draw awareness briefly to these phenomena, and let him make of them what he will. Quite often, if my timing is good and my perception of increasing saliency accurate, the patient can make quite good sense of these, and gain in awareness of what he is doing. Some brief, concrete clinical examples might be helpful here.

A woman in individual therapy is going over, in a very complaining voice, some examples of how she was recently mistreated by her mother-in-law. I am impressed in her account by her lack of awareness of how much she invites this, and how she underperceives her capacity to interrupt this behavior, but say nothing. My attention is caught by a rapid repetitive movement of her hand against her other arm, though I can't make out the movement.

T: What are you doing with your hand?
P: (slightly startled) Uh, making a cross.
T: A cross?
P: Yes. (Pause)
T: What might you do with a cross?
P: Well, I certainly hung myself on one this weekend, didn't I?

She returns to her account, with more awareness of her martyr attitude and its contribution to events.

A couple in marital therapy are going over their problems rather repetitiously and fruitlessly. The wife is staring past me quite fixedly.

T: What are you looking at?
W: The tape recorder.
T: Can you describe what you are seeing?

W: 　　It's just going round and round.
T: 　　Round and round?
W: 　　Yes.
T: 　　Is anything else going round and round?
H&W: 　(simultaneously and rather impatiently) We certainly are.

They return to their discussion, but more fully aware of their sterile circularity, and they begin to take more productive steps to break out of it.

A paranoid woman in her first group therapy meeting on the ward begins by telling the group in a flat affectless voice that her husband had tried to poison her. As she goes on and on to enumerate her delusional complaints, she also mentions a severe pain in the back of her neck. Asked to describe this, she indicates finally that it is as though she had been struck a judo blow; she indicates that her husband knows judo. Able then to say that she feels as though her husband had actually struck her, she can then go on when questioned to begin to talk about ways in which her husband symbolically hurt her and very quickly she is telling the group, with appropriate tears and anger, how her husband slights her, ignores her, and flirts with other women. She has temporarily abandoned the paranoid solution to her problems.

There are several important characteristics of the kinds of therapeutic interventions described above that attempt to help the patient integrate attention and awareness. The intervention builds on actual present behavior; some present concern of the organism is involved, though neither patient nor therapist may have any idea what it is when the intervention is made, and it may turn out to be quite unrelated to the verbal material concurrently expressed. Ideally, and usually, the intervention is non-interpretive. I ask what is going on or what he is doing; where we go from there depends on the patient's answer. If he makes connection with the verbal material, or achieves some understanding of what he is doing, he has done it for himself in his own language. If he denies any connection or experiences nothing in his behavior, that is up to him; typically I let the matter drop. My timing was bad or he was not ready. If I push for a response or give my interpretation, he may only mobilize more defense against me. If the behavior is important, it will happen again. A third important characteristic of this style of intervention is that it continu-

ally operates to enhance and expand the patient's sense of responsibility for his own behavior. Responsibility here means not the broad
sense of social responsibility, but rather the feeling that "I, here and
now, am aware of doing thus and so." (However, I feel that true
responsibility in the broader sense is rooted in this feeling of being
the actual agent.) Thus, throughout the course of therapy, whatever the content, the patient is learning to do for himself, and to face
indecision and make choices—on a small but increasing scale.

The questions that introduce these interventions are almost exclusively *what* and *how* questions seldom *what for* and *why*. Most
people most of the time don't really know what they are doing fully,
and it is considerable therapeutic contribution if the patient can
achieve a vivid and ongoing awareness of his moment-to-moment
behavior and surroundings. In a sense, the achievement of such full
awareness is all that therapy need do; when a person feels fully and
vividly what he is doing, his concern about why usually fades away.
If he does remain interested, he is in a good position to work it out
for himself.

In keeping with this bias of Gestalt Therapy in favor of what and
how questions, the next step in this presentation will be to consider
in more detail some of the ways in which areas of self-functioning
are kept out of awareness, and some of the consequences of this
blocking. Four of these ways will be considered: Retroflection, Desensitization, Introjection, and Projection. All of these can be seen
functioning from moment-to-moment in the here and now, to
block awareness of current behavior or as repetitive residuals of earlier attempts to avoid awareness. A brief discussion of these may
leave the impression that they only rephrase existing concepts, and
certainly there is extensive overlap with related concepts from psychoanalysis and general psychiatry. The difference in emphasis is
often quite subtle and would require a fairly extensive discussion to
clarify. This is particularly true of projection, which is used in a
very similar sense as in general psychiatry. There is perhaps more
emphasis in Gestalt Therapy on the less seriously pathological forms
of projection in which the individual does not distort reality seriously but shows his over-concern only in his perceptual selectivity of
certain phenomena from the whole range of his surroundings.

Retroflection is an impulse or idea rooted in organismic sensorimotor tension, shaped partly by inner drives and focused on environmental events or objects. Retroflection describes the general process of negating, holding back, or balancing the impulse tension by additional opposing sensorimotor tension. The concept includes most of what is often referred to as repression and inhibition, and emphasizes the how of the processes involved. Since the net effect or resultant of all this cancelled-out muscular tension is zero—no overt movement —there is no particular increase in activity at the contact boundary, and awareness doesn't develop. Later, perhaps, since there is increased activity at the points of muscular opposition, awareness may develop there as pain or discomfort. As indicated, this process of retroflection can be transitory or chronic. The cry of distress begins with moistening of the eyes and a characteristic facial expression. The *stiff upper lip* and the literal holding (squeezing) back of tears constitute the retroflection. This can last a moment before the tears break through, or—as Tomkins (1963) describes so vividly—a lifetime.

Perls' debt to W. Reich is most clear in the development of this concept. Reich's *character armor* is chronic retroflection. It is important to note that the organism is expending energy in maintaining the tension of both the impulse and resistance, and both are quite typically alienated from the self and awareness. In therapy, both need to be reclaimed and made available for organismically satisfying, constructive use.

Desensitization is the sensory analog to motoric retroflection. Scotomata, sensory dullness, frigidity, visual blurring, chronic "not hearing," etc., are equal in importance to retroflection in the blocking of awareness. They are more dependent on verbal report and hence less accessible to direct observation and study than motoric phenomena.

Introjections consist of complex, integrated ways of behaving or being that are adopted wholesale by the developing organism from significant others, *without assimilation or integration with the self*. They correspond quite closely to Eric Berne's *parent* or *exteropsychic* ego states (1961). They can be detected by the repeated concurrence of a certain voice quality, type of verbal content, and gesture-posture style, and by the similarity with which others respond to this unified complex of behavior. The details of the process by which these introjects are taken in are complex and unnecessary for this paper. Our interest here is primarily in the role they play in current life. There they are the chief actors in the endless self-nagging and inner argument between ideal and real self in which so many people fritter away their lives. They also clutter up relations, when the self plays out one of these roles with significant others, or projects one of them on another person. Introjects are one of the main transmitters of pathology across the generations. An individual who may have successfully minimized his use of introjects in other areas of his life still may activate them when he functions as a parent with his own children.

Insofar as the individual relies on these means for the transitory or chronic blocking of awareness, he leaves himself with vast areas alienated and inaccessible, interfering with rather than facilitating the flow of life. He feels—and in a sense is—weak and divided, feeling pushed and pulled by forces outside himself. His behavior tends to be graceless and awkward; breathing and vocal expression are crippled. And with so little energy left over to live with, a great deal of unfinished business piles up.

The unfinished business is perhaps the major consequence of the blocking of awareness. Need cycles cannot be completed; tension is aroused but not reduced; affect mounts and is unexpressed. The flow of behavior is clogged with unexpressed action; little new can happen in the ensuing constriction and frustration. The individual becomes hung up on the unexpressed; life slows down into despair and boredom with lack of autonomy, spontaneity and intimacy. The neurotic's life is not a happy one, even if he does not happen to develop one of the specialized symptoms, such as phobias, obsessions, anxiety, etc., but remains merely grey and unfulfilled. Frequently, the neurotic's conscious ego is not in very good touch with what is wrong, and his verbal account of his problems is often quite wide of the mark. He has successfully distracted himself from even knowing where he hurts, and his problem of presenting complaint is not the meaningful place to start therapy. Quite often the patient would be only too happy to talk indefinitely and abstractly about The Problem, keeping in safely at a distance. If he is trained as a patient, he may come in ready to ruminate his current fantasies about his childhood, with the same distancing intent and result.

Fortunately, the general strategy of Gestalt Therapy does not depend on the patient's accuracy in self report. We simply tell him, in effect, to sit down and start living, then note where and how he fails. The therapeutic value we implicitly ask him to accept is that he will probably be more effective and comfortable in his life in the long run if he is more fully aware of what he is doing from moment-to-moment, and accepts responsibility for this behavior. He may have to accept this on faith for a short time, but we hope very soon to demonstrate the advantages of this orientation directly and concretely.

In this situation the organism will immediately turn in some way to whichever of its store of unfinished business is pressing and more or less relevant to the current situation. His techniques for blocking awareness will immediately come into play, he will begin to show us in his projections, tension, and dissociated activity the portions of his self that are alienated and inaccessible. The therapist can choose the most salient of these with which to begin. I have become impressed with the importance and probable centrality of the *very first* opening gambit—verbal or not—of the patient. Where he sits, at whom he glances, the sigh, the smile, the posture, the idiosyncratic image in his opening remark, anything he says before he formally begins to talk about The Problem, are the rich leads to the most deeply involving material he is likely to be able to get to, if the way can be found to use it nonthreateningly. The beginning can be—indeed should be—some trivial surface event, such as a smile at the therapist. When this is expressed more fully and awarely, he is ready to go on to the next, slightly more involving fact that he is, now that he thinks about it, also a little angry at the nice therapist. And so on, through layers of resistance and impulse—each one dwelt on as long as necessary, and hopefully not left behind until the energy invested in it is available for use, and the patient not too anxious about the next step into the unknown and unexpressed. Resistances are not overcome, but identified with and made one's own. Affect or impulse is not balanced or blocked in expression, but encouraged into more intense and full expression, finishing the business, and leaving decks cleared for new action. No attempt is made to keep the patient on to any topic as verbally presented, but a systematic and aggressive attempt is made to keep him in constant contact with *what he is doing.* He is then encouraged to do whatever this is as fully and completely as he can, with growing awareness of what he is doing. If he blocks himself from doing it, we then turn attention to how he is blocking himself and encourage fuller and more aware expression of this. The therapist spends as little time and energy as possible speculating on what is likely to emerge from each step the patient takes but instead concentrating on timing of the step and listening as fully as possible to what the patient is doing. This is perhaps the most significant gain of a non-interpretative therapy. The therapist is liberated from his endless fantasies about what is going to emerge from the patient in the next few minutes (with associated anxiety about whether he is right or wrong) and instead can simply listen and help the patient find his own way through the pauses and blocks.

The basic assumption of this therapeutic approach is that people can deal adequately with their own life problems if they know what they are, and can bring all their abilities into action to solve them. Our task is to unblock awareness by helping them relax their retroflected energies, restore sensitivity, assimilate introjects, and change projection into direct expression. Once in good touch with their real concerns and their real environment, they are on their own.

So far, an effort has been made to present techniques of Gestalt Therapy that are generally applicable to all modes of therapy—individual, group and family. Some of the techniques and tactics presented can be more powerful when we ask the patient to sit down and start living in a group with these new people he must learn to deal with, or in the family, to sit down and continue living with these significant but frustrating others. In a group, abstract problems can more quickly and readily be brought to earth. A patient who complains that he can't speak up and criticize his wife might be asked to address a critical remark to each group member present, thus experiencing immediately his difficulty instead of talking about it. A patient who claims to have an inferiority complex might be greeted with the request to indicate to whom in the group present she feels inferior, and how. With many more people available, the range of unfinished business that can be quite readily contacted is much greater. More people provide more screens on which projections can be cast, and the work of reclaiming and expressing them can be more easily done. Thus, a patient who comments that another patient is "looking contemptuously at the group" might be asked himself to try looking contemptuously at the group to see if he can make contact with his own feelings of contempt, and express them directly instead of through projective over-sensitivity.

In addition to the enhancing effects of getting several patients together, there are certain techniques that are specific to people in a group. In addition to the therapeutic value of awareness and responsibility already mentioned, we ask the group or family patient to accept another group-specific value. This is, that in the long run he will probably deal more effectively and better with people around him if he is direct with them, and listens to them with respect for them as individuals. Again, he must briefly accept this on faith, but we hope soon to demonstrate its validity concretely. In essence, the techniques about to be presented all follow from this value assumption and are simply ways of implementing belief about human relations. The goal we set for the patients as they sit down together in a group or family is an *I-thou* relationship in which each person is aware, responsible and direct in his own communications and listens as fully as possible to the other person as an equal.

The first technique implementing this point of view about human relations is to ask as quickly and fully as possible, in all interactions that take place in the group, that people speak directly to each other without use of the third person. A is discouraged from making a comment about B to the therapist and is asked rather to rephrase his comment in some form directly to B. This sounds simple, almost trivial, but in practice is very powerful. Patients often respond to this request first by saying that it is too simple to bother with, or that it doesn't matter, but when they try it, they go on to rebel strongly against it. The affect that is mobilized by such direct confrontation is very different from that which can be dissipated indirectly in the third person comment. Typically, a patient has considerable difficulty in making very much of a direct statement to another. The most common result of an attempt at directness is that ambivalence immediately becomes apparent, usually non-verbally, and the simple statement immediately turns out to be very complicated indeed. This ambivalence and difficulty with directness then become the focus of therapy. For example, a patient may attempt a critical statement to another, and look away from the other in the middle of the statement or interrupt it with a smile. We might ask him then what he was looking away from, or to put the smile into words. If he says he was looking away from the other's angry expression, he can get immediate feedback, and perhaps go on to find out that the anger he saw was his own, projected. As he gropes to put his placating smile into words, he becomes more aware of how he blocks and weakens his own assertiveness. As he succeeds in expressing the placation in words, he is then open to the further possibility of becoming aware of how his placating is tinged with contempt toward the other for being fooled by it, and is itself complex and ambivalent. The advantages of directness, in the form of more immediate and fuller feedback from the other and the expansion of one's own awareness, are experienced almost immediately in this approach. Since the individuals are engaged face-to-face with each other in this small scale encounter, they are learning these advantages in the most direct way possible, with the greatest likelihood of carryover into their outside lives.

A second technique which encourages the individual's awareness of responsibility for his own position is to discourage questions. A question from one patient to another usually serves either or both of two purposes. For one, it says in effect, "you speak, not me," and thus is a way of avoiding the questioner's participation. Secondly, almost all questions turn out to be implied statements, usually critical, about the other person. "Why did you do X?" almost always means "You shouldn't have done X," "I don't like it that you did X," or something to that effect. Almost never is a question a simple uncomplicated request for information. As much as possible, depending on the level of the group, we insist that a question be rephrased as a statement before the other person is asked to answer it. Then, since the statement is no longer masked as a question, B is released from the necessity of answering it (i.e. defending or justifying himself) and more easily can give his total response to A.

The second half of the group therapeutic value—to listen to others —can be implemented in a variety of ways. I often question the intent of an interruption. If people seem to be drifting off, I will ask if it is becoming hard to listen and get the group to consider simultaneously its obligation to listen, and the speaker's obligation to be worth listening to. A game of hostile and unproductive *verbal ping-pong* might be interrupted by insisting that each participant paraphrase the other to the other's satisfaction before being permitted to give his own response.

The details of technique vary; the strategy is always to keep a steady gentle pressure toward the direct and responsible I-Thou orientation, keeping the focus of awareness on the difficulties the patients experience in doing this and helping them find their own ways through these difficulties.

This strategy of Gestalt Therapy is most effective in family therapy. Family therapy differs from individual-focused therapy in that the patient's central presenting life problem is itself brought into the consulting room. The patient does not have to increase his awareness in relation to some stranger, then figure out later how to use this to modify his relations to significant others. His significant others are present with him. In a very real sense, the family is the patient, and can work on its *joint* unfinished business. The unsaid accusations, the unexpressed guilt, love and resentment that are clogging up the flow of inter-family feeling must be expressed by the family, in its own language, at its own pace. The therapist's task, as described in the paragraph just above, is to keep turning the focus of awareness on the difficulties that stand in the way of maintaining the I-Thou orientation.

There is a number of issues on which any theory of therapy must take some stand. The position of Gestalt Therapy on some of these could be induced from the above account, but it might be helpful to make its stands explicit. Six of these issues will be discussed: (1) The actual therapeutic agent as seen by Gestalt Therapy and the concept of the mentally healthy person that follows from this position; (2) the criterion for termination of Gestalt Therapy; (3) the range of applicability of the therapy; (4) the use of dreams; (5) the place of the therapist as a person in the technique, and (6) the place of the past in a here-and-now therapy.

(1) Awareness, Consciousness, Insight and the mentally healthy person

The theoretical and therapeutic core of Gestalt Therapy is awareness. This is essentially an undefined term referring to a particular kind of immediate experience, but it is possible to make some verbal description of it and distinguish it from other states of consciousness. Awareness develops *with* and is integrally *part of* an organismic-environmental transaction. It is always of some organism-environment contact in the present, and, though it includes thinking and feeling, it is always based on current perception of the current situation.

Much of the usual "content" of consciousness for many people is a flow of fantasy-imagery and subvocal speech (thinking) that is *not* deeply rooted in ongoing organismic behavior, but only partially and tangentially related to it. Occasionally, this fantasy-thinking is focused, in necessary anticipatory problem solving, working on some problem or unfinished business that is important, but not currently represented in the environment. More frequently this detached thinking-imagery is a more unfocused, pointless, dreamlike reverie, obsessing about, without particularly working on, unfinished business and serving mainly to distract and attenuate awareness of the actual. The difference between awareness and this unfocused reverie is most clear in the process of eating. Awareness of eating would be of the appearance, smell and taste of the food, the kinesthetic sense of the destruction of the food through chewing and swallowing, and the associated affects of pleasure or disgust. In fact, of course, most people while eating are engaged primarily in the above mentioned thought-reverie. They engage, perhaps, in revenge fantasies about some recent slight, a re-run of the latest Giant's game, or even fantasies about what they are going to eat for dessert in a few minutes—anything rather than the actual ongoing organismic activity. Many people clutter up their lives almost constantly with this internal noise of subvocal speech and fantasy that is pointless and only shallowly gratifying. Since it is not substantially gratifying, and does not successfully resolve any unfinished business, its consequences are to make the actual ongoing behavior—e.g. eating—less satisfying, and create more unfinished business. The extreme of this is represented by the obsessing student, who interrupts his studying with fantasies of the evening's date. When evening comes, and studying is not completed or well done, he ruins his date worrying about studying.

No implication is intended that in healthy life awareness is particularly big, grand or ever-exciting. It is simply there, flowing along with behavior. In therapy, however, when awareness develops where it has been previously blocked, it does tend to be accompanied by a sense of release of tension and a feeling of increase in energy. The experience is in a sense pleasurable. Even when the developing awareness is of a painful affect such as mourning or anger, it is accompanied by a feeling of "I want this; I'm glad it's happening even though it is painful." This gratifying aspect of therapeutic awareness is crucial, since it is the internal regarding and motivating factor that permits and encourages the patient to press on even into very painful feelings.

Awareness needs particularly to be distinguished from introspection. In introspection, the self is split; part is "looking at" another part as object, self-consciously. Awareness is the self, conscious of that to which the organism is attending. Introspection is effortful, forced concentration; awareness is spontaneous concentration on that which is exciting and of organismic interest. Introspection, being relatively detached from ongoing total organismic concern and being out of touch with the actual environment, can never discover anything very new, but only rearrange and rehash the verbally remembered and hence unnourishing past. Awareness being in contact with the current environment and organism always includes something refreshingly new. Genuine awareness is always a little bit of a surprise since neither the organism nor the environment is ever quite the same. (A person who claims that an experience is the same as a previous one is telling us, thereby, that he is actually replaying a fantasy rather than attending with awareness to his actual experience.) Awareness as it develops in therapy almost always follows a sense of taking a chance or taking a step into the unknown —of grouping to say the unsayable or beginning something without being sure of the ending. When this experience is not present, almost certainly the insight being presented is a sterile rehash rather than an expansion of awareness.

It would be impossible in the scope of this introduction fully to articulate this fundamental concept of awareness with its analog in Psychoanalysis—insight, but a brief consideration of their relation might be helpful. Quite early in the history of Psychoanalysis, its theoreticians and therapists became concerned that insight did not always produce the expected and desired therapeutic changes. One insight would seem to work; another remarkably similar-seeming one would lead nowhere. A distinction introduced in the attempt to account for this difference was between intellectual and emotional insight, the latter being the insight that worked. The Gestalt therapist would say that the emotional insight (whatever its verbal form—past, present or future) was based on an expansion of awareness of an ongoing organism-environment relationship with its associated positive effect and sense of discovery, while the intellectual insight lacked this crucial rootedness in the actual. This is an over-simplification of a very complex matter, but hints at the relationship of these two central concepts.

A complete theory of therapy should indicate some image of the healthy functioning it purports to help people achieve. In the Gestalt Therapy view, the mentally healthy person is one in whom awareness can develop without blocking where ever his organismic attention is drawn. Such a person can experience his own needs and the environmental possibilities fully and clearly from moment to moment, accepting both as given and working toward creative compromises. He has his full share of inner conflicts of needs, and environmental frustrations. However, being in close touch with these developing needs and the environment, he is capable of achieving reasonably adequate solutions quickly and does not magnify his real problems with fantasy elaborations.

Since he is carrying around much less of a filtering cloud of thought-fantasies to obtund the world, his sensual world is vivid and colorful, and his interpersonal world relatively uncontaminated with projections and unreal expectations. He can perceive and respond to others much more as they are and become from moment to moment rather than as fixed stereotypes. He has a clear sense of the relative importance of things, and can do what has to be done to finish situations. Since unfinished business does not pile up, he is free to do and be quite fully and intensely whatever he is doing or being, and people around him often report a sense of his being much more *with* them when he is with them. Seeing people reasonably clearly and without excessive fantasy, it is easy for him to be quite direct with others and appreciate them for what they are. Again, he has his share of conflicts with others, but he can resolve those conflicts that are resolvable, and let go of those that are not. (And he can usually tell the difference!) He is self-respecting in every sense, including an appreciation and enjoyment of his body with consequent physical grace.

(2) Criteria for the termination of therapy

A central characteristic of Gestalt Therapy is that throughout the sessions the patient, as much as possible, carries out his own therapy, with the therapist standing by as observer-commentator and occasional guide. The patient makes his own interpretations, formulates his own direct statements to others and achieves his own awareness. We see this not as thrusting the patient's responsibility for his own behavior onto him, but rather refusing to permit him to thrust it onto us. It rightfully is his, and we do him a disservice if we do something for him, depriving him of the learning experience and enhancement of ego functions consequent on his doing it himself.

It is quite consistent with this general orientation to ask the patient as quickly as possible to take over the responsibility for deciding to continue therapy, for deciding what he is getting from it and if he values this sufficiently to continue. We show him very quickly what we have to offer; he experiences in microcosm the rewards of increased awareness, and evaluates for himself if this is valuable and meaningful to him.

This can be implemented in many ways. I ask individuals and families almost from the first meeting if they would like another session, and end almost every group session by asking the members how they feel it went. Doubts about progress—verbally or non-verbally expressed—becomes the focus of discussion, and the patient is asked in effect what he intends to do about his discontents.

Not surprisingly, many patients find this request to make their own decision rather startling. It often brings quite precipitously into the foreground some otherwise quite concealed fantasies about magical cures and what the therapist is going to *do for* him. In the very process of exploring these, the patient can sometimes get glimmers of his own potential strength and capacity for self-direction. Issues of responsibility, choice, goals of therapy and autonomy often then become the beginning foci of therapy.

The whole course of therapy goes differently when termination is a central issue from the beginning. The patient cannot reasonably terminate without evaluating his progress, and cannot do this without being aware of his goals. Goals can—indeed, usually do—change, but the danger of both patient and therapist losing sight of goals and drifting is minimized. Occasionally there are practical consequences of this approach in the form of quite irregular schedules as some patients, finding it very difficult to say directly "I want an appointment next week," come more sporadically. Though these patients will have fewer contacts over a given time span, perhaps, for them, this is best.

(3) Range of applicability of Gestalt Therapy

It is clear from the above discussion that Gestalt Therapy in pure culture is not for every patient.

Basically, it is designed for someone who is dissatisfied with some way that he is and willing to expend some effort to be different—or to be more content the way he is. Many of the specific techniques and principles can be applied to less willing patients—children, some psychotics and some character disorders—but it is beyond the scope of this introduction to discuss the modifications necessary for such applications.

(4) The therapeutic use of dreams

Since Freud's brilliant work, any system of therapy must either provide a way of working with dreams, or a justification of avoiding them. Gestalt Therapy meets this challenge with a totally non-interpretive approach and which permits the patient to progress at his own meaning in his dreams. Every image in the dream, whether human, animal, vegetable or mineral, is taken to represent an alienated portion of the self. By re-experiencing and re-telling the dream over and over again in the present tense, from the standpoint of each image, the patient can begin to re-experience and reclaim these alienated fragments, accepting them, living with them and expressing them more appropriately. A restless, domineering, manipulative woman dreams of walking down a crooked path in a forest of tall, straight trees. As she *becomes* one of these trees, she feels more serene and deeply rooted. Taking these feelings back into her current life, she then experiences both the lack of them and the possibilities of achieving them. *Becoming* the crooked path, her eyes fill with tears as she experiences more intensely the devious crookedness of her own life, and again, the possibilities of straightening out a little if she chooses. The role of the therapist is simply to suggest the order in which the images might be contacted—usually going from the less to the more vivid ones. He also helps deal with the resistances—the tendencies to talk about and interpret instead of entering the experience of the image—and occasionally suggests when to carry the dream images and feelings back into the context of the patient's current existence.

(5) The place of the "therapist-as-a-person"

A major issue between current theories of therapy is: "Is the therapist a technician or a person?" Does he greet the patient's gambit with a professional technique, or his own spontaneous human response? Gestalt Therapy takes no stand on this. Anything goes if it contributes to the patient's expansion of awareness. In the small ranks of Gestalt therapists, I have encountered both extremes. I have found myself moving slowly but steadily in the direction of more open revelation of my own feelings of boredom, pleasure, annoyance, embarrassment, etc. Strictly speaking, this is still technique. If the patient is talking in a monotone, staring at the floor, and I am getting a little bored, I might ask him if he is aware of his voice, or what he is looking at. I might also help him to the same awareness of his withdrawal by commenting that I am finding it hard to listen closely to him. Though this is indeed my human response, it is hardly spontaneous if I pause to decide between these approaches! (In any case, I steer clear of the presumptuous interpretation, "You are trying to bore me." This may well be true, but I want him to discover it himself if it is so, and I want to set a model of responsibility by starting only with what I know to be true—that I am finding it hard to listen.)

(6) The place of the past in a here-and-now-therapy

Any here and now system of therapy must have some way of dealing, both in theory and practice, with the past. In theory, after all, the past caused the present. In practice, the patient often comes in fully expecting, in fact bound and determined, to deal with the past. This is especially true now that the popularization of psychoanalysis is pretty much complete.

Frequently, a preference for talking about the past—either on the part of the patient or therapist—is a maneuver to maintain distance from current potentially threatening concerns. The patient would rather blame her mean daddy for past deprivations than upbraid the therapist here and now for withholding the here-and-now goodies (advice, cure, insight, or whatever). The therapist would far rather talk about the patients "incestuous fantasies" than about her here-and-now coy flirtatiousness (and perhaps his own growing organismic response to it). So a conspiracy of verbiage about the past is quite frequently purely defensive and distancing, and should be short-circuited as rapidly as possible. At times, the patient presents some past events in a genuinely involved and concerned manner. At these times, I respect this concern and listen. I still view this language of the past as a fable wherein the patient is telling me allegorically about some present concern, but at least the discourse is concernful rather than defensive. At times like these, I treat the material very much as a dream, listening in it for the parallels to the patient's current existence, and trying to help make the transition when appropriate. Almost never do I find it fruitful to inquire into the details about "what really happened." The fable then turns into a just-so story that can be used to prove anything the patient wants to prove.

This tendency to limit the discourse to the present is feasible only because in Gestalt Therapy we are listening to the *total communication* rather than the strictly verbal. The relevant past *is* present Here and Now; if not in words, then in some bodily tension and attention that can be hopefully brought into awareness. It is impossible to overstress the importance of this point. For a purely verbal therapy to remain in the Here and Now would be irresponsible and disastrous. It is only the aggressive, systematic and constant effort to bring the patient's total communication into his awareness that permits a radical concentration upon the Here and Now.

This is an appropriate place to take up the fundamental psycho-analytic concepts of repetition compulsion and transference, to articulate these with the concept of unfinished business and discuss the Gestalt Therapy alternatives to the use of these concepts. This is again a complex and subtle task and this presentation will only attempt to suggest the nature of the relationships of these concepts. Gestalt Therapy does not deny that the hand of the past has, to a large extent, shaped the present, but in addition points out two facts.

One is that the past-shaped present nevertheless does exist in it own right, with all the relevant past actually present in some form. The other is that there is always something a little new in this current instance of the repeated compulsion or in this recurrence of the transference relationship. The organism may be very rigid but the environment at least is always a little different. This particular here-and-now relationship may be 99 percent determined by transference but nevertheless have a one percent leeway for creative variability following from the fact that the therapist *is not* the father and cannot be exactly like him. Gestalt Therapy attempts to expand that one percent and draw the patient's awareness to the discrepancy between his transference expectations and the reality sitting in front of him. This can be implemented sometimes very directly by asking the patient to describe physically the therapist or the group member involved in the transference and helping him see and experience in vivid concrete detail the discrepancies between transference and fantasy. In doing this, we are asking him simply to come to his senses; to cut for a moment through the filtering fog of fantasy which he maintains around himself and experience for a moment the reality of the person who sits across from him. Simple as it sounds, when this is done at the actual moment of distorted perception, it can be effective in jarring the person into closer touch with the real world of his own senses.

REFERENCES

Berne, Eric: *Transactional Analysis in Psychotherapy.* New York, Grove Press, 1961.

Kempler, Walter: Experiential Family Therapy, *Int J of Group Psychother, 15*:57-71, 1965.

Perls, Frederick S.: *Ego, Hunger and Aggression.* London, Allen & Unwin, 1947; New York, Random House, 1969.

Perls, F.S., Hefferline, R.F., and Goodman, P.: *Gestalt Therapy: Excitement and Growth in the Human Personality.* New York, Julian Press, 1951; New York, Dell, 1965.

Tomkins, Silvan: *Affect, Imagery, Consciousness.* New York, Springer, 1963, Vol. II, p. 57.

CHAPTER III

I AND THOU, HERE AND NOW: CONTRIBUTIONS OF GESTALT THERAPY

CLAUDIO NARANJO

Introductory Remarks

GESTALT THERAPY is a label that makes reference to the psychiatric approach and procedures developed by Dr. Frederick Perls. This approach, practiced by his trainees all over the United States, is fragmentarily described in his books (Perls, 1966, Perls, 1965). Essentially a form of existential psychiatry,[1] it is also characterized by the relevance of the holistic and gestaltist conception as well as many notions derived from psychoanalytic theory. Its most specific link with psychoanalytic therapy lies in its concern with body language. In this concern Perls has expressed his indebtedness to Wilhelm Reich. The uniqueness of Gestalt Therapy does not lie in a theory of personality of the neuroses, nor, for that matter, does it lie in theory at all. It is essentially a nonverbal creation, an approach to people in the therapeutic situation which has developed out of understanding, experience and intuition, and continued to be transmitted nonverbally.

I think the essence of therapy is more than an application of ideas, a living fact to be explained aposteriori, and Gestalt Therapy is no exception. I see a unity among its different devices, and can elaborate on their rationale, but someone else might look at the same facts

1. Gestalt Therapy is one of the three psychiatric schools which have arisen from phenomenology and existentialism, the other two being Frankl's logotherapy and Binswanger's Dasein Analyse. Of these, the latter does not and cannot claim to be a therapeutic procedure. Van Dusen, in his discussion of existential analytic therapy, claims that "There is a psychotherapeutic approach which most closely fits the theory. In fact, a close adherence to the theory demands a particular approach. The approach has been called Gestalt Therapy, and considerable credit for it is due Dr. F. S. Perls" (Van Dusen, 1960).

from a different point of view and in terms of a different conceptual framework. I will, therefore, in the following pages, focus on therapeutic methods, restricting the more abstract comments to what is of immediate relevance to the description of procedures.

I believe the techniques of Gestalt Therapy can very well be conceived as exercises for individual use. However, it is in this context that Perls has described most of them in his books. When he describes "concentration on eating," "undoing of retroflexions," "body concentration" (Perls, 1966), "feeling the actual," "sensing opposed forces," "attending and concentrating" (Perls, 1965), etc., he is addressing the reader and not a psychotherapist, and he assumes that anybody can set himself to experiment with the procedures.

True as this may be, I have chosen to describe the techniques in the context of the two-person therapeutic situation, since the overt dialogue between patient and therapist lends itself well as an example of the inner dialogue in him who wants to be his own therapist. I also believe there are advantages in the two-person situation, and I think the average person would be in a better position to proceed on his own after an initial contact with someone more *awakened* than himself, or who may at least supplement his own awareness. Parenthetically, I may here state that I also believe this to be true of all spiritual exercises: that though we can only tackle certain inner struggles by ourselves, we may get there faster with the help, support and challenge of somebody ahead of us in experience. Nevertheless, it is up to the reader to decide what he may do with the ideas in this chapter, and I would emphatically advise him to try them out at least twice before pronouncing judgment.

The immediate aim of Gestalt Therapy is the restoration of awareness. The ultimate goal is the restoration of the functions of the organism and personality, which will make an individual whole and release his potentialities. It assumes that awareness by itself will bring about development and change.

It is an agreed-upon concept of depth psychology that the essence of healing lies in the process of becoming conscious of the unconscious. The emphasis of Gestalt Therapy on awareness rather than consciousness or understanding points further to the importance of contacting the immediate ongoing process Here and Now and better suggests the sensory and feeling basis of such processes.

Accordingly, the intervention of the therapist is essentially noninterpretative, and directed to the awakening of the patient's own awareness of what he is doing and feeling. The emphasis definitely doesn't lie in explaining behavior, in understanding why, but in perceiving how it proceeds. This awareness by itself brings about a new experience and a new challenge to awareness.

Staying in the Continuum of Awareness

A basic procedure in Gestalt Therapy is that of staying in what Perls has designated "the continuum of awareness." The patient here is asked to simply express what he is experiencing. Here the emphasis on *experiencing* makes the situation very different from free association of thought, in which not only abstractions but memories and anticipations constitute much of the verbal output. In fact, most persons will discover to their own surprise that they have enormous difficulty staying in awareness of their experience for more than a few seconds. At a given point they will turn to thinking (computing in Perls' jargon), to remembering, or to fantasies about the future. All of these, in a situation in which the task is to stay with the present experience, are regarded to be forms of avoidance. It is important to contact the experience that led to the avoidance, by returning to the points at which there was an interruption in the awareness of the present. It will then be found that there was at that point some discomfort or fear that prompted the subject to establish a distance by thought or to escape from the instant. Furthermore, awareness may possibly extend into the underlying experience at the time of thinking, so that the patient notices that he is explaining himself in fear of not being understood, justifying himself to counteract his feeling of guilt, offering an interesting thought or observation to be appreciated, etc. In the same way the awareness of fantasies can be deepened to the point of contacting what the *subject is doing* with them, and to the discomfort at the root of the urge to do what he is doing. Not only the activity of thought and fantasy are stimulated by the need of avoiding or counteracting an experience, but physical activity as well. Posture, movements of hands and feet, facial expression and intonation of the voice, all convey either the feeling that was excluded from awareness and the effort to ward it off or counteract it, or both. The function of the therapist is to redirect the patient's attention to his experience of himself: Are you aware of what you are doing with your hands? I noticed your voice sounds different now, can you hear it? Can you see where you stopped, and began to make a case, and so on. The expression of experience is not a matter of an all-or-none response. For example, the patient's form of reporting may be at any point between real expression and *talking about* himself as an outside observer, and he will be unaware of his implicit avoidance of identifying with himself (and taking responsibility for it). The therapist may choose to concentrate on this at the beginning, so that the patient becomes more aware of what is the basic experience and what is his elaboration or his diluting of it in irrelevant words and concepts. For example:

T: What is your experience now?

P: I feel there are several persons I don't know in the room and perhaps they may not understand what I say.

T: That is a thought, and an expectation, not an experience. Try to express your experience now.

P: It is like what I feel when . . . I guess it could be called fear.

T: Can you describe what you are feeling now?

P: My hands are trembling. My voice quivers. I am afraid.

Directness is often dimmed in English by recourse to *it* and related figures of speech on occasions in which either *I* or *you* are implied (and avoided). It may be fruitful to point out such alienated statements and ask the patient to reword them,[2] e.g.:

P: My hand is doing this movement . . .

T: Is *it* doing the movement?

P: I am moving my hand like this . . . and now the thought comes to me that. . .

T: The thought "comes" to you?

P: I have the thought.

T: You *have it?*

P: I think. Yes. I think that I use "it" very much, and I am glad that by noticing it I can bring it all back to me.

T: Bring it back?

P: *Bring myself back.* I feel thankful for this.

T: *This?*

P: Your idea about the "it."

2. "Everytime you do apply the proper Ego-language you express yourself, you assist in the development of your personality" (Perls, 1966).

T: My idea?

P: I feel thankful towards you.

Perls conceives personality as comprising three layers: The surface is constituted of the roles we enact in manipulating the environment, the *games* we *play*. When we do away with such phoney personality we are confronted with an area of deadness, nothingness, emptiness (the *implosive* layer) and only by working through, and giving in to that deadness can one come to real life—the *explosive* layer of true feelings and strivings. The exercise in staying with awareness will eventually lead the individual to an impasse, a nothingness in which the forces of resistance are equal to what he is resisting. So the next stage is working on the impasse. Here again the aim is to restore awareness to the activity that there *is* in the apparent paralysis. The patient that seems to be unmoved is being pushed or torn by opposing forces of equal strength, and must be brought in contact with them. More than that, he has to recognize that these opposing forces are himself, his own potential. In psychological terms, the Ego has to identify with the alienated functions as processes.

An example may make this more clear:

> When the therapist asks the patient to pay attention to his own voice, the patient becomes aware of it and reports a sad intonation. As he does this there is a change in his facial expression. The therapist comments on this, too. "Yes, I feel some moisture on my eyes." The therapist then asks, "What would your tears say if they could speak?" The reply is, "We feel shy. We would like to come out but we don't dare." Since a conflict has been exposed, the therapist now instructs him to alternately take sides in himself with the desire to cry and "with the desire to resist the crying." This leads to a dialogue between the little tender baby and the *tough man* in the patient, and to an acceptance of both, and an understanding between them.

Enacting

It can be seen in this example that each statement of the therapist leads the patient to *identify*, to *become* his unconscious and alienated activity. His voice first, then his tears, finally the desire to refrain from weeping. The greatest resource for this purpose is that of dramatization, and in this we find the second tool of Gestalt Therapy. As awareness leads to some action, so does deliberate acting lead

to expanded awareness. Through the attitude of taking sides and acting out any alienated movement, feeling or thought can be developed, contacted and reassimilated by the Ego. It can be one's own
voice, a gesture, a fleeting suspicion, a figure of speech, an imagined
attitude of the therapist, a fantasy. The therapist will typically propose this at the moment in which he notices an inconsistency between the verbal and nonverbal expression of the patient, suggesting
to him to *be* his posture, to develop a movement of the fingers, to
put into words a smile, or to impersonate the therapist and answer
his own question. An illustration here may be helpful:

P: I would like to understand . . .

T: I hear a wailing in your voice. Can you hear it?

P: Yes . . . There is a trembling . . .

T: Be your voice now.

P: I am a weak, complaining voice, the voice of a child that doesn't
dare to demand. He is afraid . . .

T: *I* am . . .

P: I am a little boy and I am afraid to ask for anything, can only ask
for what I want by showing my sadness, so that mommy will
have pity and take care of me . . .

T: Could you be your mother, now?

Here we see in succession the enacting of the voice, of the child
and the mother. A dialogue between the two eventually showed the
actor how he was manipulating others by playing the helpless child
and how he was hating himself for his deviousness. This awareness
was not achieved by analyzing the past or talking about his present
but rather by letting his behavior develop and, so to say, speak for
itself. The individual is not encouraged to become an observer of
himself (alienating himself further from his doings) and compute an
interpretation, but to merge with his actions, and have them say what
they want.

The Handling of Conflicts—Reversal, "Taking Sides" and Encountering

The strategies discussed thus far—the exercising of awareness and
that of acting, impersonating one's self—are the two aspects (the con-
templative and the active) of one indivisible process: we can only

become really aware of what we do or perceive while doing it, and we can only have the experience of being the actor, the doer, the perceiver, when these functions are in our awareness. In other words, there is no real distinction between being aware, contacting our experience, becoming ourselves, entering our bodily or mental processes and becoming one with them. The alternative to this, the state in which we think of ourselves as removed from ourselves and our experience is one in which we are creating an artificial boundary between self and not-self, and therefore asserting an illusory separateness from the stream of life—our life. In this duality lies the root of all inner conflicts.

We may be no more aware of the extent of our intrapsychic conflicts than we are of our sleepwalker-like restriction of awareness or our estrangement from ourselves, yet the lack of unity in neurotic functioning is as pervasive as the lack of awareness or the lack of identification with ourselves. And, again, it is no more than a facet of the same happening. In the same way that total awareness involves opening up to the bliss of the eternal Here and Now, and the end of our alienation involves the realization of the Upanishadic "That art thou," "Thou art God," so the end of conflict—the synthesis of opposites—involves being one with life, surrendering to the push of its stream and being *it* at the same time, relinquishing any individual will other than the will of life through us—our true self.

The strategies of Gestalt Therapy in dealing with conflict—reversal and encountering—constitute an elaboration of those discussed thus far and are among its most original contributions to psychiatry.

Whenever a conflict is experienced as such ("I would like to but I don't dare," "I am not sure whether I like it," "I feel like crying but I cannot," etc.) it is generally easy to take sides with the alternatives and become involved in the fullest possible experience of each at a time. It may be that either one or both conflicting tendencies are being experienced as *non-self*, so it has to be reassimilated by the Ego through the active effort to impersonate it, to become it by living it from the inside. It is an assumption of Gestalt Therapy that hardly ever or never will the solution be an either-or. Since both tendencies are living forces in the individual, "each element of the self style must be experienced so that the person can use it when necessary. Freedom is the choice and responsibility taken for the style element used."[3] In other words, the approach is not one of doing away with the elements of the personality (such as resistances or the commands of the Super-Ego) but of reassimilating them into the Ego. Becoming aware of what happens in us is to become aware that *we do it*, and by so *becoming* it, we have both the potential and the control. "Do not be tempted to give up your style until you have experienced it. Otherwise you give up one false God to worship another."[4]

Reversal

Whenever a conflict is not experienced as such, it may not be so easy to act out and experience its sides, yet a therapist may see enough of the contradiction to point it out. If the patient smiles while being critical, for instance, he may suggest to him to act critical and severe, first, and then, after having expressed his attacking side, to develop that ingratiating smile. Or if the patient is feeling critical towards her own relaxed, lazy posture, the therapist may guess that she is only avoiding the awareness of the other half of her experience: that she wants and enjoys this posture, since after all she is assuming it. So he may instruct her to exaggerate and give in to her laziness, until she is able to be one with her unacknowledged urge. In a similar fashion, he may propose to someone who is feeling guilty, carrying the *well-deserved blame*, to act resentful in face of *undeserved criticism*, thus trying out a reversal in his perception of the situation and himself. Or he may tell a little old lady to say nasty things and yell, if it is obvious to him that she is not acknowledging and expressing her hostile reactions. The principle involved in all such instances is that of taking up attitudes which are opposite to those the person has been assuming.

We live in only a fragment of ourselves, holding on to a pre-established self-image and rejecting as non-self all that is conflicting with it or that we expect to be painful. In this island of personality we feel impoverished and helpless, subjected to the pulls and pushes of impulses or compulsions. Gestalt Therapy suggests that we regard the self-image as the figure in the figure-ground relationship that is involved in all perception. In order to regain from the background what has been rejected from the self, this therapeutic approach in-

3. Gene Sagan: unpublished manuscript.
4. *Ibid.*

vites us to reverse the figure-ground relationship involved in this self-perception, and start experiencing ourselves as the background: not the one that is being depressed, but the one that depresses himself; not the one that feels guilty, but the inner judge condemning himself; not the one that feels half dead, but the one that does the chronic self-rejection and kil'ing. Only by sensing how he does this can a person stop doing it, and put to better use his energies than engaging in fruitless battles.

The principle of reversal can be applied not only to feelings but also to physical attitudes. Opening up when in a closed posture, breathing deeply as an alternative to a restraint in the intake of air or exhalation, exchanging the motor attitudes of left and right, etc., can eventually lead to the unfolding of unsuspected experiences. The following is an example of this kind:

> The therapist notices that while expressing his ongoing experiences the patient often interrupts what he is saying and feeling, and in such moments he swallows or sniffs. The therapist suggests that he do the opposite of sniffing and swallowing. The patient engages in a forceful and prolonged exhalation through nose and mouth, that ends with what he reports as an unfamiliar and surprising feeling: ". . . somewhat as if I were sobbing, but also pushing against a resistance, and my muscles are tense, as when I stretch in yawning; I enjoy this tension when trying to exhale to the very end of my breath, which also feels somehow like an orgasm."
>
> Later, he discovered that he had been living with this feeling for a long time without being aware of it: "It is like wanting to burst, wanting to explode from the inside, tearing down a sort of membrane in which I am wrapped and limited. And I am at the same time this straight jacket and I am squeezing myself."

This short experience was the starting point of a spontaneous development which took place in the coming months. The muscular tension and concomitant feelings were always very much in his awareness from then onwards, and he felt more and more inclined to do physical exercise. He then discovered the pleasure of dancing and becoming much freer in his expression, both in movement and general attitude. Finally, he could sense the anger implied in his muscular contractions until he would be aware of it in his reactions to people to a degree he had not been before.

Encountering

Taking sides and merely experiencing the tendencies involved in a conflict may sometimes be enough to precipitate a spontaneous synthesis or resolution. If not, this integration of the opposites may be brought about by their encountering.

The term *encounter* is being used with increasing frequency to describe a form of direct communication *between* people, but Perls has extended its use to include communication between intrapsychic entities or processes. These could be, for instance, the two sides of a conflict, or the experienced Ego and any specific mental content, such as a fantasy, an urge, a feeling. To him, as to Buber, the essence of the encounter is the I-Thou relationship: one in which neither party is deified by talking about you or me, but one in which the speaker directs his own activity to the other.[5]

In the interpersonal relationship the therapist may encourage the encounter by bringing to awareness all avoidances of the relationship, such as looking away, indirect speech, etc. In the situation of group therapy, the members may be encouraged not to talk in third person of anybody present, but express any feelings or thoughts directly to the person they refer to. Also, in the same situation, when faced with a question, individuals are encouraged not to answer but rather to respond. Regardless of the answer to a question, we do have a response when confronted with it in a given situation: indifference, eagerness to answer, fear of being exposed by the answer, annoyance, etc. Expressing this response is closer to self expression, encounter and the I-Thou relationship than an answer would generally be.

Here are some examples of how the principle of encountering can be carried into the intrapersonal domain:

Example 1

A lady explains she would like to remember last night's dream. She is instructed to call the dream, to address it directly, and she says in a very low, monotonous voice, "Come dream, I want to remember you." When her attention is drawn to the lack of feeling in her calling she tries again several times with no success. In doing so she is able to experience the fact that she really does not feel an urge to remember. She feels rather indifferent towards the issue and has been misinterpreting herself assuming she had such a desire. She can now see

5. Says Buber, "There is no *I* taken in itself, but only the *I* of the primary word *I-Thou* and the *I* of the primary word *I-it*."

that she has been playing the "good patient."

I perceive something. I am sensible of something. I imagine something. I will something. I feel something. I think something. The life of human beings does not consist of all this and the like alone.

This and the like together establish the realm of *It*.

But the realm of *Thou* has a different basis.

When *Thou* is spoken, the speaker has no thing for his object. For when there is a thing there is another thing. Every *It* is bounded by others; *It* exists only through being bounded by others. But when *Thou* is spoken, there is no thing. *Thou* has no bounds.

When *Thou* is spoken, the speaker has no *thing*; he has indeed nothing. But he takes his stand in relation. (Buber, 1958).

Example 2

A woman had a dream in which she saw herself crawling across a room. Somebody asks what she is doing, and she answers: "I want to have a confrontation with that wall."—"Why don't you rather have it with a person, then?"—She answers, "People are walls."

Not only was the person replaced in the dream by a wall, but the wall itself was never reached and confronted. When told to do so in a session, the woman did so in the same position as in the dream, on her knees and bowing. "I want to go through you, wall." Taking the role of the wall, now, her reply was distant, hard and disdainful towards her meekness and docility, her posture and weak complaint. After several reversals of roles, she stood up, and further, she adopted the attitude of the wall, herself, firm, erect and hard, so she was visualizing two walls in front of each other. This felt to her like the confrontation she was seeking. A week later she reported that she had for the first time been able to confront a man in the same attitude.

A great many and perhaps the most significant encounters are particular forms of the widespread split in personality: the *I should* versus the *I want*. It may take the form of a dialogue with an imagined parent, with a disembodied self-accusation, with people in general, etc., but the parties appear again and again with distinctive feature that inspired Perls (in his inclination for a phenomenological nomenclature) to call them Top Dog and Under Dog.

Top Dog can be described as righteous, bullying, persisting, authoritarian, and primitive . . .

Under Dog develops great skill in evading Top Dog's commands. Only half-heartedly intending to comply with the demands, Under Dog answers: 'yes, but . . .,' 'I try so hard, but next time I'll do better,' and 'manana.' Under Dog usually gets the better of the conflict.

In other words, Top Dog and Under Dog are actually two clowns performing their weird and unnecessary plays on the stage of the tolerant and mute Self. Integration, or cure, can be achieved only when the need for mutual control between Top and Under Dogs ceases. Only then will the two masters mutually listen. Once they come to their senses (in this case listening to each other), does the door to integration and unification open. The chance of making a whole person out of a split becomes a certainty. (Perls, 1961).

The following encounter (written by the patient in a therapeutic encounter) does not lead to full integration, but nevertheless illustrates the procedure:

Here and Now

C. says might try encounter between the monk and the beast.

Monk: Terrible, terrible, the pains of the flesh.

New I: No pain necessary right now—listen to "Trout" and enjoy grok[6] the sunshine, grok the trembling, which is for opening the Door, man.

Monk: You make me feel so lonely, Charles.

New I: Thanks for naming me. Now I can proceed to fuck or at at least *feel* something down *here* between the legs.

Monk: That is a dog, that puts his tail between his legs.

New I: Then you are a dog, sir.

Monk: *How dare you!*

New I: Now you're acting like Miss Henrietta. Reach down there, man, and feel your balls, for a change.

Monk: Don't use such vulgar language.

New I: Just for that, sir, I sentence you to 90 days and nights of extreme pleasure.

Monk: *Anything*, so long as you don't play the Japanese music. (Just the mention of that makes me tremble clear up to the armpits.)

New I: I am going to play that, man, exactly as soon as this fucking "Trout" quintet peters out.

(This Japanese music is very pleasant—rather innocent. *Well, that's the way to start*, in innocence. *Puer aeternis* is thyself and every other beautiful person.

6. Neologism introduced by Robert Heinlein in his novel, *Stranger in a Strange Land*: a martian word originally signifying "to drink," "Grok also means to understand so thoroughly that the observer becomes a part of the observed—to merge, blend, intermarry, lose identity in the group experience."

Yes, it's cruelty of myself, to my body. The monk
tortured and killed my body. No wonder I put the
Crucifix above the bed: "the man who died.")

Monk: I became what I am because you left your playmates behind in Minnesota.

New I: Makes no sense.

Monk: "Lose your mind and come to your senses."

New I: You're getting pretty sharp, man.

Monk: Thanks for calling me that, son.

New I: I'm not your son, thank God.

Monk: I see you recognize me.

New I: You mean, I presume, that every man who oppresses the
body is my mother. By the way, are you aware of the fact
that we have reversed positions?

Monk: Wasn't so important as we thought, was it?

This last sentence sprang from the feeling that the two characters
were not in antithetical roles any more. Both have changed to the
point of sharing the same traits. (The "New I" does the torturing,
the monk feels victimized), so that now it does not make much difference who is called by what name or who is in what position.

Focusing on Dreams

The procedures discussed thus far constitute the embodiment of
three principles: (a) that of bringing the spontaneous activity into
awareness, (b) that of identification or taking sides with such spontaneous activity and (c) the integration of personality functions or activities by bringing them into a relationship or encounter. Though
any experience can be the object of such approaches and procedures,
a special place must be granted to our most spontaneous activity,
which is dreaming. In fact, dreamwork is one of the most original
contributions of Perls to the therapeutic traditions.

As in the case with Gestalt Therapy in general, its approach to
dreams is non-interpretative, and yet it views the dream as an existential message that is to be understood. Understanding in this context refers to the direct experience of the dream's content rather
than to an intellectual influence, in the same way that awareness
stands in opposition to an intellectual insight. The road to awareness,
here too, is letting the experience speak for itself rather than thinking

about it, entering the dream rather than bringing it to mind. In accordance with this, it is important that the dream be not only remembered, but brought back to life. Only by experiencing it *now* can we gain an awareness of what it is conveying. It is therefore advisable to begin by narrating the dream in the present tense, as if it were happening at the moment.

The mere change in wording implied in the use of the present tense instead of the past may be enough to bring about a great difference in the process of recall, which now, to some extent, becomes a returning to the dream and the feelings that go with the fantasy. This may be an adequate moment to sense its metaphorical language by thinking or saying before every sentence: "This is my existence." Thus, saying: "This is my existence: I am rolling a peanut with my nose," made a dreamer aware of how in her life she was adopting an overly humble role, kneeling down and preoccupied with menial tasks instead of standing up and facing the important issues. In another instance, by saying, "This is my life: I am driving on a freeway and would like to pull off and sleep," he realized how he was feeling caught in a conflict between a compulsive, stressful and lifeless race for power and the wish to relax, enjoy and dream.

It may not be easy for some to produce anything more than a dry recall of dream images, in spite of the effort to re-experience, and this only indicates the strength of the tendency to alienate the dream from the individual's own experience. This alienation is, to some extent, present in every dream, so the task of Gestalt Therapy is that of reassimilating it into the Ego and having the person take responsibility for his unacknowledged forces, now projected *out there* as *strange* images. When the attempt at actualization and contemplation of the dream does not lead to more than verbal formulas, such reassimilation may be effected through the acting-out of the different elements in the content.

The acting-out of a dream necessarily entails a creative experience of interpretation or translation into movement, and as such it involves an extension of the creative activity expressed in the dream itself. But this is not the only way in which the dreamwork can be expanded. It may be fruitful to fill in the gaps with fantasy or finish the dream where it was forgotten by waking up. In being faced with this task the individual necessarily turns into a dreamer again, and

becomes one with his dreaming self. Or he may give words to characters that only felt unspoken emotions in the dream, so that they
now engage in a dialogue. This is only feasible if the individual really
listens to his dream by becoming part of it.

A man relates a dream in which he sees himself in a corridor full of
lockers. He is looking for some books that he has kept in one of them,
but does not remember which. An attendant approaches him and tries
to help him, but with no success. Here the alarm clock rings and he
wakes up. When told to go on dreaming, he fantasies that he finally
finds the locker and opens it.

When instructed to *sense* this image as his existence he reported that
he was actually feeling "in a corridor full of lockers." His life felt
grey, enclosed, impoverished, boring, and unsatisfactory, as if he were
searching for something with no success.

The following are some excerpts of the play-acting that followed:
(Here comes the attendant. He takes the key and wants to help me.
I know better than he where I left my books . . .)
T: Tell him.
P: You can't help me. I know better than you and can do best when
undisturbed. Leave me alone.
T: What does he answer?
P: I am sorry sir. I only wanted to help you. . .
T: Be the locker now.
P: Here I am, a grey locker. I have a number on me. People come
and use me. They open me and close me; they put things in and
take things out of me. I am pretty tired of this. I am sick and
tired of it! How I would like to disappear, not to be found again!
. . . I know now . . . I know I can play a trick on this fellow; I
can have him be deceived so he doesn't find me! Yes, I will have
the attendant "help" him, so he is mislead and does not find me.
T: Be yourself opening the locker, now.
P: (He goes through the movements in a pantomime and exclaims:
So it was you! *You*, trying to deceive me!)
T: What does the locker answer?
P: Ha, ha, ha, ha, ha!
The patient ends expressing that triumphant mockery in a dance,
turning slowly and powerfully at the center of the room while he
laughs.
T: Do you still feel grey and like a number?
P: Not any more.

The illustration shows how meaningful it can be to identify with
objects, and not only human or animal characters, in a dream. This,
too, was an instance of a figure-ground reversal, by means of which

the patient came to experience himself as the one playing hide-and-seek with himself, and not merely the searching victim. When his self-defeating wish was enacted and channeled into the dance he was not in an impasse any more but creatively expressing himself and feeling himself as a living being.

The integration of these selves—the full acceptance of how one *is*, rather than how one *should be* leads to the possibility of change. As long as people persist in remaining split and not fully acknowledging (taking sides with and experiencing) what and how they are—real change—I believe—is impossible (Simkin, 1965).

Although I believe all of the techniques described in this chapter can be advantageously used by the individual, I think the procedure that lends itself best to the therapeutic situation may be the exploration of dreams. Not only is the dream "the royal road to the unconscious," so that it can be a guarantee of starting off with a very significant theme (however insignificant it may appear), it also provides a convenient blueprint to follow when applying the diverse exercises of Gestalt Therapy. For the one who is willing to explore on his own, here is an outline to follow:

1. When you wake up in the morning, write down the dreams with the greatest possible detail.

2. Look in the dream for unfinished situations or anything that you have been avoiding, and finish the story in the spirit of *not avoiding*.

3. Say the dream aloud as if the action in it were actually happening in the present, and be aware of yourself and what you are feeling while you do so: is the intonation of your voice compatible with the reactions you are reporting: What is your breathing doing? etc.

4. Go over your dream once more, still in the present tense, and contemplate it as a picture of your existence: Does it make sense?

5. List the elements in the dream: human characters, animals, objects, elements of nature (wind, earthquake, fire, etc.)

6. Act out the completed dream story from the point of view of yourself in it, placing special emphasis on the avoided situation (falling, dying, being caught, etc.)

7. Play each of the other elements, giving them a voice and

letting them speak for themselves and their wants ("I am a hard rock, a very old rock polished by the centuries," "I am the wind, powerful, free, invisible, uprooted," etc.)

8. Look for pairs of opposites and engage them in encounter. In doing this, you may want to write down a sketch, and then play it to the best of your dramatic ability. While giving words to your characters, (including yourself) do not just make up sentences, but try to impersonate them, enter the situation, and honestly express your reactions in each role.

9. While doing all of this, *be aware!*

10. Did you get the message, your dream's message, *your* message, *yourself?*

The four visions that I include as a final illustration are particularly relevant to the application of the foregoing suggestions outside the two person therapeutic encounter. The poetess who wrote them had been deeply affected by the Top Dog—Under Dog confrontations in a few sessions with me, and was particularly impressed by the effect of reversing roles with a sadistic mother image. This reversal and becoming the other in the encounter, as well as the enacting of her fantasy images in general, soon became spontaneous attitudes to her, and led to the ecstatic merging with the elements while writing the following lines:

Four Visions

I

We swim together
in a clear pool of water
like two tadpoles
close to each other
face to face
ready to mate
and we stop swimming
and tread water
and the water slowly turns
blue blue blue
cherulean peacock blue
and slowly we too
turn the same blue
our arms our bodies
our necks and finally
our faces
and we merge with the water
into the water
and we merge with each other
into each other.

II

Among the big green leaves
of the plane trees
I make my bed
on blue sheets of air
the wind rustles the leaves
against my white voile gown
lifts the gauze
the leaves caress my limbs
through the thin veiling
enfold me in their hands
and I dissolve
to liquid smoke or fog
and merge into each leaf
become a flock of
small gray birds
that sing and sing and sing
from inside each leaf
with high thin delicate voices
the whole tree sings
with every leaf.

III

The eastern sky is pale
yellow air
and I a traced line
in morning sungold coming
with many other girl graces
toward the light
by banks of thin clouds
below the whole earth
where sleep all
now the rolling red ball
fire comes toward us
burns through our air bodies
reflects rosy below
sweats smiles
as he rises smiling giant
climbs to the sky
drops tears and sweat
of hot sungold
down to us we glide
down to it on earth
it becomes sunshine
our traces part of it
we fall with it
rest on fields of grass
and sway on each head
of wheat on each blade
and we become laughter
of pure light and colour.

IV

A black tall slim shadow
against the blue-grey
water coming in small waves
in from faded sky
the shadow flat
not molded round like
sculpture or man
shallow or hollow
as a shadow
or a mirror dark
entrance to another world
where it is the beast
I come but do not fit
the shadow
my yellow hair flies soft
in the bare wind
my shadow white and round
against blue-black water
the shadow shrinks
down to my size moves
as if to embrace me
shrinks more
into my white arms
into my white thighs
into my belly
into my head until
I finally sink
into the dark beast shape
and become one
with its dark world beyond
fill the space and
finally am one with the world.

REFERENCES

Buber, M.: *I and Thou.* New York, Scribner, 1958.

Perls, F.S.: *Ego, Hunger and Aggression: A Revision of Freud's Theory and Method.* San Francisco-Big Sur, Orbit-Esalen, 1966.

Perls, F.S.: *Gestalt Therapy and Human Potentialities.* Esalen Paper No. 1, Big Sur, Esalen Institute, 1961. (mimeographed)

Perls, F.S., Hefferline, R.F., and Goodman, P: *Gestalt Therapy: Excitement and Growth in the Human Personality.* New York, Dell, 1965.

Simkin, J.S.: *Introduction to Gestalt Therapy.* Los Angeles, Gestalt Therapy Institute, 1965. (mimeographed)

Van Dusen, W.: Existential analytic psychotherapy. *Am J Psychoanal, Vol. XX,* No. 1, 1960.

CHAPTER IV

ON LOVING ENCOUNTERS: A PHENOMENOLOGICAL VIEW

JOSEPH C. ZINKER

Introduction

EVERY WRITER AND POET worth his name has written things in praise of love. Scholars and psychoanalysts have spoken on the meaning of love and on different forms of love. But psychoanalysis of love cannot substitute for the experience of it and every person must discover for himself the joys of giving himself fully to another. These notes were written in the spirit of self discovery in the process of my own growth. They were written over a period of two years. They grew out of many experiences both joyous and painful. I am presenting them to you in their original chronological order. The pieces seem to flow naturally into each other. You will notice that in the beginning, my language is more formal, didactic and theoretical. Later I speak in the first person. My language and the issues dealt with become more concrete and purely experiential; it is in this sense that I refer to these writings as "Phenomenological."

You fill me with a kaleidoscope of liveliness
Open me up and pour the world in—
Make me overflow into the world:
    Contactful sponginess
Hallucinations of the world-starting-all-over-again
    With its purity, brilliance
Yet twirling around as in coitus or birth labor:
    Going in and out of focus
Hallucinations of world-coming-to-an-end:
    Heart torn out of me
Yet all is well: Better than ever
Permeability will never kill me; it will purify and
    Cleanse . . . tears cleanse
She-God-is-totally-loving
    And never impatient

And her love sifts through me
Warming all the world . . . (Zinker, 1966-1969)

Letting the World Come In

The experience of feeling loved is one of acute receptivity, of taking in the gift of the other. It necessitates one's readiness to let the other person penetrate one's deepest stratum of feelingful experience, of openness and lack of defensiveness and suspiciousness that the loving person will be injurious. In the experience of letting the other person love us, we willingly take the risk of being hurt. The fact that the loving other has the power to hurt (to reject) and chooses not to, gives the experience a sense of magnetism and tension.

Because letting the other love us is a receptive experience, the feeling of being truly known and understood is accompanied by a heightening of sensation in all bodily modalities, not only in response to the loving-other but to the whole world at the moment of encounter. When we truly let the other love us, we experience hot and cold sensations, trembling, heightened breathing, *goose pimples*, hair-standing-up-on-end, burning and itching and fluidity and softness in our eyes, fullness in the abdomen, breasts, and genitals, and perspiring. Our body addresses itself to the loving other, saying, "All of my powers of receptivity take you in. You are so marvelously beautiful that I feel all of me taking you in." We feel soft and as a sponge we want to let the whole world seep deeply into our being.

Moreover we say it to the rest of the universe: "World, you are beautiful, I have never seen your beauty so clearly, so brilliantly, so ecstatically." We rejoice in the magnificence of all the world.

In order to receive the world fully, we put ourselves in a position of reverent passivity predisposed to wonderous admiration. We feel like a baby in its mother's arms. We symbolically assume the position of pliable femininity—we take the loving one into us without questioning or reservation. Lovers *surrender* to each other, regardless of their sexual identity.

When we feel totally loved by someone who really matters, the receptive experience makes us feel beautiful, perfect, graceful, profound and wise (Maslow, 1962). This feeling brings us back to our earliest experience of being hugged and cradled by mother, experiencing our mother's implied statement "you are the most lovely, the most beautiful baby in all the world." Lovers call each other "baby."

We take ownership of this statement and we say "yes" to it, "I am beautiful."

The experience of being loved may be described separately from loving; loving the other has special experiential characteristics.

Spilling into the World

The experience of loving the other is not only one of acute internal sensation but of overflowing of sensation into motility, expression and activity. Loving the other is an active statement of the self, not merely a passive aesthetic appreciation of the loved one's beauty.

Authentic love for the other is experienced as ecstacy in the very being of the other, rejoicing in the loved one's very existence; it is as if you say to her or him, "I'm glad you are," or "I'm glad you were born," or "I love your mother and father for begetting you."

Authentic love is not manipulative, guilt-making, or clinging. We let the other be. We do not wish to violate his or her unique integrity.

The physical expression of loving the other ranges from rapture to tenderness to passion, to sexuality, to seduction, even to violence. The fullness of sensation spills over into words of love and into crying, trembling, moaning, sighing, heart palpitations and sexual orgasm. These physical experiences are accompanied by feelings of floating, flying, merging, dancing. We feel we can do anything; we can climb trees, float over villages, kiss the moon. The artist Marc Chagall expressed this imagery beautifully in his paintings. We can change any situation which may hinder our expression of love for the other; "love conquers all." We feel holy, pure. We feel as though we can be the loved one's mother and father—we can take care of him or her forever; we are always hovering over the other.

As Erich Fromm (1956) has pointed out, loving is not necessarily equivalent to passion, sexuality, and seductiveness. These may be particular expressions of love, but they are not necessary ingredients of it. The purest kind of love (purest not in the puritanical sense of being clean, but in the sense of prerequisite clarity of rejoicing in the other's being) involves the total experience of the internal tension or energy which is part of one's responsiveness to the loved one. Staying with this tension and letting it permeate one's whole being is an enormously difficult task to accomplish, particularly since, in our society, there is a tendency to sell immediate canned pleasure and immediate satisfaction. With respect to sex, however, girls are taught not to *go all the way*, and I think that for this reason, they have more tolerance for experiencing the tension of loving (or childbirth or pain) much better than men are able to.* In the loving encounter, staying with the tension of internal sensation accentuates all processes of liveliness and creativity and results in a kind of internal overflowing and finally, a temporary exhaustion. Freud discovered that maintaining his patients' celibacy accentuated their feelings for him, their intellectual productivity and finally, speeded up the psychotherapeutic process. I think this is one reason why, in some religions, those who seek total fulfillment remain celibate: Here carnal love is sublimated to the love of God.

Thus we can speak of love as a kind of creative tension as well as of love as a manifestation of passionate sexuality culminating in coitus and orgasm. Without the above described experience of loving the other, sexual contact results in an unfulfilled sensation of emptiness, oblivion and depression; with it, however, sexual gratification is experienced as a total fulfillment of a human relationship.

> I give to you with soul, guts
> ask no questions, make no requests
> Nothing matters but the act of moving toward
> you
> Flowers in hand.
> Floating over the hamlets at
> daybreak
> I feel a thrust within—
> it says,
> give all, give all!
> Lovely
> Exhilarating—
> I move toward you, my being touches
> you with its gift—
> You move
> ever-so-slowly so gracefully in
> response to me,
> almost floating in slow-motion-
> picture fashion

*I will not go into the negative, constrictive effects of such conditioning here.

We mingle in the act of giving
and taking.
No witness could tell who gave and
who received.
(Zinker, 1966-1969)
July, 1968

Making the World Over Again

The loving encounter is transcendent. We feel lifted beyond the confines of the immediate, concrete world. We feel as though we are being reborn, and that the world around us is also transformed. The peak experience of touching another's being is akin to the fulfillment of all our wishes, it is like being in Heaven. All our fantasies of being fully actualized suddenly seem to come true—to come to life. We have found the *mythical him* or the *mythical her* (Tucker) —the person of our childhood dreams, our prince or princess. We experience our own sense of godliness, holiness, creativity. We feel born again, cleansed, pure, transformed. Union with the loved one is life, and loss of him (or her) is death.

The World Coming to an End

When we give up our self and experience total union with the other and the universe, it is a cataclismic experience which may be accompanied by feelings of the end. A suicidal patient once told me that after she fell in love, she realized that the feeling of the world coming to an end returned in her total fulfillment with her husband —that in a sense, it was just fine to die now for all is well. She mentioned that while reading Shakespeare she realized that he used the expression to die both when lovers actually physically died as well as when they culminated their lovemaking.

Heightened sexual encounter with the loved one is simultaneously an accentuation of life and an experience of death. It is as though the whole life cycle is condensed into one encounter.

Another dimension of love-destruction, the sense of millenium, exists with respect to losing the loved one or to having our overtures of loving rejected. We feel that life is not worth living. This goes back to the primordial need for total love from our mothers. If the infant does not get it, he dies (Spitz, 1941-43). It is well known that most people who commit suicide are either single, divorced, or separated from loved ones. Suicidal notes often express dismay over being rejected by loved ones. The person's experience is that no other human being can give him the love that in his fantasy his loved one alone was capable of giving. Because the loved one is experienced as the only and the ultimate fulfillment of all one's dreams and fantasies of immortal union, rejection is a cataclysmic destruction of one's life, the end of the world (Spande, 1962).

Becoming the World

In the ecstacy of the loving encounter, the world comes to an end in another sense—in the sense that we lose ourselves in the other, in the experience of the other and, finally, in all the world around us. We give up our personal identity. This is the height of the peak experience, the experience in which we no longer have motives, needs, aspirations, defenses, and demands from the world. We let go of all that is worldly and concrete. Nothing matters. All is well. We are totally with the other person and the other person knows this deeply. We are accepting of all, we are totally non-judgmental and forgiving. We experience a kind of quiet, deeply warm bliss. Our eyes feel warm, deep, ageless. Time no longer matters. Nothing matters but the experience of being fully there.

> I think
>   yes,
>   that I am walking
>   with a man-child
>   very tall
> I think
>   he is touching me:
>   sharp sometimes
>   but sharply soft
>   soft sometimes
>   but softly sharp
> I weep
>   because the pain
>   and the joy
>   are very close
> and I know that they are good.

(Conklin, 1967)

The Longing for Total Union

Mama and Papa did not fulfill all our needs because they are human beings and they have their own hangups just as we do.

Deprivation is an organic part of life. Partial deprivation energizes us and propels us toward more contactful, more fulfilling relationships. Even a psychotic person hasn't given up the hope of finding idealized union with a loving other.

In spite of our sophisticated protests and intellectualized rationalizations, we have an insatiable longing for being truly and totally understood, loved and embraced by another. Our primordial voices cry out: "Fill me with your love and striving and contact and keep filling me over and over again." In this sense we are ever expandable containers, love being as basic as food for us; when our bellies are filled we feel satiated and all appetite is gone, but when the hunger comes again, it is as though we hunger for the first time in our lives.

Our dream of the perfect love is delightful and it is propelled by the original primordial energy of having been one with mother (Fromm, 1956).

Our whole being scans the universe for the perfect love, the perfect encounter, the perfect beauty in another. Each one of us has a unique fantasy of total union and salvation. Culture has formalized this perfect union in theological terms; in Christianity total salvation is our ultimate individual union with Jesus Christ.

Loving Other as Catalizer of Self-Awareness

When we look with eyes full of private fantasies at the person we *want*, we can get so flooded with the anticipation of our own fulfillment that our vision may blur and we can't experience or see the other's being or his need. Yet, at other times, we can experience the other person in great depth and with great sensitivity.

We say, "Good friend, you speak well," and unconsciously we mean, "I like the sound of my language when I speak to you because you take me in willingly and you have a way of making me aware of myself." We say, "I love you," and we mean, "Thank you for making me aware of my worthiness." We say, "You are beautiful," and we experience, "Thank you for helping me become aware of my own beauty." We say, "I see your glow," and within, we experience, "Your warmth lights me up."

Our deepest, most profound stirrings of self-appreciation, self-love and self-knowledge surface in the presence of the person whom we experience as totally accepting. It is as though we say, "When I know your total acceptance, then I can show you my softest, most penetrable, delicate, vulnerable self" (Rogers, 1961).

Real Contact Is NOT a Mere Byproduct of Loving

Later, when filled with the other's love, we gently push away until we hunger for more.

What do we see? How much do we *touch* the other? And how much do we care to discover the details of the other person's being? We feel penetrable and penetrated but do we ourselves penetrate? The dangers are always there of two scripts reading lines to each other: the people are absent, their souls hungering and yet not knowing how to eat, chew, swallow, and digest.

We set up stereotyped rituals which resemble total union in order to help ourselves touch each other more fully: thus dance or sexuality is often a lonely, empty, meaningless rite because we lose ourselves in the *thingness*, the image of it instead of the other person existing Here and Now with us.

When the ultimate love finally arrives, it never satiates all of our internal life for we are in danger of losing the other person's humanness by deifying him in our fantasies.

Working at Real Contact

Because of our basic narcissism, as well as cultural alienations, real contact does not and cannot come by itself at all times. We have to start by working at contact when we begin taking each other for granted:

> . . . I think
> he is touching me
> sharp sometimes
> but sharply soft
> soft sometimes
> but softly sharp . . .

Daily contact is not the ultimate fulfillment of total union with God. Rather it is the use of one's total resources, one's total being touching another person; it is the concrete, thoughtful and simple application of a narcissistic dream.

Once we break through each other's stereotyped social games, and no longer need our own, contact becomes infinitely richer and more delightful. There is no end to such contact. And it has intrinsic loveliness and temporal integrity. It has rhythm (Polster, 1960-1968).

Confrontation

The possibilities of confronting another with a total awareness of him and of staying with the rhythm of the confrontation is frightening, for not only is it a difficult relationship for us to start, but we are also taking the risk of hurt and rejection. The wonder and intensity of contact is also frightening because it will never fulfill our childish dreams of the infinite, immortal union. Finally, no matter how stimulating and productive the confrontation, we need to stop, rest, and face solitude.

> All day I have bathed in deeply stirred
> souls,
> My eyes glowing, my body moving with the
> spring winds,
> And now, at midnight, I rest in the lines
> of your body,
> My soul sinking into nothingness.
>
> We spoke well, my dear love and
> We touched each other with wisdom
> born of the moment
> But now the snow has fallen and all
> is silent.
>
> (Zinker, 1966-1969)

Resistances to Confrontation

Confrontations are multidimensional. Confrontations are difficult to achieve because we set conditions on the manner in which they ought to take place.

> Don't tell me how I am to touch you,
> To touch you gently, with whispers
> or sexually
> or asexually
> or quietly.
>
> I will touch you as the spirit moves me:
> with words and movements
> or yelling,
> with violence or
> with sentiment,
> with tears or

with eyes penetrating the depth
of your fragility.
(Zinker, 1966-1969)

Confrontations are not just interpersonal—they are also intrapersonal and they take place with a thousand media surrounding and
encircling us. All creativity is confrontation, but no matter how
great the paintings, the books, the poems, the music and the archi-
tecture is that we produce, no matter how exhilarating it is to create,
we still need affirmation from the loving other of our own uniqueness, beauty and goodness.

We continue in our longing for total union, in our hoping that
the other person will liquify us and pour us deeply into his soul.

Self Affirmation

When we confront another person with responsive acute sensitivity, we make a statement of self-affirmation. We can only confront another after we have experienced our own incisiveness, after
we have appreciated the vicissitudes of our own internal power. We
believe that our response, our impression, our feeling has validity and
that it is capable of moving the other, and because we feel this way,
the other person does take us seriously. It is this self-affirmation that
is the dynamic stimulus to contact: self-affirmation gives us presence.

> I don't believe in anything or anyone; only in Zorba. Not because
> Zorba is better than the others; not at all, not a little bit. He's a brute
> like the rest. I believe in Zorba because he's the only being I have in
> my powers, the only one I know. All the rest are ghosts. I see with
> these eyes, I hear with these ears, I digest with these guts. All the rest
> are ghosts, I tell you. When I die, everything'll die. The whole Zor-
> batic world will go to the bottom.

(Kazantzakis)

Experiencing My Primordial Mother

For me, a man, to be fully with you, a woman, I must know the
woman inside me. The woman in me is the primordial mother who
loves you because you exist. She loves the words you say, your si-
lences, your embarrassments, your angers, your movements, your
body. The primordial mother inside me loves you now at this moment so fully that you will know her love forever and you will pass
it on to those who touch your life.

This mother-woman inside me loves me, too. She gives me a sense of naturalness in the world. She lets me be as I am. She lets me be a wrathful lion, a panther, a thinker, a child, a playful boy. She sees the goodness in my mistakes and celebrates my constant change. To her, I am always growing up even if I am seventy years old.

I move toward you, woman, from this feeling about myself. I move freely, openly, gently, acceptingly, strongly, weakly, playfully, childishly, manfully, receptively, reverently. When I move toward you, I am and you are all living things in the universe—an enormous, quiet universe which does not judge its own existence—it merely is. You and I live this moment in our mutual sweet isness.

Experiencing the Man-Father in You

Even if you don't think it in your head, you too know your primordial mother and father. Your mother is for you what she is for me. And I experience her in you when you move toward me. The father in you, man in you, has enormous power, a volcanic power. I feel him in your lusty laugh, in your playful attacks on me—when you growl and bite and scratch. These feelings I take for granted in myself. Man in you knows my sensitivity, my questioning, my wondering, my philosophizing and my need to withdraw and renew myself. Man in you is also critical of my careless thinking, my imperfection.

Union as the Archetypal Mother-Father Experience

And so, in this spirit, you and I move toward each other. I am your mother and you mine. I am your father and you are mine. My own feeling—this feeling that I know so strongly—is that your simple physical closeness by itself is the greatest, most ecstatic experience in my lifetime. It is existence itself. The endless universe cradles us together with such overwhelming power. How beautiful we are. I know most fully that I exist. I am. And I know also the infinity of all organic things. At the same time that I know my own existence fully, I give it to you completely and unquestioningly. I live and die, and live and die and live. . .

I penetrate you and you welcome me. I am engulfed by your sweetness and you by my power. You are engulfed by my sweetness and I by your power.

You are so totally dear to me—that when we separate, this feeling of dearness stays with me—and it spreads itself toward all things. When I walk on the beach and pick up a rock or weed, we have a loving dialogue with each other. For me, this dialogue is stronger with human beings because of our experience—and most of all it is stronger with women. My primordial self loved them a long time ago, but you make it a concrete experience for me, a real part of my daily life.

I offer you no ethics, no philosophies, no lessons, no answers. I am not making implicit demands or requirements. In celebrating our union, we assert our infinite goodness.

> Love gives us naught but itself and takes
> naught but from itself.
> Love possesses not nor would it be posessessed;
> For love is sufficient unto love.
>
> (Gibran, 1960)

Young Love

Loving you for the first time was volcanic. Loving you was recovering the curiosity of my childhood, the energy of ancient warriors, the passion of passion without end, the joy of rejoicing in your existence, in my being, and in the being of the stars and galaxies. Loving you for the first time was a great adventure. To adventure you was not like climbing mountains or sailing the oceans; it was discovering the essence of life over and over again in a thousand ways, groping for the discovery of the mysteries of life in you—and with every discovery of you I found a bit of me. Loving you for the first time was an obsession which took all my energy and all my time. Not wanting to let you go for a moment, I would gaze into your eyes, watch you doing simple chores, discover the shape of your toes and just talk about everything that popped into my head. There were no traditions for us or precedents or habits—no history— we had no history to hash over or turn against. We were fresh and new not only in our mutual chemistry but in the knowing of ourselves. We were children on a new continent, not knowing exactly what we would discover but having a naive confidence that the discoveries would be substantial.

Our new continent didn't have any street signs or streets or designated methods of getting places. It was vibrant, wild and sometimes frightful. The excitement was at times so great that I knew my feelings were greater than both of us, that we were participating in the birth joys and pains of generations of living beings before our own births. We laughed, cried, and knew it was good. We awakened in the middle of night and discovered each other's freshness and beauty anew. We were children. We knew no ugliness and when it assaulted our lives, it was unbelievable to us because everything we knew in each other was good and pure. If you were clumsy or if you lisped or if you made a blunder, you were somehow even more charming than before.

We wanted to know each other's thoughts, feelings, beliefs, sentiments, moods, angers, sorrows. We really wanted to know them! We were simple. We had no tactics or sales pitches or defenses or games. We offered each other the very best of ourselves. We didn't know then how to hurt each other or close each other off, or set each other up. We simply were. We turned to each other for love, comfort, understanding and sheer contact. We even gave up—at least temporarily—our individual historical problems for the sake of being good human beings for each other. How this giving up of our own preceding problems for the creation of something greater than both of us takes place is a mystery for me.

What we didn't know about each other seemed to add to our mutual excitement. Our mutual ignorance enabled us to daydream into each other's beings only the finest attributes of character and motivation. At a deeper level the empty spots in the other could be filled with imagined fulfillments of primordial wishes for total acceptance, total grace, total care, total softness, total goodness. The empty spots of the other became the most concrete experience of the presence of God in our lives. Everything was good—even ignorance of each other's being had its place in our young growing love.

April Dream

Last night my house was burning. Could not find one precious thing to grab and find comfort in. And when the torrential rain hammered out the flames, I was angry with its self-righteous interference.

My house is still burning. And where it is whole, I have not found all the rooms, closets and old garbage. There is no longer a complacent order. Havoc has its own integrity. Charred walls accept young vines and holes in roof allow the fragrant spring to freely visit.

My house is not my castle. It is not the precious final coagulated fulfillment of ironed-out dreams. It is a plant, a tree swaying in the evening wind.

(Zinker, 1966-1969.)

Marriage as Deadness

Then we lived with each other. The talk diminished and lost its freshness. We stopped looking at each other with interest and curiosity. Slowly and insidiously we became objects in each other's lives. We used each other. Oh, God, it is unbelievable how we turned all our young goodness into dullness and deadness! And at that time we didn't even know what was happening to us. The old wishes for fulfillment remained deep in our souls but they became isolated from the realities of our daily lives.

How did we abandon each other? Engrossed in our individual life struggles (careers, children), we didn't seem to have the wisdom or insight or energy or awareness to once again turn to each other for feelingful sharing. We didn't become involved in the meaningful events—*gut type* events—of each other's lives. We became cautious and afraid of injuring each other.

You decided without telling me, that I was not what I had been, that I, unlike your tender, ever embracing lover, was really like another man who was selfish, crude, insensitive and critical of everything in you. You proceeded to perceive only those characteristics in me and the rest of me seemed to become weaker in your vision.

I failed you because when you silently resented the imagined or real cruelty in me, I did not question you long enough or persistently enough to get a satisfying answer from you. I took comfort in your silence for it permitted me to daydream or deal with my own struggles without amplifying new problems and conflicts with you. I did not understand the beauty and usefulness of conflict and conflict resolution. Your silence left me feeling vaguely guilty and somehow helpless in my attempts to contact you. You didn't help me and I didn't help you.

The only way I could feel whole with you was in the darkness of night when I could encounter you simply and silently. I knew my power as a man and must have known somewhere in my soul that I could reach you, penetrate you and make it possible for you to renew your love for me. How helpless I felt when your silent crying would awaken me at night! And how guilty—if it was the bastard you knew in me best, perhaps I could be your bastard then. I wanted to be tender. Tenderness never left me and I wanted to explode with anger also. Remember I once did explode but we failed to turn this experience into a real contact with each other. I think you wound up apologizing to me and I stayed righteously indignant and perversely victorious. I did not know that the object of conflict is not individual victory but understanding and the coming together of two people. And I didn't even come close to the understanding of your deep loneliness, self-hate and enormous anger with me.

Yes, we lived together but not with each other or even inside our own selves. We became robots, executors of habits, routines and by now, historically reinforced mutual resentments and emptiness. Marriage. We never fought. We both suffered alone—nothing was said. A death of two spirits. You never told me how you felt about me or how you felt inside. I told you about my creative accomplishments on the outside but I could not manage to be creative with you. You resented my growth because you experienced it as a dimunition of yourself.

> I'm a sleek, sharp piece of wood; my life pounding me into the ground. I watch horrified at my smiles. A lazy brainless primordial protoplasm. I suffer from juices of spring, longing for life more than life—some special transcendent dizziness beyond all beauty.
>
> (Zinker, 1966-1969.)

Marriage as Struggle to Come to Life

Now we come together again. We assault each other angrily. We speak quietly and with great weariness. We renew our enormous and never dying passions. We endure. I have gone into the world; you have not. I have rediscovered myself in the world and you are rediscovering yourself in your new Ulysses. I am your vicarious new lover.

The whole world is my new passion. And although I often feel boundless energy and spirit, I also feel heavy with weariness. I'm a whole man and I'm a fragmented being. I think I still take comfort in retreat, aloneness and silence. I am afraid to work at loving.

We sit, drink, and talk quietly into the night. There are simple remembrances, embarrassed confessions, revelations of secrets long guarded, explosions of re-experienced resentment and bitterness, renewed challenges, hypotheticated *if onlys, what ifs* and *could haves.* We sit or move in silence. We embrace quietly, almost shyly, almost embarrassed to look into each others' faces because they may not know how much two persons have changed.

Then we approach each other with infinite gentleness as if to re-discover each other with the greatest sensitivity possible. Old and familiar touches become rich revelations; new levels of understanding and feeling are reached, like rediscovered paintings or novels.

There is little drama. We make no promises to each other. No re-newed vows. We don't enjoy each other's past mistakes or take gamey advantage of apologies. There are not pacts or conditions or contrived sessions to make things smooth again. We don't even know where this silent rebirth of feeling will lead us, but I feel honest and I experience honesty from you. I enjoy hearing the vi-gnettes of the feelings you have just shared; you are refreshing.

And then you are a woman. How you have grown that way! When we make love I feel for the first time that you really care about every subtle response from me. You want to please me.

Yes, now at this moment we come together and we tap into each others' deeply moving rivers of feeling. Our love is alive again but it will never be the young love of passion without end, of dramatic discovery. Perhaps it will be like the savoring of a newly discovered classical guitar sonata. We will never be children again, my love, and sometimes that feels most comforting.

> I've stopped thinking all the time of what happened yesterday. And stopped asking myself what's going to happen tomorrow. What's happening today, this minute, that's what I care about. I say: "What are you doing at this moment Zorba?" "I'm sleeping." "Well, sleep well." "What are you doing at this moment Zorba?" "I'm kissing a woman." "Well kiss her well, Zorba. And forget all the rest while you're doing it; there's nothing else on earth, only you and her."
>
> (Kazantzakis)

* * *

> When I experience the other fully, acceptingly, when I experience the flow of his feeling, the beauty of movement, of expression, of longing, then I know the meaning of reverence, holiness and the presence of God.
>
> (Zinker, 1966-1969.)

Coming Together

When I take your face into my hands and my fingertips and palms know your hair and your cheeks, I feel as though I am holding all of you. Feeling exquisitely sensitive to your inner life, I also experi-ence a kind of joy that language can't describe; I can only give you some approximation of the word-ingredients of my joy. It says, we are lovely, good, pure, holy, true, real, fulfilled, whole, floating and in touch with all of mankind, past and future. I feel understood and understanding, appreciated and appreciating, adored and adoring (Maslow, 1962).

Looking into your face peacefully and without asking for anything or demanding or even feeling like I must give you something, I become aware how special, unique and rare you are. My sense of your beauty transcends all social norms and aesthetic values.

In this moment of contact between us, I am overcome by the feeling that no one in the universe is like you or like me and the special way I feel right now has never happened and will never occur quite the same way.

Condensation of Life-Cycle

This simple act of holding and gazing is a condensation of all that life is for me; I approach you and you want to be approached. I touch and we both feel deeply. I may speak special words and you hear me. My touching and gazing and words and inner feeling make you feel graceful. Later you may tire of my holding your face or I may choose to move away from you. We move toward some other contact or some other experience.

We came, stayed, felt intensely and we left. And that is life for me. It is the cycle of arriving, experiencing aliveness and departing. This tiny condensation may take only moments and yet it feels panoramically enormous. We have encountered each other (Selver, 1966, 1968).

Holiness

In this moment of complete engrossment, of tranquil-liveliness, when I take you in fully—when I gaze at you with all of me and when every detail of your being gladdens and enhances us—in this moment I know our holiness. We are consecrated, pure, blessed, sacred. In our utter reverence of each other we give recognition and praise to all which exists beyond our lives, to Jehova, God, Buddha, Christ.

How is this moment different from other contacts, casual contacts with people, I ask myself? I can only say what I experience as I will never know precisely what you are experiencing. The feeling is of infinite patience, a kind of serene slowness, looking without examining, touching without exploiting, feeling deeply without protecting or rationalizing, allowing experience to occur without censoring, giving without reservation. I give up my intellect, my computing. I am simple, childlike, naive (Suzuki *et al.*, 1960). This feeling of mine and your tranquil participation in it, your leaning into the process of our union affirms this special sense of blessedness, of holiness.

Sense of the Magic

What we do together is very simple, a gaze, a touch, or a word. Yet the concomitant experience is monumental, rare, unforgettable, religious. Although these simple acts do not define all we experience together, they seem to make the experience. Simple acts are powerful. (In the beginning there was the word. The word was God). Language is powerful. A gaze can hypnotize. A touch can convert deadness into intense liveliness. We perform magic with our gazes, touches and words in this tiny moment because we create a majestic transcendent encounter which moves beyond all recognizable and verbalized ingredients of our experience (Maslow, 1962, 1964).

When I take your face into my hands, my fingertips and palms knowing the shape of your face, I am filled with the sense of magic and holiness. I am no longer simply my*self* and you your*self*. We become part of the cosmos, magical and consecrated.

REFERENCES

Conklin, Holly: Poem (unpublished). Painesville, Lake Erie College, 1967.

Fromm, Eric H.: *The Art of Loving*. New York, Harper & Bros., 1956.

Gibran, Kahlil: *The Prophet*. New York, Knopf, 1960.

Kazantzakis, Nikos: *Zorba the Greek*. New York, Simon and Schuster, 1952.

Maslow, Abraham: *Toward a Psychology of Being*. New York, Van Nostrand, 1962.

Maslow, Abraham: *Religious Values & Peak Experiences*. Ohio State University Press, 1964.

Polster, Erving: Conversations of author with Erving Polster, 1960-1968. Cleveland, Ohio. Also, Polster's Lectures; Gestalt Institute of Cleveland, Cleveland, Ohio.

Rogers, Carl: *On Becoming a Person*. Boston, Houghton, Mifflin, 1961.

Selver, Charlotte: Report on work in sensory awareness and total functioning. From Otto, H. (Ed.): *Exploration in Human Potentialities*. Springfield, Thomas, 1966.

Selver, Charlotte: Workshop of author with Charlotte Selver, Cleveland, November, 1968.

Spitz, Rene: Studies of Children Separated From Parents, London, 1941-43.

Sponde, De Jean (Nugent, Robert, trans.): *Sonnets on Love & Death*, Painesville, Lake Erie College, 1962.

Suzuki, D.T., Fromm, E., and De Martino, R.: *Zen Buddhism & Psychoanalysis*. New York, Harper & Bros., 1960.

Tucker, Gregory: Personal Communications.

Zinker, Joseph C.: Poems. 1966-1969.

CHAPTER V

GESTALT THERAPY AND HUMAN POTENTIALITIES

FREDERICK S. PERLS

G ESTALT THERAPY is one of the rebellious, humanistic, existential forces in psychology which seeks to stem the avalanche of self-defeating, self-destructive forces among some members of our society. It is existential in a broad sense. All schools of existentialism emphasize direct experience, but most of them have some conceptual framework: Kierkegaard has his Protestant theology; Buber his Judaism; Sartre his communism; and Einswanger his psychoanalysis. Gestalt Therapy is fully ontological in that it recognizes both conceptual activity and the biological formation of *Gestalten*. It is thus self-supporting and truly experiential.

Our aim as therapists is to increase human potential through the process of integration. We do this by supporting the individual's genuine interests, desires and needs.

Many of the individual's needs contend with those of society. Competitiveness, need for control, demands for perfection, and immaturity are characteristic of our current culture. Out of this background emerge both the curse and the cause of our neurotic social behavior. In such context no psychotherapy can be successful; no unsatisfactory marriage can be improved. But more importantly, the individual is unable to dissolve his own inner conflicts, and to achieve integration.

Conflicts extend to the external as well. In demanding identification and submission to a self-image, society's neurotic expectations further dissociate the individual from his own nature. The first and last problem for the individual is to integrate within and yet be accepted by society.

Society demands conformity through education; it emphasizes

and rewards development of the individual's intellect. In my language I call the intellect a *built-in computer*. Each culture and the individuals composing it have created certain concepts and images of ideal social behavior, or how the individual *should* function within its framework of reference. In order to be accepted by society, the individual responds with a sum of fixed responses. He arrives at these responses by computing what he considers to be the appropriate reaction. In order to comply with the *should* demands of society, the individual learns to disregard his own feelings, desires, and emotions. He, too, then dissociates himself from being part of nature.

Paradoxically, the more society demands that the individual live up to its concepts and ideas, the less efficiently can the individual function. This basic conflict between the demands of society and one's inner nature results in tremendous expenditures of energy. It is well known that the individual ordinarily uses only 10 to 25 percent of his potential. However, in times of emergency, it is possible for the conditioned responses to collapse. Integration becomes spontaneous. In such situations the individual is able to cope directly with obstacles and, at times, achieve heroic results. Gestalt Therapy seeks to bring about integration with the urgency of emergency situations.

The more the character relies on ready-made concepts, fixed forms of behavior, and computing, the less able is he to use his senses and intuition. When the individual attempts to live according to preconceived ideas of what the world should be like, he brackets off his own feelings and needs. The result of this alienation from one's senses is the blocking off of his potential and the distortion of his perspective.

The critical point during any development, both collectively and individually, is the ability to differentiate between *self*-actualization and the actualization of a *concept*. Expectations are products of our fantasy. The greater the discrepancy between what one can be through one's inborn potential and the superimposed, idealistic concepts, the greater the strain and the likelihood of failure. I give a ridiculously exaggerated example. An elephant wants to be a rose bush; a rose bush wants to be an elephant. Until each resigns to being what they are, both will lead unhappy lives of inferiority. The self-actualizer expects the possible. The one who wants to actualize a concept attempts the impossible.

In responding to *should* demands, the individual plays a role not supported by genuine needs. He becomes both phony and phobic. He shies away from seeing his limitations, and plays roles unsupported by his potential. By seeking cues for behavior from the outside, he computes and responds with reactions not basically his own. He constructs an imaginary ideal of how he should be and not how he actually is.

The concept of perfection is such an ideal. In responding, the individual develops a phony facade to impress others what a good boy he is. Demands for perfection limit the individual's ability to function within himself, in the therapeutic situation, in marriage as well as other social situations.

One can observe in marital difficulties that either one or both of the marriage partners are not in love with the spouse but with an image of perfection. Inevitably, the partner falls short of those expectations. The mutual frustration of not finding perfection results in tension, increased hostility which results in a permanent *status quo*, an impasse, or at best, a useless divorce. The same condition applies to the therapeutic situation. Either a status quo of many years or a change of therapists occurs, but *never* a cure.

By turning his perfectionistic demands toward himself, the neurotic tears himself to pieces in order to live up to his unrealistic ideal. Though perfection is generally labeled an ideal, it is actually a cheap curse which punishes and tortures both the self and others for not living up to an impossible goal.

At least two more phenomena interfere with the development of man's genuine potential. One is the formation of character. The individual then can act only with a limited, fixed set of responses. The other is the phobic attitude which is far more widespread than psychiatry has been willing to recognize thus far.

Freud was the genius of half-truths. His investigations of repression, blocks, and inhibitions reveal his own phobic attitude concerning phobias. Once an impulse becomes dangerous, we turn, according to Freud, actively against it and put a *cordon sanitaire* around it. Wilhelm Reich made this attitude still more explicit in his armor theory. But danger is not always aggressively neutralized.

More often we avoid and flee from it. Thus by avoiding the means
and ways of avoidance, we miss half the tools for a cure.

The organism avoids actual pains. The neurotic avoids imaginary
hurts such as unpleasant emotions. He also avoids taking reasonable
risks. Both interfere with any chance of maturation.

Consequently, in Gestalt Therapy we draw the patient's attention to his avoidance of any unpleasantness. We work through the
subtle machinations of phobic behavior in addition to working
through the blocks, inhibitions, and other protective attitudes.

To work through imaginary pains and unpleasant emotions, we
need a fine balance of frustration and support. Once the patient
feels the essence of the Here and Now and I and Thou, he begins
to understand his phobic behavior.

At first the patient will do anything to keep his attention from
his actual experiences. He will take flight into memory and expectation (past and future); into the flight of ideas (free associations);
intellectualizations or making a case of right and wrong. Finally,
he encounters the holes in his personality with an awareness of
nothing (no-thing-ness), emptiness, void, and the impasse.

At last, the patient comes to realize the hallucinatory character
of his suffering. He discovers that he does not have to torture
himself. He acquires a greater tolerance for frustration and imaginary pain. At this point, he begins to mature.

I define maturity as the transition from environmental support
to self-support. In Gestalt Therapy, maturity is achieved by developing the individual's own potential through decreasing environmental support, increasing his frustration tolerance, and by
debunking his phony *playing* of infantile and adult roles.

Resistance is great because the patient has been conditioned to
manipulate his environment for support. He does this by acting
helpless and stupid; he wheedles, bribes, and flatters. He *is not*
infantile, but plays an infantile and dependent role expecting to
control the situation by submissive behavior. He also plays the
roles of an infantile adult. It is difficult for him to realize the
difference between mature behavior and *playing an adult*. With
maturation the patient is increasingly able to mobilize spontaneously his own resources in order to deal with the environment.
He learns to stand on his own feet thus becoming able to cope

with his own problems as well as the exigencies of life.

Human potential is decreased both by inappropriate demands of society and by the inner conflict. Freud's parable of the two servants quarreling, with the resultant inefficiency, is again, in my opinion, but a half-truth. Actually, it is the masters who quarrel. In this case the opposing masters are what Freud named *Superego* and *Id*. The *Id* in Freud's concept is a conglomeration of instincts and repressed memories. In actuality, we observe in each and every case that the Superego is opposed by a personalized entity which might be called *Infraego*. In my language I call the opposing masters Top Dog and Under Dog. The struggle between the two is both internal and external.

Top Dog can be described as righteous, bullying, punishing, authoritarian, and primitive. Top Dog commands continually with such statements as "you should," "you ought to," and "why don't you?" Oddly enough, we all so strongly identify with our inner Top Dog that we no longer question its authority. We take its righteousness for granted.

Under Dog develops great skill in evading Top Dog's commands. Only half-heartedly intending to comply with the demands, Under Dog answers: "yes, but . . .," "I try so hard but next time I'll do better," and "manana." Under Dog usually gets the better of the conflict.

In other words, Top and Under Dogs are actually two clowns performing their weird and unnecessary plays on the stage of the tolerant and mute self. Integration, or cure, can be achieved only when the need for mutual control between Top and Under Dogs ceases. Only then will the two masters mutually listen. Once they come to their senses (in this case listening to each other), does the door to integration and unification open. The chance of making a whole person out of a split becomes a certainty. The impasse of the *status quo*, or the eternal conflict, of the non-ending therapy can be overcome.

A Gestaltist integration technique is dream work. We do not play psychoanalytical interpretation games. I have the suspicion that the dream is neither a fulfilled wish nor a prophecy of the future. To me, it is an existential message. It tells the patient what his situation in life is, and especially, how to change the nightmare of his existence into becoming aware of, and taking his historical place in life. In a successful cure, the neurotic awakens from his trance of delusions. In Zen Buddhism, the moment is called the great awakening (*satori*). During Gestalt Therapy the patient experiences a number of lesser awakenings. In coming to his senses, he frequently sees the world brightly and clearly.

In actual practice I let the patient act out all the details of his dream. As therapists we do not imagine we know more than the patient does himself. We assume each part of the dream is a projection. Each fragment of the dream, be it person, prop, or mood, is a portion of the patient's *alienated* self. Parts of the self are made to encounter other parts. The primary encounter, of course, is between Top Dog and Under Dog.

To illustrate the method of integrating Top and Under Dogs by working through a dream, I relate a case of a patient who impressed everybody with his psychotic eccentricities. During one of my group sesisons, he related a dream in which he saw a young man enter a library, throw books about, shout, and scream. When the librarian, an elderly spinster, rebuked him, he reacted with continued erratic behavior. In desperation the librarian summoned the police.

I directed my patient to act out and experience the encounter between the boy, (Under Dog), and the librarian and police (Top Dogs). In the beginning the confrontation was belligerent and uselessly consuming of time and energy. After participating in the hostile encounter for two hours, the different parts of my patient were able to stop fighting and listen to each other. True listening *is* understanding. He came to recognize by playing crazy he could outwit his Top Dog, because the irresponsible person is not punished. Following this successful integration, the patient no longer needed to act crazy in order to be spontaneous. As a result, he is now a freer and more amenable person.

When Top Dog feeds Under Dog expectations of success, results, improvements, and changes, Under Dog generally responds with pseudocompliance or sabotage. The result is inefficiency and spite. If the Under Dog sincerely tries to comply, he has the choice between an obsessional neurosis, flight into illness or nervous breakdown. *The road to Hell is paved with good intentions.*

Externally, Top and Under Dogs struggle for control as well. Husband and wife, therapist and patient, employer and employees play out roles of mutual manipulation.

The basic philosophy of Gestalt Therapy is that of nature . . . differentiation and integration. Differentiation by itself leads to polarities. As dualities, these polarities will easily fight and paralyze one another. By integrating opposite traits, we make the person whole again; for instance, weakness and bullying integrate as silent firmness.

Such a person will have the perspective to see the total situation (a *Gestalt*) without losing the details. With this improved orientation, he is in a better position to cope with the situation by *mobilizing his own resources*. He no longer reacts with fixed responses (character), and preconceived ideas. He doesn't cry for environmental support, because he can do for himself. He no longer lives motivated by fears of impending catastrophes. He can now assess reality by *experimenting with possibilities*. He will *give up* control-madness and let the *situation* dictate his actions.

The ability to resign, to let go of obsolete responses, of exhausted relationships, and of tasks beyond one's potential, is an essential part of the wisdom of living.

CHAPTER VI

FRAGMENTS OF GESTALT THEORY

RAINETTE FANTZ

WHENEVER I AM ASKED to talk briefly on the subject of Gestalt Theory, I think first of two things, the word Gestalt, itself, and the concept of figure-ground. What is a Gestalt? It is a cohesive one. It derives from the German word, gestalten, which signifies form and means to *make a form* or a *comprehensive one.* If, for example, you think of a melody as a Gestalt, you become aware that any number of things may be done to it without changing its cohesive oneness; you may vary the key in which it is written, you may vary the rapidity with which it is played, you may play it loudly, softly or on a series of different instruments and yet retain unchanged the melodic line. It remains recognizable. So too does an individual. He may vary his mood, he may vary his responsiveness, his clothes or his words. He still remains John or Jeremy. There is more to a melody or a person than its various components—there is a wholeness.

It is important to remember that the way in which this gestalt is perceived is a function of a figure-ground relationship and the direct result of the focus of attention. Let me try to make this more clear. All happenings, or perceptions, occur in a field with various elements in the field shifting from foreground to background to make different forms or gestalts.

Say, for example, that I am talking to you. If the things I say to you are interesting or important, you will perceive me as figural and yourselves as background. If on the other hand, you do not find me interesting or are preoccupied instead with what is going to happen to you when this workshop really starts rolling, your own feelings of discomfort and/or apprehension will become figural—in other words attended to—and I or my voice or words will become background. Even my image may blur.

I can illustrate this phenomenon perhaps more graphically with a simple set of parallel lines. If you look at the lines in one way, you will see:

which probably appear to you as five pairs of lines set a short distance apart from one another. The lines because of their proximity to one another are seen as figural upon a white background.

If I quickly add another series of lines, the figure becomes:

which then appears to be a series of four rectangles. As you can see, what was formerly figure has become ground, blank spaces between the series of rectangles. The incomplete rectangles at the ends of the rows may be completed in the mind's eye thru the principle of praegnanz—or becoming. The same sorts of changes in perception occur in human relationships.

Now the academic Gestalt psychologists never applied the principles of Gestalt formation, the principles of similarity, symmetry, proximity and praegnanz, to organic perceptions, namely, those perceptions which pertain to one's own feelings, emotion, or body awareness. Nor did they integrate the problems of motivation with those of perception. It remained for Frederick Perls to do so. By conceiving of the need-fulfillment pattern in the individual as a process of Gestalt formation and destruction, he was able to make the role of perception, so useful to the academicians, available to the field of human behavior—always retaining as a critical element the factor of attention.

Let us go back to our musical example. Say that it is fairly late in the evening, that I have had dinner a number of hours ago and that I am sitting in a comfortable chair, in a softly lit room listening to Beethoven's Ninth, the third movement. The room, the chair, my own body are background. My felt need is for music and the music is figural. As I listen, however, I become aware of slight rumblings in my stomach and a feeling of emptiness. I ignore this and return to the music, but Beethoven has lost some of his savor; my attention becomes divided between my ear and my stomach and now a new phenomenon occurs—I suddenly see a vision—a jar of pickled herring unopened in the refrigerator. This is followed by a new sensation, my mouth begins to water and I can almost taste the onions on my tongue. Needless to say, Beethoven is quickly becoming background. I get up, walk into the kitchen, put some herring and a piece of rye bread on a plate and happily fall to. At this moment the food has become figural. Finished with it, I walk back into the living room where the Ode to Joy is now filling the house, sink happily back into my chair and allow the music again to fill my consciousness.

In Gestalt psychotherapy we describe this process as the progressive formation and destruction of perceptual and motor gestalts. As you can see, the need tends to organize both the perceptual qualities of the individual's experience and his motor behavior. In other words, the need energizes behavior and organizes it on the subjective-perceptual side and the objective-motor side.*

Once we become aware of how this process works, we find ourselves possessed of an autonomous criterion of adjustment. We need no longer decide whether an individual is mature or immature by certain cultural standards. We need not decide whether the individual conforms to society. The important thing is that in the integrated person this process is always going on without interruption. New figures are constantly being formed; when the needs which organize their formation are satisfied, these figures are destroyed and replaced by new ones. But we must remember that unless the need is clear, it cannot energize the fruitful behavior necessary for biological or psychological survival.

Only as the individual can extract from his environment the things which he needs in order to survive, to feel comfortable, to be interested in the world around him, will he be able to live on a satisfactory biological level on the one hand and a satisfactory psychological level on the other. One cannot breathe without breathing in the environment; one cannot get affection without the

*Richard W. Wallen, *Gestalt Psychology and Gestalt Therapy*, Paper presented at the Ohio Psychological Association Meeting, 1957.

knowledge that one wants it, nor without the ability to communicate this want. This necessitates that the individual be sufficiently aggressive to interrupt his environment. In other words he may be impolite and healthy or polite and neurotic.

It is good to know that there are clues available which tell us that all is going well in the formation and destruction of gestalts. For one thing, when this process is proceeding smoothly, the figure and ground become sharply differentiated; the individual knows what he wants; his field is not cluttered and only one thing draws his attention. For another, his motor behavior becomes well-organized, unified, coherent and directed toward the satisfaction of his need. The perceptual system and the motoric feed one into the other.

One of my most vivid memories of this kind of integrated behavior goes back to the time when my daughter, Lori, was first being toilet trained. At that time I had an office in my home and saw most of my patients there. Lori had learned very early that when my office door was closed she was not, under any circumstances, to come into the room, and up until that time she had never tried to do so. But she was also very involved with the idea of dry diapers and accomplishment. On this particular day she had finally used her potty successfully and was so enraptured of the idea and so motivated to tell me all about it immediately that she came running down the hall, banged wildly on my closed door and shouted again and again, "Mommy, Mommy, Lori made trickle in potty!" Obviously none of the shoulds had as yet forced her to repress her exhuberance and spontaneity, nor to interrupt her need satisfactions.

All of us know, however, from our own experiences, that the smooth progression from formation to destruction of gestalts breaks down at times, often because the aforementioned shoulds get in the way. Again we are provided with clues which point up this failure. These clues can be seen both subjectively by the individual and objectively by the therapist or other interested observer. From the point of view of the subject there is confusion. He does not know what he wants; he does not know what is important; he cannot decide among alternatives. Since there is no sense of clarity, his attention is divided among fuzzy non-choices.

The observer on the other hand is presented with fixed and repetitive behavior. It's as if the subject were saying, "If at first you don't succeed, try the same thing again." The observer is also faced—or not faced—with lack of interest and signs of effort as if the subject were saying "nothing is really exciting; I have to force myself to do anything at all." Accompanying this perseveration and lack of affect is, not unnaturally, a poor level of organization of both thought and speech.

Before we can deal constructively with the interferences that prevent need—fulfillment, we must examine what they are. We have found these interferences to be of three kinds. In the first place our subject is plagued by poor perceptual contact with the external world, that is to say, the space he inhabits, the people and things that he encounters incompletely and the sounds, smells and sights which infringe on him from outside the self. At the same time or at alternating times, this same subject may maintain poor contact with his own body. A therapist may observe that the individual with whom he's working does not look at him directly nor at other significant portions of his immediate environment. He may not be aware of what he is doing with his hands nor of how his own voice sounds.

Because of this lack of awareness of both inner and outer stimuli, our subject is kept—or keeps himself—from encountering his own needs. If he does not encounter the need, he prevents himself in turn from giving any open expression to it. By failing to express it, he militates against its ever being satisfied. Obviously, if it does not get satisfied, it cannot get discharged but remains lurking somewhere in the person's global field interfering with whatever other need might be able to organize the field in a clear-cut, coherent way.

One of the chief mechanisms for preventing the awareness of one's own needs is repression. Repression is seen by the gestalt therapist as primarily a motor process, a muscular phenomenon. In order for a need to be expressed, some movement normally has to take place, either a gross body movement which moves one from one place to another or a fine and subtle movement which may only involve the twitch of an eyebrow. Any response—be it to the outside environment or to one's own inner climate—tends to play itself out on a motor level and can only be inhibited by contracting antagonistic muscles.

This can best be illustrated by using some emotion such as anger or, in other words, the need to get angry. When one thinks of anger one envisions a frown, or the pulling down of the muscles of the mouth, clenched teeth, and the hand striking out in the urge to hit. But when anger, appropriate or otherwise, is somehow unacceptable to the person beginning to feel it, it is stopped by the smooth brow, the smiling mouth and the tightly clenched hands. If this muscular response to an emerging feeling is indulged in habitually, the person using it eventually becomes quite unaware of his own original impulse. He ultimately becomes unaware as well of the grimace on his face which started out to be a smile. In this way all sorts of impulse unawarenesses are maintained by chronic muscular contractions which, in turn, have been forgotten by the individual using them.

Very well then. Given the individual's poor perceptual contact with the external world and his own body, given the individual's difficulty in allowing open expression of his own needs or even the ability to experience them because of chronic muscular contractions, where do we as therapists find ourselves? Happily, I can say that the Gestalt therapist works almost exclusively in the present. Instead of saying, as did the Freudians, "Where Id was, let Ego be," we are inclined to say, "I and Thou; Here and Now." Although the past is important in special circumstances, particularly when the individual is so stuck there that he cannot confront current realities, usually the therapist is able to work with what is immediately in front of him. He has the opportunity to see the confusions as they arise and so see what the person is doing to cause his own confusion. Even dreams and fantasies which were used chiefly as interpretive tools by the analysts may be used as guides to the subject's present life by dealing with the different facets of them as if they were the subject's own projections.

Much of the therapist's activity is directed to the breaking up of the individual's chronically poorly organized field. He does this by isolating portions of the field into smaller sub-units which better allow for direct attention. To do this he may employ what we sometimes call a shuttle technique, that is, a technique which permits the person to move from the event he is talking about to the pain in his own gut, to his fantasy about the therapist's motives, back to the feeling he may be having about himself at that particular moment in time.

As each new figure emerges, the therapist will attempt to heighten it, perhaps by having the subject exaggerate a movement which may accompany it, perhaps by examining the resistances which the subject affords himself. Let us say for example that the person looks sad, that his eyes are misty but that he never quite cries. The therapist may ask not "Why don't you cry"—because very likely the person doesn't really know, but "How do you prevent yourself from crying?" In trying to answer this, the individual may discover that he's been holding his breath or that the muscles of his face are rigid from smiling. The object of this is not to take away the resistances of the resistor if he still has a real need for them, nor to destroy his ability to control his own behavior, but to make him aware of what he is doing so that he may choose what he does.

Finally, it must be remembered that just as the client is there with his frailities and hang-ups, so is the therapist there with his. Both are there together as real human beings whose only live point of contact during that hour is the significant other. Initially, as in all human contact, there is a barrier, more or less permeable, which can only truly be bridged through feelings shared and emotions bared—not only by the client but by the therapist as well. Therapy is not a one-way street.

CHAPTER VII

POLARITIES: DIFFERENTIATION AND INTEGRATION

RAINETTE FANTZ

ONE OF THE AREAS that lends itself with great richness to the therapist who enjoys setting up experiments is that of polarities. I find it extremely interesting that in four books written wholly or in part by Frederick Perls, there is no notation in the indices which pertains to this concept. And yet it is a concept which permeated much of his working style and which contributed heavily to his theories about dreams.

Of course, the concept and use of polarities did not originate with Perls although he placed great emphasis on it. The opposites of Good and Evil, of God and the Devil, were certainly prevalent in the Christian bible as were the antitheses of ying and yang in Buddhist thought. In psychology I encountered polarities first in my readings of Jung, primarily in his presentation of the archetypes. If you recall, Jung described his archetypes as the structural components of the collective unconscious, a universal thought form or idea which contains large elements of emotion. Among these archetypes, he described the eternal compassionate mother as opposed to the devouring witch, birth as opposed to death, the hero contrasted with the child, and God as antagonistic to the devil. He posited that all these characters existed within us as more or less well-delineated facets of our personality. Jung stressed that the basic aspects of the psyche which the person has denied in his conscious living tend to grow in the unconscious as a shadow tends to reflect the mass of the *real* thing. For example, the person who typically thinks without feeling casts a long shadow in the feeling area. Because it is kept unconscious, Jung felt that the feeling area tended to remain primitive and so could grow to monstrous proportions. Therefore any eruption of feeling would tend to be experienced as fearful.

Jung believed that personality contains polar tendencies. He believed that a psychological theory of personality must be founded on the principle of opposition or conflict because the tensions created by conflicting elements are the very essence of life. Without tension he felt there would be no energy and therefore no personality. Nor did he believe that the contest between rational and irrational forces of the psyche ever ceased.

It is important to remember that polar elements not only oppose one another, they also attract and seek one another, and that a balanced and integrated personality can only result through a synthesis of these polar traits. Now whether or not Perls' idea about polarities derived from those of Jung, they both stressed the same principle, namely differentiation and integration. As Perls describes it, "The basic philosophy of Gestalt Therapy is that of nature—differentiation and integration. Differentiation by itself leads to polarities. As dualities, those polarities will easily fight and paralyze one another. By integrating opposite traits, we make the person whole again."*

Now Perls' favorite technique for getting at these opposing traits was the Top-Dog, Under-Dog experiment. He equated the Top Dog essentially with the super-ego and characterized it as the autocrat or dictator, the part of the self which judges and tells one what to do. The Top Dog is always righteous, has the right to criticize, to nag, to put one on the defensive. Yet in spite of Top Dog's apparent power, Perls felt that the Under Dog always won out—usually through sabotage, evasion, postponement, just as do the masses under the heel of the dictator. But the winning was basically a negative thing since the person merely succeeded in stopping himself from doing what one part of himself wanted to do. Perls felt that the solution could be found in a dialogue between the two selves represented by the Top Dog, Under Dog, a dialogue that could lead to integration.

Interestingly when the two parts of the self start talking, almost always at first neither side listens. One possible reason for this is

*Frederick Perls, *Gestalt Therapy and Human Potentialities* (Esalen Paper No. 1, June, 1965), p. 8.

that one dog or the other is often an introject which the individual has neither fully incorporated nor spit out. Not so oddly, then, the person is often unaware that there is someone else living in his skin. In a recent workshop I did, there was a very attractive young divorcee who wanted to get married again, but who discovered that she was unable to do so because the moment she became really important to a man, she not only lost interest in him but started treating him like dirt. She found this terribly upsetting but was apparently impotent to do anything about it. Now it was obvious that there were two parts to this woman in conflict, and my theory was that the lonely *wanting a man* self was essentially valid but that there was a highly potent Top Dog that was somehow sabotaging her moves toward union. So I asked her to engage in a dialogue with herself which, after some demurring, she proceeded to do.

U. D.: I'm so lonely, I wish I had someone to come home to at the end of the day.

T. D.: You have the children; that should certainly be enough for you.

U. D.: I'm all right during the day as long as I'm busy and at night I'm all right if I'm tired enough, but . . .

T. D.: Don't be such a baby; you should certainly be more self-sufficient than that!

U. D.: But I don't want to be self-sufficient! I want a man to take care of me, and make some decisions for me, and . . .

T. D.: Decisions, ha! What man is really strong enough to make your decisions? They're all weak—you'll end up taking care of him!

U. D.: I won't! Paul was wonderful about decisions, he made everything so easy for me, I really loved him until . . .

T. D.: Yah, until! Until he couldn't make a move without you; until you could do nothing except worry about his falling apart. You aren't any good for a man.

U. D.: But I want to be! I hate myself when I turn on men this way, when I can't give them the time of day after they've been so wonderful.

T. D.: Forget it baby; go it alone. You can do it; there's something wrong with all of them!

By this time my gal was practically in tears and it was evident that her Top-Dog, Under-Dog dialogue had tapped some other source of pain. I asked her who her Top Dog reminded her of and she said that it was her father who had died some years ago but who had treated her like a princess. He had taken her out instead of her mother, had taken her to concerts and opera and had planned to take her to see the world. Instead he had died in agony in her arms.

So I had her change the experiment and play her father in dialogue with herself. This part was fun. Because once her father was outside of her she was able to see him as the loving but very clever man who with great finesse managed to sabotage every relationship she briefly entered into. She did a beautiful job imitating his deprecating attitude toward her boyfriends, his building up of her ego, and his fostering of her dependency on himself. She was also able to see how she played along with this, because, in essence, he gave her everything she wanted—except sex—which while he was still alive she hadn't acknowledged as important. In addition, she became aware in the course of the experiment that she *still kept him alive* inside of her where he (as her Top Dog) was desperately interfering with her life. It was time for her to say goodbye.

But this, by herself, she could not do. She could only dissolve in tears. So I once again changed the experiment and had one of the men in the group play her father, which he did with great skill. He was able somehow to convey all the wants of the father, his desire never to be supplanted, his need to go on living in her, without in any way removing from her the necessity of making a decision in regard to him. She in turn was able to say that she still loved him, that he had been very important to her but that he no longer really gave her anything. She could say that her only choice was to keep him alive and never have anyone else or allow him to die so that she could discover someone who in some way could fill her emptiness— if not as he had, at least with some measure of fulfillment. And she finally did choose to say goodbye.

Now the experiments I just cited point up several things quite clearly. The Top-Dog, Under-Dog stage illustrates how two parts of the personality can emerge with some vividness. It also illustrates the fairly easily detectable presence of an introject. Finally, it shows how an introject, once recognized, can be dealt with and either digested or spit up. It is well to remember, and I cannot stress this too strongly, that it is difficult, if not impossible, to give up something which you do not know is there.

I find it quite fascinating that so often in the Top-Dog, Under-Dog experiments one finds an introject as representative of one of the dogs. These introjects, however, need not always be spit out; sometimes it is incumbent on one to thoroughly digest them so that one can utilize one's untapped power. An excellent demonstration of this occurred in another workshop I conducted somewhat earlier.

One of the girls in the group was a very pretty, sweet-looking youngster who consistently sat just outside the circle of events. Occasionally she appeared on the verge of tears but practically never said anything unless asked directly and then only briefly. On the last day of the workshop, fearing that she would leave more depressed than she was when she came in, I tried to get with how she was feeling. She was feeling miserable. She was angry and unable to vent her anger; she wanted to scream and couldn't allow herself to scream. She had spent three days being very nice to very nice people when all she wanted to do was rail at them loudly and, failing this, go hide in her room.

Again I had her start with Top-Dog, Under-Dog dialogue and play her *nice* self against her *bitchy* self.

U. D.: What makes you so nasty all the time? I don't even like the sound of you.

T. D.: I hate nice people; I just want to strike out at them, tear them limb from limb.

U. D.: You're shitty when you're like that. I don't see how anyone can stand you! Why don't you go hide away till you're bearable?

T. D.: Talk about bearable! Wow! Do you put on an act—sugar wouldn't melt—who do you think you're fooling?

U. D.: There you go again—always claiming to see right through me. Man, I need you like a hole in the head. At least people like me!

T. D.: Like you! They don't even know you! At least I'm *real* even if I'm miserable. All you do is smile or cower in corners. No guts!

U. D.: Oh, you have guts all right! But where would you be without me? Alone, that's where! No one could stand you for two minutes! I can't stand you. I hate you!

By this time both dogs were screaming at one another, and it rather looked as if they could continue to do so for some time to come. So I asked Janey who she *really* wanted to scream at. And she screamed at me, "My mother! She's terrible—you can't believe how terrible. Oh, I can't stand her; I can't stand her; I can't *stand* her!" At which point she buried her face in her hands and shuddered. It was obviously time for the dialogue with mama, so we switched to that, Jane playing both parts.

Mama: Jane, you'd better go speak to your math teacher tomorrow, or you'll never get an A in that course.

Jane: I don't care about the A, Mom. I'm doing fine.

Mama: (Whiny voice) How can you say you're doing fine? All you want to seem to do is have fun! After I worked and slaved to send you to school. And what school do you choose? A silly little college in Indiana instead of all the good places you could go. With trash!

Jane: Mama, I'm not coming home this summer. I don't want to drown this summer at home with you.

Mama: But I expect you home; everyone expects you home. Why, I've sewed three new dresses, and I want everyone to see you in them.

Jane: I don't want the dresses! I want to do things for myself. I hate you taking care of me. Ever since I was little you wanted to live my life for me.

Mama: I want you to live up to your potential, I want you to do the things I didn't do, have the things I didn't have. You're all I have! I want you to be a lady!

Jane: That's all you ever say! Mind your manners! Mind your grammar! Mix with the right people. Be sweet; be nice. I could die of it!

Here, she turned to me and said, "You're so sweet! How can you be so sweet? I don't understand it!" Whereupon my co-leader cleverly said, "Jane, you be Rennie and, Rennie, you do Jane." So, sort of blinkingly, we switched.

Me: Good grief, you're sweet! Ugh.

Jane: Well, it's easy when you understand everyone.

Me: Understand! You just sit there and absorb—with that kind look on your face. It turns my stomach.

Jane: (smiles and nods her head)

Me: My God, you sit there like some damned powder puff with no guts. I could just blow you away.

Jane: I'm not really a powder puff, I'm. . .

Me: So okay, not a powder puff, a pillow maybe; one you can pound and pound and it always goes back into shape! I'm so tired of pounding on you.

Jane: You could always stop.

Me: I won't stop! I'll make you budge somehow. You're killing yourself! You're sitting there damping all your fire and vitality; you're making yourself in a nothing, a shadow, and if you keep it up, you'll die!

Jane: Are you still me, or are you *you* now?

Me: I'm both. I'm the part of you that can't tolerate being stifled, I'm the part of you that's fighting for your life. I'm your power that's bubbling up and being quashed by your mama in you. But I'm also myself, my self who believes all the things I'm saying to you.

Jane: I like that. I like you when you talk like that. Maybe I could like myself if I could do it too.

So, perhaps we had got through the impasse. You may have noticed, though, that the pathway was at no point particularly straightforward. To begin we had the polarities of nice versus bitchy, but it was quite unclear what generated either the niceness or the bitchiness. Gradually, with the shift to mama, who incidentally was not quite the kind of *terrible* I would have expected from Jane's tremendous expressed rage with her, we discover that the bitchiness comes from mama but is disguised as caring. But also from mama comes the introject of nice, which mama, the Superego, has demanded from her for years. So we have two introjects, both acquired from mama, and both impossible to digest since she cannot stand mama, nor allow herself to be in any way like her. Consequently, she cuts herself off from her own power by cutting herself off from her own aggression. Happily in this instance she could identify with my bitchiness and possibly allow herself the prerogative of using it since she had enjoyed it in me. If she becomes able to do this, she may also end up by enjoying her own niceness.

Needless to say, experiments with opposites do not always work out so neatly. Just a week or so ago, I was seeing a fairly new client in therapy and trying to get some kind of a fix on the aggression which he took great pains to keep under wraps. He had an almost constant tremor in his right hand which two neurologists had labeled psychological and due to tension, but I had no clear idea of what the tension was about. On this particular day he had related to me a dream which was largely a melange of color. In it he was aware of a blob of red-orange which he could only conceptualize as Aquarius —Aquarius being the zodiacal sign of his beloved. Next to it was a blackish snake-like form which he identified as Scorpio and, to finish off the triumvirate, a red crab-shaped form which he interpreted as Cancer, his own astrological sign.

Unwilling to get caught up in all the symbolism the dream presented, I asked him to describe himself as the different parts of the dream and to start with the snake-like form. He began, "I am the personification of evil. I am out to get you, Mary, (the red-orange blob) and to bend you to my will. I will drag you in the dirt and then cast you from me." All of which was said in a low, level voice with little expression. I remarked about the incongruence of his words and his feeling tone and asked him if he could make himself sound more evil and more gleeful. Which, to my surprise, he proceeded to do. "I will use you for my own satisfactions; I will degrade you and revile you and then grind you in the dust! There is nothing you can do to resist me! I will besmirch you, defile you and then toss you aside." His tone throughout this second attempt had become more and more unctuous; his expression had become more gloating. He had started to rub his hands together in satisfaction; his tremor had all but disappeared. I applauded his characterization and then asked him to be the red crab.

He again began in a somewhat droning sing-song, "Never fear, fair maiden, I will rescue you! I am your knight in shining armor and I and my trusty steed will ride to your defense. I will slay the villainous dragon and restore you to honour and chastity." I remarked that he certainly sounded peaceful for someone about to go into battle, to say nothing of sounding dull. He explained to me that he was having all kinds of trouble (indeed, his hand was trembling again) and that although he could think about going into battle and even consider having won, he could not get with the actual battle at all. So I said, "Fine, why don't you really try to do that? Be both the evil serpent and the stalwart knight and have a dialogue one with the other." He made several abortive attempts to do so, all the time getting tighter and less and less real. When I commented on this, he looked particularly troubled and began to stammer. "I can't do it. I just can't do it; I'm getting more and more panicky!" In truth he appeared unusually upset, and I asked him what he was afraid might happen. He responded, "I don't know—I just feel as if I'll explode, as if something in my head would just burst, and I'll, I'll . . . ." "As if you'll flip your lid?" I asked. He sort of nodded and I was quiet for a minute with fantasies of broken crab shell all over the room and shining armor (note the analogy) falling in shards and a possible serpent triumphant. But I didn't push it. A part of me respected his very real fright, and I withdrew. Nevertheless I did share with him, a little later, my feeling that all his vitality and power were bound up in what he considered the evil part of himself and that we would have to search out constructive ways to let it emerge.

As you can see, we arrived at no simple denouement; we never got around to working with the third part of the self, the part openly vulnerable to attack, and we even ended the session on a distinct note of uneasiness. Still, I have received no frightened phone calls in the middle of the night as is sometimes his wont, and I have a somewhat clearer picture as to where to move. Needless to say, I also have a hodgepodge of symbolic and metaphorical material which I can, if I choose, use in different sorts of experiments.

Which brings me in a somewhat roundabout way to what Perls talked about as integration. He stated that in psychotherapy we look for the urgency of unfinished—or perhaps even undeveloped situations in the present situation. By present experimentation with new attitudes and new materials from the experiment, we aim at new unities. It is not that the patient remembers himself as the Freudians might posit, but rather that he discovers and shapes himself.

As I have indicated, the resisting part of the personality has vitality and strength and often many other estimable qualities which are mired down in a host of introjects. Although it may take a long time and much energy to form a complete whole out of the disintegrated parts of the personality, to fail to do so would be to accept a depriva-tion in the self which is unnecessary and painful. It often seems to me that work with polarities is the tool par excellence for integration.

CHAPTER VIII

JACKIE: AN EXPERIENCE IN SELF-APPLIED GESTALT THERAPY*

JACQUELINE SNYDER

TONIGHT I am going to try an experiment about using Gestalt Therapy on myself. I made a remark the other day to Doug Stephenson that Jim is putty in my hands and Doug said, "Why don't you be the putty." I'm going to try and do this, and I am going to try to be me and the putty, and me talking back and forth and see what happens. Now let's see if I can get into it. I'll start with me. (Jackie)

Jackie: Jim has always been able to manipulate me extremely easily. I have allowed him to manipulate me. I have, as I said before, been putty in his hands. I feel like putty in his hands. He tells me, in his manipulative way, to do something for him, and I just do it. I don't even stop to think about how I'm feeling at the moment, I just simply do it.

Putty: I'm a blob, a blob of putty. I can be molded, shaped, worked, flattened out, rolled into a ball, tossed around, thrown on the floor, scraped off the floor, picked up again, slammed around the room, spread across anything. (Pause) I can be molded into a figure of a waitress, the dishwasher, the banker, the bookkeeper, (Pause) the worker of any kind, (Pause) that Jim needs. (Pause) He wants me to be the putty that he can mold in any shape or form that is beneficial to him.

Jackie: I'm Jackie, I don't want to be putty. (Pause) I don't want to be putty. (Very sternly) I don't want to be shaped, formed, manipulated into something I don't want to be.

*A verbatim transcription of tape recorded session.

Putty: That's bullshit; you love it. Where he is concerned you love it. He can easily trap you into anything he wants to do. (Matter-of-fact voice, dogmatic) You can stand by and you can say I'm not going to, I'm not going to, I'm not going to, but you (emphatically) do it. You always do it. You love it!

Jackie: You're right; I do it, and I do seem to love it. I don't understand it. (Sigh, pause) I don't understand why I like it. Because when he isn't here and I'm on my own and I am independent, I can be a strong person. I am a strong person (definite). I am doing the things I want to do; I have forced myself into independence; I've worked hard at it; I don't like it sometimes. I don't like my independence (Quietly).

Putty: No you don't like your independence. You loved it when you could depend on your dad. (Pause) He could make your big decisions for you. He handled your money for you; he gave you money when you wanted it; you never had to go without; you were spoiled. (Silence) You were independent up to a point. You were free when you were independent; you were free, free to do the things you wanted to do. (Pause) Oh, you had your ups and downs with him but nevertheless, he did allow you a lot of freedom, and he also gave you the security you needed. The security that you were loved, that you had a home and a place that you belonged, a place to hang your hat, money when you needed it. (Pause) He was always there to help you when you needed it.

Putty: (Whispering, self-pitying voice) . . . and now you don't have anybody, girl, to help . . . just yourself. (Long period of crying and sobbing)

Jackie: This is ridiculous. (Trying to laugh with heavy breathing)

Putty: Shit, what are you going to do about it?

Jackie: It's just, shit, I don't know, I'm afraid. (Silence) I guess I am going to think about my strengths . . . yeah . . . my strengths . . . I sure got myself this far on my own strengths. Pretty damn good. (Sigh) Oh, boy. (Pause) I sure don't feel like putty. Not when I knew I could do it, do what I have done, to bring me this far on my own. (Pause) (Sigh) (Clear the throat) Yeah, hell, I feel pretty good, now that I think what I have done for myself. (Silence) Yeah, I've been able to stick it out here. Yeah, I've been able to stick it out here. (Sigh) Scrimping, saving, saving hell! I don't save a thing; it all goes. Boy, I'm grateful for Jimmy to send me what little he sends. And I am grateful, grateful for dad to have left what he left. God, if he hadn't (Pause) ... If he hadn't been able to be strong and do the things that he did, he wouldn't have gone as far as he did and he has taught me an awful lot and helped me with my strengths. (Sobbing) When it comes right down to it, what I've learned is to be strong through him. (Crying) Shit! There I go again. (Sobbing and sighing) (Silence) Damn, I am strong . . . and I've got; . . . I am a person with a lot of good ideas . . . and a pretty good head on her shoulders. I'm beginning to straighten a whole lot of things out that I've wondered about for a long, long time. (Pause) And I have come this far, by damn I can keep on going! (Pause) I can somehow gather the strength that I need, and go along with my feelings and express my feelings . . . and I realized today when I finally got myself together to sit down and write that letter to Jimmy, that I was headed in the right direction as far as my relationship is concerned with him. I expressed my feelings . . . I expressed my feelings toward Jim about the things that he failed to do that *I* want him to do, if we are going to be able to continue this relationship. I want him to be able to express his feelings towards me and open up communication between us. I don't know if he will be able to or not, but at least he knows what I want. And I also told him about his unkept promises that I have been listening to for 13 years. How I, . . . how I despise his unkept promises, and I won't put up with that crap. Well . . . (Pause) . . . I guess I'm not so much putty in his hands—at least when he's away—it's pretty safe this way . . . letter writing . . . maybe by the time he gets back here I will have gathered enough strength to be able to carry on in a strong way. I think I will.

CHAPTER IX

THE GROUND RULES IN GESTALT THERAPY

JERRY A. GREENWALD

Introduction

THE GROUND RULES in Gestalt Therapy constitute an invitation to the person, if he is willing, to accept a certain attitude in working with the therapist. They are not intended as *musts* or *shoulds*. Following the ground rules in a mechanical manner or dutifully playing good patient is in itself a negation of the philosophy of Gestalt Therapy. The purpose of the ground rules is to create an atmosphere and attitude toward working in therapy that lead to greater awareness of the reality of oneself and how one interacts with others, and how one functions in the Here and Now. The ground rules are intended to enhance awareness and make obvious what he does that is his authentic self and what he does that is phony, manipulative or avoids being his own person. This emphasis on increased awareness is intended to confront the person with the full responsibility for all of his behavior, to increase authentic self-expression and relating, and to minimize self-deceptive, evasive, self-frustrating and meaningless behavior.

Much of the work in Gestalt Therapy involves increased awareness of obsolete attitudes and behavior patterns which were learned in the past and which continue despite their frustrating effect on the person's well-being in the present. While he adopted these as the most effective way he could find to cope with conflicts in his past life, he may begin to see that they no longer fit present reality. As he becomes aware of these archaic responses, he may begin to experiment by taking risks in letting go of them and discovering new, more effective attitudes and behavior. The energy that had been diverted into frustrating or non-nourishing activities is then freed and available for more meaningful experiences in the Here and Now.

100

The goal of Gestalt Therapy is growth. This involves movement away from what a person no longer wants for himself and movement in new directions or an interest in exploring different behavior patterns and experiences. The growth process *is* awareness and the willingness to experiment with different self-initiated behavior.

In Gestalt Therapy, there is no preconceived concept into which an individual should fit. There are no goals as to how he *should* be, nor is there a fixed concept of what a mature person is like. The emphasis is on growth through self-discovery—becoming aware and experimenting with what fits and what does not fit the unique self of each individual. This respect for the integrity of the individual applies whether the person experiences himself as fully functioning or as confused, bewildered or baffled about his identity.

Nothing supersedes the self-regulating capabilities of the individual; this basic principle always take precedence. No one is pressured or coerced to do anything or to participate in any way. Anything the leader suggests or asks of anyone is an invitation. The rule is specifically stated that it is up to each person to say yes or no to any invitation by the leader or any approach from others in the group. The participant is responsible for not allowing others to intrude on him by pressuring him into something he really objects to doing. He is also encouraged not to pressure himself into doing something he really doesn't want to do. This attitude is often stated as follows: "Say what you want to say and don't say anything you don't want to say." Similarly, each participant is asked not to push, urge, or coerce others to work or otherwise participate more actively. All such attempts to be helpful are considered to be intrusions on the other, even when motivated by a feeling of caring and well-meant intentions.

The Group Setting

There are two methods of working in a Gestalt group. The first involves work between the leader and a single participant within the group setting. When one-to-one work occurs, the rest of the group is usually asked to refrain from interaction until the work is finished. Then the other participants share whatever they wish about what they experienced and how they reacted while the one-to-one work was taking place. This feedback is a source of much group interaction. It becomes apparent that others relate to (identify with) the participant who is working with the therapist and do a great deal of silent self-therapy, becoming aware of unfinished situations or fragmented parts of themselves. Experiencing the work of someone else frequently has the effect of helping other group members to recognize their own frustrating attitudes and behavior patterns. Often the leader will make an explicit statement to the effect that each participant, *if he is interested*, can relate to anything that is happening when another person is working.

The second method of working in a Gestalt group includes all other interaction within the group. There are definite limitations to what can be considered valuable or meaningful ways of interacting and relating. Intellectualizing, psychologizing, and advice-giving are considered wastes of time and energy. Any kind of *talking about* which has any flavor of a lecture, a case history or story-telling about oneself or someone else is considered dead material which avoids or dulls awareness and aliveness.

All attempts to fit someone's behavior into a theoretical framework—to analyze or explain it on the basis of psychological theory—are irrelevant. Usually, this becomes an explanation game. It focuses on *why* questions and answers. In Gestalt this process is considered endless and without growth potential. Why questions avoid the Here and Now and are explanation games. In Gestalt therapy, *explanations* are translated to mean *excuses* for not living in the present. Participants are encouraged to make statements in the first person singular about what they are experiencing and how they are reacting in the Here and Now.

In Gestalt Therapy, the group setting has the advantages of providing an atmosphere of the *safe risk-taking*, in letting go of obsolete behaviors and experimenting with new ones. The attitude of open self-expression within the group enables the participant to experience honest interaction between himself and others. For each person, there is no substitute for the experience of expressing himself to others and checking out catastrophic fantasies of how people will react if he shows who he really is.

Each participant is encouraged to express himself *primarily* to satisfy his own need for self-expression. Attempts to convince, persuade or sell another participant on his own opinion or viewpoint are considered manipulations which detract from authentic relating.

Frequently the leader will suggest group games or other procedures. These include exercises for enhancing awareness and focusing on the Here and Now, as well as a number of techniques to encourage authentic interaction and relating within the group.

A meaningful growth-enhancing group atmosphere minimizes interaction which is meaningless, time-wasting or poisonous. The ground rules restricting behavior are intended to minimize ineffective activities which avoid awareness and aliveness in the Here and Now. Usually the only outright prohibition is against physical violence.

The Continuum of Awareness

Being in touch with one's flow of awareness is an essential aspect of the Gestalt method. Participants are encouraged to tune in to what they are experiencing from moment to moment. The emphasis is on non-intellectual awareness as opposed to thoughts and speculations. The person is asked to focus on the sensory data, feelings, emotions and reactions to experiences from within himself and from his environment.

Reality Is the Here and Now

Because the past and future are considered fantasy, to be in touch with reality *is* to be in touch with the Here and Now. This is reflected in the rule that each person is asked to speak in the present tense. Various techniques are used to implement this rule. When a person is in touch with something that happened in his past, he is asked to bring the memory into the present using Gestalt techniques. For example, referring to a childhood episode with a parent, he may be invited by the therapist to put the parent on an empty chair and talk to him as if the episode were happening now and to express the feelings he experiences now. *Any* experience—a past episode, a future fantasy, a dream—can be brought into the present by various Gestalt methods.

Everything I Say or Do Is Part of Me

Every thought, feeling, verbalization, action, etc., is an expression of the person's identity at the moment. In order to become more aware of his identity, the person is asked to *own* everything he says and does by speaking in the first person singular and avoiding abstractions and impersonal statements. Instead of saying, "There is a funny feeling in my stomach," the person is asked to own the funny feeling by saying, for example, "I feel funny in my stomach."

A person can realistically make only first person singular statements about what *he* experiences or how *he* reacts. A person who becomes restless at the empty verbalizing of another may say in irritation, "You are very boring to us"; he speaks for the whole group. He fantasizes that everyone present is reacting with boredom as he is. People often generalize by using the pronoun *you*. A participant will say, "You can't go around telling everyone how you feel." He is asked again to personalize and own his statement by saying *I* instead of *you*. For example, "I am very bored with you," or, "I can't (won't) tell everyone how I feel."

Speaking in the first person singular avoids the endless *talking about* which tends to be impersonal and intellectual. First person statements enhance awareness of the emotional aspect of what is being said.

Meaningful Dialogue

Interaction between participants is also on a first person basis; each person makes statements about himself to the others. Meaningful dialogue involves a sequence of first person singular statements in which what one person says to another is reflected in the response of the other. The result is ongoing feedback, and it is obvious in the responses of both that each person is reacting to the other and really hearing him.

An essential aspect of the *make-first-person-statements* principle is that the person makes his statement *primarily* for the purpose of self-expression. When this is his attitude, he sounds as if there is a period at the end of his statement. He feels finished and satisfied. While a person usually wants a favorable response to what he has said, this is the prerogative of the person to whom the statement is made. In authentic dialogue, no one attempts to sell anything to anyone else. To respond as he chooses, or not to respond at all, is respected as being the other person's right.

No Gossiping

The no gossiping rule applies to talking about another person, regardless of whether he is present. To enhance feelings of contact and interaction, each person is asked to make statements directly to the other person. For example, instead of saying to the group leader about another participant, "He makes me angry with his intellectualizing," the person is asked to make the statement directly to the participant toward whom he feels angry; i.e., "I am angry at your intellectualizing."

To avoid talking about people who are not present, various role-playing techniques are used so that the absent person may be spoken to as if he were actually present.

Questions

Questions are generally discouraged. They avoid meaningful interaction. Questions frequently ask a person to explain, defend or justify some aspect of himself or of his existence. Questions often are attempts to manipulate other people; they can usually be restated as first-person statements. The leader often asks a participant to check with himself to see if there is a statement behind his question. When someone does ask a question of another member, the other person is asked to take the responsibility for deciding whether he wants to respond and *how* he would like to answer. In general questions are considered to be an evasive way of interacting without revealing anything of oneself to the other.

Relevant Subject Matter

A participant may work on any attitude or behavior pattern relative to his functioning as a human being. These conflicts may concern the person's past, present or future. There is no aspect of behavior which is considered more or less desirable in terms of what the person should work on. Rather each participant decides for himself what he feels is most important of those things he is willing to work with or share in the group.

What and How

The achievement of greater awareness involves getting more in touch with the *whats* and *hows* of behavior. The focus is on *what* a person does and *how* he goes about doing it. *Why* questions are avoided. Gestalt Therapy is non-interpretative and avoids any kind of explanation of behavior. This is usually called the *why merry-go-round*; it is the psychoanalysis game. In Gestalt, explaining why one behaves as he does, even when the explanations are valid, is considered an intellectual exercise which does not lead to behavior change. Furthermore, explanations about oneself or one's behavior serve as excuses for one's frustrations and are considered poisonous. They are often attempts by a person to justify his existence or to defend himself rather than encouraging change or growth. Such activity enhances stalemated behavior.

Taking Risks

By trusting the self-regulating potentials of the individual, the therapist affirms that he has neither the desire nor the willingness to push or in any other way work at getting the person to open up. The individual is responsible (and free) for whatever self-expression he decides to initiate. In Gestalt Therapy, taking a risk refers to a person's fears—grounded in his past—that if he reveals himself, he invites a catastrophic reaction. He will elicit scorn, contempt, rejection or even annihilation from others. Frustrated self-expression usually reflects a person's fear that he will inevitably experience rejection if he shares his feelings with others. When he is willing to check out his fears and anxieties in the reality of the *now*, he is open to the possibility that these squeezed-in parts of himself are acceptable and will not lead to the catastrophes and rejection he anticipates as a result of his past (particularly childhood) experiences.

Can't vs. Won't

The *won't* attitude emphasizes the Gestalt philosophy that a person has the potential power (and freedom) within himself to change when he is genuinely interested in doing so. Can't means that whatever change the person wants is impossible. This is rarely realistic with respect to a person's attitudes and behavior patterns. *Won't* means, "I don't want to," or "I am not willing to." Often a person is asked to change his statement by using the word *won't* instead of *can't*. This confronts him with taking responsibility for what he is willing or unwilling to do on his own behalf.

Psychological Interpretations

Interpreting behavior is contrary to the Gestalt approach. When a person makes a statement about how he experiences the behavior of another, that is self-expression. When one makes a statement interpreting the *meaning* of another's behavior, that statement implies that the interpreter knows what is motivating the other—which is fantasy. Statements intended to answer a *why* question are often interpretations. Statements by one person about how he is *experiencing* another person reflect *his* observations about how or what the other person is doing.

When a person is interested in self-expression, he is willing to own everything he says. When he is interpreting to another person, his attitude is that he believes his statement fits the other person. The interpreter puts his statement on the other person, and in so doing violates the integrity of the other by not allowing him to decide what fits him and what doesn't. When someone is interpreting, his attitude usually has the flavor of manipulation of the other to accept his statements. The more persistent the interpretation, the more obvious the he *should* do.

Don't Push

Trust in the self-regulating potentials of the person, a respect for each individual's integrity, and the attitude that each person is responsible for himself, are reflected in the ground rule that no one pushes or pressures anyone in a Gestalt group. The leader does not challenge individuals to work nor does he criticize them when they are non-verbal, withdrawn, or appear bored. In stating the ground rules each person may be asked to mind his own business. If he wishes to express his resentments or irritation at the behavior of another, or his own disappointment that another person is not working, he is asked to do this as an expression of his self at the moment. This is in contrast to expressing oneself for the primary purpose of manipulating the other person into responding in some particular way. All pushing is considered manipulation and violates the integrity of the other by not allowing him to be where he is. Pushing implies a judgmental attitude that the person is failing to do something *selling* becomes.

Gestalt Games

There are endless variations in the techniques the therapist may use in the working process itself. The games constitute invitations by the therapist to a person to say or do something relating to what he is working on at the moment. These procedures are called games because they are initially artificial; that is, the person is asked if he is willing to do something that comes from the therapist rather than from his own spontaneity. He may initially feel the suggestion is pointless or his compliance is phony. This is part of the risk-taking procedure. The meaningfulness of the game to the participant depends upon what he actually does experience for himself as real when he decides to go along with the therapist's suggestion. The purpose of the game is to focus the attention of the person on—and to enhance his awareness of—some aspect of himself or his behavior.

The Hot Seat

When one-to-one work is occurring and the rest of the group is observing, the person working is described as being on the hot seat, since he is obviously the center of attention and the focal point of the group.

In front of the hot seat is an empty chair. The person working is often asked to role-play by speaking to a significant person in his life, past or present, as if that person were actually sitting in the empty chair. Usually the person working is asked to be the other person too. He may be asked to develop a dialogue, writing his own script as he goes along, and actually changing seats each time the person speaking changes. Or, the dialogue may be between parts of himself. For example, in a decision-making conflict, he may be asked to have a dialogue with *pro* and *con* occupying the two chairs. Similarly, in working with dreams, he may be asked to be any person or object appearing in his dream and to give each a voice.

Making Rounds

This involves a participant making some kind of contact with the other members of the group. The leader may invite a participant to make a specific statement to each person. The variety of rounds is limited only by the ingenuity of the leader. Making a round may utilize the Gestalt principle of figure and ground developed into a technique to enhance awareness. By making the same statement to each person, the meaning of that statement can become focused in the center of the person's awareness. For example, a person may feel at ease expressing anger and resentment but be quite unwilling to express warmth and affection. He might be asked to make a round and express his resentments *and* his appreciations to each person in the group.

Dreams

In Gestalt, dreams are a statement of the Here and Now existence of the dreamer. The person is asked to bring the dream into the present by telling it aloud as if he is describing a movie which he can see and the group cannot. Every detail of the dream is part of himself. He is all the people, all the things, all the places, all the actions in his dream. In theory, if he were to work with every aspect of a dream, it would be a comprehensive statement of his existence. Because of time limitations, the person is usually asked to focus on one or a few outstanding aspects of the dream. In dreamwork technique in Gestalt Therapy, the person is asked to animate his dream: to give voices to the people or objects, to write his own script of monologues, or dialogues between people or objects or any combination of these in his dream. No interpreting of the dream or symbolism is used or recognized as valid.

It does not matter whether the dream occurred recently or years ago. When a person remembers an old dream, he is still holding on to the unfinished business of his dream.

The therapeutic value of the dream is based on the increased awareness which comes from owning every aspect of the dream. Fragmented parts of the personality are often revealed by what happens (or by what is avoided) in the dream.

Growth Is a Process of Small Steps

The ongoing process of adjustment and growth involves gaining and assimilating new awareness in small steps. A person is encouraged to stop working when he is in contact with some increased awareness that he is interested in holding onto (assimilating). Or the therapist may state that he would like to stop working at that point.

The Gestalt Therapist

The therapist rejects any kind of authority position toward the person with whom he is working. The therapist does not attempt to lead, guide, advise, or in other ways take away the other person's responsibility for himself. Rather, his attitude is that each person knows best what he needs for himself and how to get it; even when he is stuck, he is more capable of finding his own solutions than anyone else. The therapist accepts the premise that each person is the center of his own existence and the most important person in the world to himself. This attitude of respect for the integrity and individuality of every human being is essential. The therapist uses the ground rules for the sole purpose of creating an environment in which the philosophy of Gestalt Therapy may most readily evolve into an awareness-increasing, growth-enhancing experience.

A popular statement reflecting the Gestalt philosophy emphasizes the respect of the therapist for the integrity of the individual: "Right now I cannot be any other way than I am right now." For example, if a participant decides to criticize himself for not following the ground rules, this is what *he* needs to do. The therapist is not interested in evaluating or criticizing him for this. The therapist *is* interested in helping the participant become more aware of what he is doing. Respect for the other person means that the therapist recognizes and allows each person to be where he is.

The therapist is explicit in stating that he is available to work if the other person is interested. Nothing is excluded as a potential source of work. This includes any kind of problem or symptom. The therapist emphasizes that anything he initiates while working with the other person is an invitation or a suggestion, and it is the other person's responsibility to decide whether he is interested in accepting the offer or not.

The therapist seeks to be continuously in touch with his own awareness of how he experiences others and what he observes them doing. He does not respond with his knowledge of psychology; he does not use case history data. He does not make interpretations of the *whys* of behavior. He does not try to *fit* the person into a theoretical orientation. He shares his experiencing and awareness at the moment, and interacts in an I-and-Thou dialogue. It is the responsibility of the therapist to work this way. The therapist is an observer, not a mind reader. He *offers* his observations to the participant; he doesn't try to *sell* them. He respects the right of the participant to accept what he experiences as meaningful and to reject what he doesn't want from what the therapist shares with him.

In essence the therapist's attitude is:

> I won't help you by trying to gratify your needs or trying to live up to your expectations (whatever your fantasy is of what I *should* be able to do for you). I am not interested in doing this. Whatever your past experiences have been, your behavior in the Here and Now of

your life is your responsibility. Your attempts at manipulation of yourself or others lead to further frustration when you fail and to stalemate of your own growth when you succeed. I am interested in helping you become more aware of when you are taking responsibility for yourself and when you are being manipulative. It is my responsibility not to manipulate you even if it brings temporary relief or gratification.

I *am* interested in helping you become more aware of how you cut off your potentials for greater self-reliance. I am interested in working with you in this direction as long as you are interested. This is how I show my caring for you as a person and my respect for your integrity as an individual. It is my responsibility to openly and honestly share with you how I experience you. It is your responsibility to take from me what you decide is valuable, or meaningful, to you. It is also your responsibility to reject what you feel doesn't fit you.

Our goal in working together is to increase your awareness of your needs, behavior patterns and responsiveness to yourself and others. As you become aware of these it is your decision what, if any, behavior patterns you wish to change and what you wish to keep or develop. The goal is discovering through increased awareness how you hamper your ability to satisfy your needs, grow as a person, and fulfill more of your potentials. From that point, you're on your own.

SELECTED READINGS

Enright, J.B.: An introduction to Gestalt Therapy. Unpublished, The Langley Porter Neuropsychiatric Institute.

Enright, J.B.: Thou art that: Projection and play in therapy and growth. Accepted for publication in *Psychotherapy: Theory, Research & Practice*.

Greenwald, J.A.: An introduction to the philosophy and techniques of Gestalt Therapy. *The Bulletin of Structural Integration*, 1969.

Greenwald, J.A.: The art of emotional nourishment: Nourishing and toxic encounter groups. Unpublished, Beverly Hills, 1971.

Keleman, S.: The body, eros and consciousness. Unpublished.

Kempler, W.: The experiential therapeutic encounter. *Psychotherapy: Theory, Research & Practice*, 1967.

Levitsky, A., and Perls, F.S.: *The Rules and Games of Gestalt Therapy*. San Francisco, Lodestar Pr. (Reprinted by permission of publisher) from Joen Fagan and Irma Lee Shepherd (Eds.): *Gestalt Therapy Now*, 1970.

Levitsky, A.: The rules and games of Gestalt Therapy. Unpublished.

Perls, F.S.: *Ego, Hunger and Aggression*. London, Allen & Unwin, 1947; New York, Random House, 1969.

Perls, F.S.: *In and Out of the Garbage Pail*. Lafayette, Real People Pr., 1969.

112   *Gestalt Therapy Primer*

Perls, F.S.: Gestalt therapy and human potentialities. Esalen Paper No. 1, June, 1965.

Perls, F.S.: *Gestalt Therapy Verbatim.* Lafayette, Real People Pr., 1969.

Perls, F.S.: Workshop vs. individual therapy. This paper was delivered at the American Psychological Association Convention, New York City, 1966.

Perls, F.S.: Gestalt therapy and human potentialities. In *Explorations in Human Potentialities,* Springfield, Thomas, 1966.

Perls, F.S., Hefferline, R.F., and Goodman, P.: *Gestalt Therapy.* New York, Julian Pr., 1951. (Republished: New York, Dell, 1965.)

Pursglove, P.D. (Ed.): *Recognitions in Gestalt Therapy.* New York, Funk & Wagnalls, 1968.

Resnick, R.W.: Chicken soup is poison. Unpublished, Beverly Hills.

Shepherd, I.L., and Fagan, J. (Eds.): *Gestalt Therapy Now.* Palo Alto, Science and Behavior Books, 1970.

Shostrom, E.L.: *Man, The Manipulator.* Nashville, Abingdon Pr., 1967. (Republished: New York, Bantam, 1968).

Simkin, J.S.: An introduction to the theory of Gestalt Therapy. Cleveland, Gestalt Institute of Cleveland.

Simkin, J.S.: Innovations in Gestalt Therapy techniques. Unpublished, 1968.

Yontef, G.A.: A review of the practice of Gestalt Therapy. Doctoral dissertation, University of Arizona.

CHAPTER X

THE ART OF EMOTIONAL NOURISHMENT: SELF-INDUCED NOURISHMENT AND TOXICITY

JERRY A. GREENWALD

Introduction

PREVIOUSLY I described relationships in terms of the nourishment and toxicity a person experiences from his interactions with others. Each individual has both nourishing and toxic qualities which he elicits in relating to others; i.e. the interpsychic level of his behavior. While no dichotomy is implied, there are those (N people) who are usually experienced as enriching and nourishing. Others are typically experienced as ungratifying, stifling or burdensome (T people). Within each individual are behavioral patterns on the intrapsychic level which are congruent with that person's behavior on the interpsychic level. Those who are nourishing in their interactions with others also tend to be good self-nourishers. Those who poison others by various toxic patterns of interaction are generally self-poisoners also. This paper focuses on these intrapsychic phenomena of self-generated nourishment and self-generated toxicity.

Self-induced Nourishment

N people have a healthy capacity to generate their own nourishment. They enjoy self-initiated and autonomous activities. While they thrive on human interaction, they are capable of experiencing many emotions and pleasures without necessarily sharing them or obtaining them from interaction with others. They enjoy solitude and find pleasure and self-nourishment in a variety of unshared activities and interests. They enjoy periods of quiet, withdrawal and isolation. They find such experiences enriching and rejuvenating in ways which cannot be obtained through relationships and interactions with others. They have a rich inner life which they find stimulating and exciting. They are eager for increased awareness and greater knowledge about themselves. They enjoy experiencing their inner world. While they may subsequently share some, or even most, of these experiences, they never share all of it. The solidness of their identity is reflected in the comfort and pleasure they experience in their happy, honest privacy which inwardly is open and without the agonies of guilt, shame or fearfulness. The core of their autonomy and integrity is firmly rooted in their own approval and appreciation of their self.

Self-induced Toxicity

Each individual, whether he is primarily N or T oriented, has his unique pattern of internally generated psychological poisons with which he toxifies himself. That this pattern may represent part of his most effective effort in adjusting to his environment makes it no less toxic. Nor is it any less poisonous if he lacks awareness of its very existence. Lack of awareness of what one does to oneself does not change the reality of the toxifying process. A person who is slowly dying under the continuing stress of a disease process will continue to die as long as the process continues whether he knows what is happening or not. Self-poisoning on the emotional level is usually quite subtle so that its deadliness tends to escape the full awareness of the person. Like the constant noise level or bad air of a large city, it saps his strength little by little. A continuous self-induced toxic pattern *must* inevitably erode the health and well-being of the organism however gradual the poisoning process may be. The only unpredictable aspects are when the breakdown will become obvious; what form it will take and what part of the organism will be the focal point.

N people nourish themselves by focusing on what they find enjoyable, what they appreciate, or what they find gratifying in an experience or an encounter. They focus on the doughnut and its nourishing qualities rather than bemoan the fact that the doughnut has a hole in the center; this latter attitude is characteristically T orientation. It is the *hole-in-the-doughnut attitude* with which T people contaminate the potential nourishment they might otherwise obtain. They obstruct their potentially self-nourishing capabilities with their own psychological excrements. Emotionally they defecate on their own experiences. It is the *T* person, for example, who spots every candy wrapper and beer can in a park or forest and becomes obsessed with this aspect of his experiences. To be sure, such debris is an unfortunate blemish, but he cheats himself of the nourishment of all the beauty which is also present. It is ironic that *T* people, who typically are so emotionally deprived and frustrated, are the very ones who are most apt to cheat themselves of the potential emotional enrichment of their own experiences.

T people lack autonomy and self-initiating abilities, or they are phobic about using these resources for their own gratification. Their relative absence or self-starting ability makes them poor self-nourishers. With their helpless attitude, they appear as if they would starve if left to their own devices. Consciously they are often fearful of being left alone or abandoned and may spend their whole lives under the black cloud of this kind of fantasy. Their constant dependency on others for nourishment becomes self-defeating and self-poisoning. *T* people tend to suck or pull the nourishment out of others and thereby destroy the desire of the overtaxed other person to continue this one-sided relationship. The *T* person's nourishment problem is further complicated by his other-oriented focus which lessens his chances of developing his latent potentials for self-nourishment. The less he has developed these capacities, the more likely he is to feel that he is lacking in them. An added tragedy of his existence is the fact that he never finds out how capable he really could be.

The *N* person uses his resources for self-gratification, pleasure and achievement. He is interested in sustaining himself. He functions in a self-enhancing manner for his own joy and growth. Being more self-satisfied, he consequently has more to give in his relationships with others. The *T* person, in contrast, abuses himself. He does things and acts in ways which he experiences as ungratifying, self-weakening and frustrating. Such self-toxifying patterns often have a compulsivity about them as if he is unable to control himself regardless of his awareness of the consequences. For example, obese people go on eating splurges fully aware from similar past episodes that the momentary gratification does not at all counterbalance the guilt and self-contempt that ensues later.

Patterns of Self-induced Toxicity

The unique constellation of toxic behavior in each person forms a hierarchy with one or more toxic patterns being dominant. Others are of secondary importance within the context of his total toxic reactions. The labeling of various *T* patterns is for descriptive purposes and does not imply categorical or qualitative differences. While they are described here as they operate on the intrapsychic level, there is in each instance an interpsychic effect which also operates. That is, self-poisoning patterns radiate their deadliness to others who are exposed to them excessively. Different types of self-poisoning patterns vary in their infectious qualities much like different diseases. Some are highly contagious, more deadly, and therefore more dangerous. Others are relatively non-infectious and less hazardous. For example, depressed people radiate their depression and permeate the atmosphere with it until those around also experience their depression in some toxic form. Similarly, greedy people tend to generate a mood of apprehension and uneasiness in others exposed to this kind of toxicity.

Self-induced toxic patterns create a condition of stress within the person. They function as a source of disruption to the health and well-being of the organism. It is for the victim an existence in a state of *dis-ease*. To emphasize the sickness-inducing effect of *T* patterns on emotional and physical health, the suffix *itis* has been added to most of the descriptive terms. It connotes this state of irritation, inflammation and infection in the person. It implies that some poisonous phenomenon is occurring which is toxic to the organism.

Approvalitis

All *other-oriented* patterns of behavior are toxic since they detour the person away from greater integration and an increasing sense of identity by growth from within. The victim of approvalitis toxifies himself by putting his well-being in the hands of someone else. The deadliness of this self-poisoning pattern is manifest in his vulnerability to being wiped out at the whim of another to whomever he has given over his power. The stability of such people runs a rocky course since they impede the natural path of growth of their identity by the psychic stoplights of the powerful others who object to their various attempts at self-determination. They subjugate themselves to a pattern of behavior reflecting the identity and needs of another person instead of their own. For example, approvalitis is a common occurrence in the man who is always mild, pleasant and likeable outside his home. This constant squeezing down of his identity by his refusal to risk disapproval is counter-balanced by a tyrant-like attitude within the confines of his home where he acts like an angry bully towards his wife and children . . . and nobody who sees him outside his home would ever believe it!

Approvalitis is not a toxic pattern in childhood but becomes toxic if it persists as the child grows to adulthood. In such cases it may take the form of congenital approvalitis in which the victim of one generation, having developed so little autonomy and self-reliance of his own, in his turn as parent dominates his children in the same manner he was dominated as a child. This cycle of chronic infection is exemplified in families where each generation is obsessed with controlling and dominating the next generation. Each generation poisons itself as it avoids the issue of its own identity by its other-oriented focus on the next generation.

Approvalitis leads to chronic self-immobilization as the person constantly squeezes himself from striking out on his own. This might meet with the dreaded disapproval from the phantom king (or queen) he worships. Instead he awaits his cues about what he should do and how he should act. He vainly hopes that, if he is good enough, he will gain the approval and get the nourishment and gratification he has so long sought. Since, at best, this comes only in spurts and at the whim and benevolence of the other, he grows steadily more desperate. At the height of his desperation and before the poisoning process has done too much damage, the effect of this T pattern may reach the intensity of a homicidal (or suicidal) rage. Gradually the toxicity takes its toll and the victim is more apt to take on the appearance and behavior of a person who literally looks like all the life has gone out of him. He burns himself out with his hoping and waiting.

Failuritis

This T pattern is characterized by the person who habitually puts himself down. He poisons himself by wearing the label *failure* on his forehead. He does this silently and by making announcements to this effect to others. When he does something well, and often such people are superior in ability, he then sprinkles his accomplishment with self-generated poison. Somehow he must do something to contaminate the potential nourishment of his achievements. He acts as if he has a phobia about enjoying himself. Similarly, he can be counted on to toxify a compliment from another by pointing out some failure or shortcoming about what he did or how he did it. This is not modesty but rather a deeper conviction that he is essentially a failure so that anything good which happens through his efforts is rejected as alien to his self. It is like the woman who wins the cake baking contest and toxifies her victory by insisting that any of the other contestants could have done as well if they had spent as many laborious years baking cakes as she had. Another example is the artist who toxifies a compliment by a self-generated put-down often in the form of a humorously self-derisive remark. For example: "You really like it! I was drunk when I did it! Maybe I would be more successful if I became an alcoholic!"

Explanationitis

T people toxify themselves by their constant need to explain themselves and their decisions to others. While this pattern is not as immobilizing as approvalitis, the victim does find himself bogged down in explanations and justifications which hamper his own freedom to act more effectively and nourish himself more efficiently. This kind of toxicity ranges from defensiveness and meekness as if he is pleading his case in court, to a belligerent or defiant explanation as if he expects to be constantly challenged but intends to fight back. Sometimes this pattern unfolds as an internal battle in which the victim fights with himself. He has a built-in tormenter to whom he must always justify himself. The effect is just as deadly and immobilizing as when his antagonist is another person. The hook in this kind of self-torture pattern is that it is so important that someone understand and accept all the *whys* of his actions and attitudes. Since no one ever finished explaining himself yet, this *T* pattern becomes a way of life.

Rebellionitis

While rebellion against a suppressive authority may be realistic and healthy, *T* people exhaust themselves by their fantasies of oppression. Frequently they act this out by a self-imposed Don Quixote role and chase their own brand of windmills. An example of this form of self-induced toxic reaction is the pseudo hippie. Lacking any real interest in nourishing himself or confronting himself with his own hang-ups, he becomes a rebel for the sake of being a rebel . . . it's better than being nothing. In the process he latches on to movements or identifies with groups which he joins but to which he never feels genuinely involved or honestly committed. He poisons himself by a double bind in which his phony rebellion ironically emerges as an ersatz way out conformity. This pattern is also observable in some members of extreme political groups, liberal or reactionary, and various fanatical religious sects. Their rebellion against everything that fails to support their dogma takes on an automatic, compulsive form. It does not primarily reflect their personal convictions and integrity. Rather, it is in essence an elaborate, disguised scheme to escape the self. As a result, there is little nourishment from the enormous energy they expend. The self-deprivation of this T pattern is reflected in the increasing rigidity and desperation of their efforts. The more they starve themselves, the more they redouble the intensity of their efforts. The end result is fanaticism which, in itself, reflects the psychological death of the victim's identity.

Appreciationitis

Those plagued with this toxic infection play boy scout (or girl scout), always doing good deeds and favors for others, usually in a compulsive manner. In turn, other people are supposed to appreciate them and respond in like manner. Typically, they keep records on who owes them how much of what. The dose of self-poison comes when the other person simply accepts and enjoys what was given him but doesn't show his appreciation by paying off. When sufficiently frustrated by this toxic pattern, the T person may blow his fuse and insist to the other that *you owe me*. This reaction is apt to be emphatically and angrily rejected by the other person unless he too is hungup with some toxic pattern of his own.

Performeritis

This is another record keeping pattern of self-induced toxicity in which the person constantly compares and measures his performance in a desperate attempt to sustain his identity and feeling of self-worth. The more he needs to prove himself by comparing, the more he toxifies himself. The poisoning effect results from the uncertainty about how good he really is since the standards he sets for himself, as measured against the capabilities of others, are merely the product of his own fantasies. Hence he is stuck on the self-proving treadmill. It is exemplified in the woman who becomes upset if she feels she is not the most attractive female in the room. She rejects the friendship of those other women whom she sees as rivals. Typically all her women friends are older, overweight or in some other way clearly perceived by her as less attractive. The poisonous aspect of this pattern is inherent in the life-long beauty contest she subjects herself to ˙ at the expense of her personal growth and self-nourishment. The process becomes more deadly when it is combined with a morbid fear of growing older as she fantasizes any diminishing of the attention and admiration of men as an overwhelming catastrophe. A similar toxic pattern occurs in men. However, their physical appearance is apt to be secondary to their anxiety about their sexual virility and toxic performeritis is most apt to show up in this area of their behavior. While anxiety about aging is normal in both sexes to some degree, in *T* people it takes on an obsessive quality. The self-poisoning centers on the energy consumed, and it can be enormous, in warding off the reality of the aging process instead of utilizing this energy for more nourishing pursuits. To the extent that the obsession demands the time, energy and resources of the person, the remainder of his total identity is deprived and disregarded.

Sexually, performeritis is manifested in concern that the other finds him or her *the greatest*. In this other-oriented *T* pattern, the meaning and nourishment of the sexual experience is greatly diminished or lost entirely. The comparing game poisons the sexual relationship to the degree that the experience is contaminated by any type of preoccupation with performance.

A classical self-poisoner is the person who suffers from the gravely toxic condition of nice-guyitis or good-boyitis. This syndrome refers to a pattern of multiple infections including several already discussed. These occur when the person is overwhelmingly other-oriented and his readiness to detour himself in order to please others is a major aspect of his personality. In severe cases, he drains his energies to an extent that he lacks sufficient remaining strength for the growth of his own identity. Driven by the demands of others, he is a ready victim of their toxicities. The dose of self-poison comes when he refuses to say "no." Instead, he functions as if he has a phobia about rejecting anyone. The inevitable consequence is the slow death when one chronically rejects himself.

I'll Out-last You

This is a frequent pattern in disruptive marriages where one or both partners are committed to some kind of war to the finish. Having, for various reasons, decided that they cannot, don't want to, or are too frightened to dissolve the marriage, they become engaged in an ongoing campaign in which each unwittingly aggravates the other. There is a pattern of mutual frustration and strong feelings of seeking revenge against the other who is, of course, "no damn good." While the *T* interaction is the more obvious pattern, the endless battle each partner commits himself to is a virulent self-poisoning process also. The winner also loses. The one who literally may end up burying the other has paid an enormous price in the neglect of his own self-nourishment and growth.

Emotional Constipation

This includes patterns often referred to as inhibitions, suppressions, or repressions. In each case, the person applies a general squeeze against his need for open expression. When this is a predominant *T* pattern, the person literally looks like he is uptight or like he's about to blow up. Visible tremors of the hands or face may warn that the fuse is lit. The more constipated varieties have achieved such control that nothing shows anymore. They look like devout people in solemn prayer on the holiest day of the year. Their mask-like outer tranquility is paralleled by an inner volcano of withheld expressiveness. Refusal to release emotional tension creates a chronic pressure which strains the whole organism. A variety of body and facial characteristics may reflect chronic emotional constipation. A pattern of hard, deep lines about the face, which give the look of a person being tortured, is one example. Or the constipation may be expressed in the squeezed-tone of the voice which is unnaturally high pitched and tense. Strongly developed jaw muscles which appear locked in tension, tightly clenched fists, and eyes which are squeezed to an habitual squinting position also reflect the general suppressive attitude as well as the constant state of pain to which the victim himself may gradually have become unaware.

Psychological Diarrhea

This pattern is the opposite of emotional constipation and is equally as toxic. The person so afflicted appears as if he can't hold anything back. He has little frustration tolerance and must discharge any kind of tension as quickly as possible. He may appear to be frightened by tensions, even of pleasurable kinds, as if any intense emotional excitement would be too threatening. In men, it frequently takes the form of premature ejaculation. The verbal form (verbal diarrhea) is more often seen in women who *must* talk incessantly. They find this mode of discharge necessary to reduce their inner tensions. Silence with another person present, even for a minute or two, generates an unbearable pressure. The self-toxifying aspect of this pattern is its effect in short circuiting nourishing experiences. Many potentially deeply gratifying experiences require a healthy buildup of tension to a full peak which is followed by a more intense discharge and more complete gratification. This is obviously true in sexual gratification but applies to other body appetites also. For example, such people miss much of the potential enjoyment and emotional nourishment of eating. Having so little tolerance for the tension of hunger pangs, they tend to eat immediately before they begin to feel panicky. Yet a good meal is more enjoyable when one is truly hungry and has had time to work up an appetite.

Controlitis

People who insist on controlling their environment to an extremely unrealistic degree poison themselves by their control-madness. They are unwilling to openly express themselves, reach out or go into ordinary activities of living unless everything is just so. The self-poisoning process centers on their chronic attitude of squeezing and inhibiting their spontaneity and naturalness. When in a position of power, they seek to afflict others with the same straightjacket. This pattern is frequently observable in *old maid* school teachers (of both sexes) who, in their need to control, select the lower grades as their choice of teaching environment since younger children are easier to control and manipulate. It also occurs in people who can't sit still, enjoy themselves or stick to one thing at a time. Instead they continuously interrupt themselves as one thought or another of some trivial item that must be done pops into their mind every few minutes. Everything must be under control or they can't relax themselves. Since they tend to be compulsive in general, there is a continuity of self-imposed disruptions to the simple, everyday activities which might otherwise provide them with gratification and nourishment.

Depressionitis

This form of chronic self-induced toxicity is also known as swampitis or wallowitis. The afflicted person does the psychological equivalent of trodding around the Everglades in huge circles, knee deep in water, continuously getting stuck in the mud and slime. His facial expression suggests a constant groaning about life and the miseries that always seem to come upon him. With a chronic gloom-to-doom attitude, he seems to rock his head in passive submission as he continues the self-poisoning process of resignation by wallowing in his swamp. He seems unable to go into his depression or mourning more fully and get finished with it. He keeps himself locked in by his mopingness and feeling sorry for himself. With his *poor little me* attitude, he refuses to open his eyes to see if there isn't some firm, dry land nearby where he might get a foothold and start to move out of his swamp. Instead, he stays with his misery, typically wearing the facial mask and body posture of the chronic griever.

The Dumping Syndrome

Some people never miss an opportunity to unload their junk on anyone who is willing to listen. The victim of this toxic pattern is caught in his own web of verbiage. He vainly hopes that if he dumps enough of his problems, troubles and anxieties on others, he will consequently free himself of them by this process. It is analogous to trying to get rid of a wad of sticky chewing gum by wiping it on someone else. He often undergoes psychotherapy with an attitude that he is in treatment to unload his conflicts onto the therapist ("After all, I'm paying you to help me!") and waits for him to do something. He insists that if he dumps enough information, memories, dreams, etc., on the therapist, he will find a solution and clean up the whole mess. In some cases he has the illusion that others enjoy (or should enjoy) his openness and desire to share. Wives sometimes use their husbands in this way. Under the virtuous banner of togetherness, she claims her right to dump her day's anxieties and frustrations on him and feels unloved if he gets bored, resentful or irritated with her need to share and relate. The self-generated toxicity comes through the passive, helpless role the person chooses for himself. In addition, he drives others away since they are apt to experience their giving as a futile attempt to fill a bottomless hole. Each day brings a new load of garbage, so why bother? In marriages burdened with this affliction, the end result is a husband who is always on his back reading the newspaper and a wife who is bitterly obsessed with his withdrawal and lays her unhappiness on his indifference.

Solitude-itis

T people confuse solitude with loneliness. Often they equate the two and develop a phobic attitude toward any prospect of being alone even for brief periods. They become anxious, frequently to the point of panic, at the prospect of spending time alone. They may drive themselves to arrange some activity every evening. Anything will do; social evenings with people who are boring and emotionally dead, attending dull lectures or meaningless self-improvement courses, or just finding someone to get drunk with. The toxic effect is usually experienced as a growing syndrome of fatigue, listlessness and depression. Their strength is drained in counteracting their phobia of being alone. They are further depleted since they deprive themselves of the energy-charging potentials inherent in healthy solitude. Frequently the final solution is an empty relationship which relieves them of their phobia of aloneness but is without nourishment or emotional meaningfulness. An adult child who lives with an aging parent is often a manifestation of this form of self-generated toxicity although the victim may cry martyr or profess deep devotion to the parent. Another common example is the dead marriage in which each tolerates the other in a chronic state of misery, but at least they are not alone.

Openness-itis

This is the opposite from the fear of solitude. It occurs in people who habitually frustrate themselves by their unwillingness to be open and ask for what they want from others. *T* people tend to be phobic about initiating activities involving others from whom they want something. The stronger their need for another person, the more phobic they become about revealing themselves. Rejectionitis plays a central role in this disabling pattern. They may be charged with energy, aware of their needs to reach out, but then poison themselves by becoming immobilized or passive. The extreme form is a catatonic-like stance frequently accompanied by violent implosions. They burn themselves out in the same sense that one would burn out a car by accelerating the engine while holding the car immobile by applying the brakes. This self-poisoning pattern frequently culminates in a chronic psychosomatic illness with definite organic deterioration.

Conclusion

The art of emotional self-nourishment requires the individual to face the responsibility for the ongoing decision-making process regarding when and how he chooses to nourish and poison himself. (We all do some of each.) It requires awareness that he cannot avoid making such choices and that he will inevitably experience the consequences of his choices—if not immediately, then later. When his choices are too inconsistent with his basic concepts about who he is, what he aspires to and what he needs for himself, he becomes fragmented and thereby poisons his primary identity . . . such fragmenting activities are *dis-integrating* to the whole person. Of the many kinds of self-induced poisons, this is the deadliest of all. It is psychologically a self-rape; the person chooses to tear himself apart rather than face his fantasy-fears that he will be annihilated by others if he dares pull the pieces of himself together (integrate) and show the world who he really is! !

The concepts of self-generated nourishment and toxicity, in their broadest meaning, reflect an orientation toward life as a whole. Explanations of why a person behaves as he does may be valid according to various developmental theories, but they only serve as excuses for the adult living in the Here and Now . . . which is the only source of genuine emotional nourishment. A person can no more nourish himself in the present by his memories of the past or hopes for the future than he can nourish his body by fantasizing how good yesterday's meal was or what he will enjoy tomorrow. Each person makes his choice. He can poison himself emotionally by neglecting his own needs and generate his choice of other-oriented toxic patterns, or he can take the responsibility for himself and learn how to stand on his own two feet as a person. In the latter instance he becomes a more effective self-nourisher. Self-nourishment is the foundation of emotional health. It leads to greater capacity to nourish others which, in turn, leads to being .nourished by others. These three aspects form a positive psychological climate for growth and development. Each person faces these choices of nourishment versus poison every day of his life.

CHAPTER XI

GESTALT THERAPY IN INTERACTIVE GROUPS*

JOHN B. ENRIGHT

F OR THE PAST EIGHT YEARS, John Enright has been applying the principles of Gestalt Therapy to groups in a new way. Whereas most gestalt therapists work with the members of a group one at a time, John works primarily with the interactions occurring between two or more group members.

John has been leading therapy groups since earning his Ph.D. in clinical psychology in 1959. He has conducted groups as a staff psychologist at Hawaii State Hospital in Hawaii, at Harbor General Hospital in Los Angeles, and at the Langley Porter Neuropsychiatric Institute in San Francisco. During 1963 and 1964 he studied under Fritz Perls, the founder of Gestalt Therapy.

We asked John the meaning of the word gestalt, and he replied: "The word means pattern or figure and comes from the field of gestalt psychology as developed by Wolfgang Koehler. Gestalt psychology was only one of the three major influences on Fritz's work, and it was probably the least important." (The others were Reichian analysis and the phenomenology of Jan Smuts—who was an existentialist before the term was coined.) But gestalt psychology was the most recent influence, and I believe he picked the term Gestalt Therapy because gestalt psychology was uppermost in his mind. He did not use the phrase when he wrote *Ego, Hunger and Aggression*, which was his first major attempt to describe his theories. When he chose the title *Gestalt Therapy* for his second book, his wife Laura objected. She wanted him to use the term existential. So I think it's rather a historical accident that Fritz

*Reprinted from *The Group Leader's Workshop*, P.O.B. 1254, Berkeley, California 94701.

used the world gestalt in naming his therapy. And it's misleading
to attach too much weight to it in understanding Fritz's theories.

"A key concept that distinguishes Gestalt Therapy from other
types is Fritz's idea of 'organismic self-regulation.' That's the notion
that the whole organism—one's whole being, which extends far
beyond the conscious self—always knows exactly what it has to
do to obtain what it needs. If the organism could somehow be left
unhindered, the process of need arousal and satisfaction would go
on absolutely naturally and spontaneously. Whatever the organism
needed at a given moment would emerge as figure (i.e. 'gestalt'—
that which stands out dominantly in consciousness). Action to
satisfy the need would occur, and a new figure would emerge.
This is the endless process of self-regulation.

"Gestalt therapy consists in finding and dissolving—or somehow
dealing with—all the barriers to organismic self-regulation. These
major barriers are learnings from other people—most often learnings
that occurred during childhood. And the present manifestation of
these past learnings is some sort of muscle tension existing right
now, a holding back or squeezing back of bodily energy that seeks
expression. Whatever happened in the past that can influence me
in the future is present right now and needs only to be activated.

"Most of our habits of perceiving and acting and thinking and
talking are mainly ways of staying out of touch with, and holding back from contact with, the wider self. When I do Gestalt
Therapy, I work with these modes of avoidance wherever they
appear—in the tone of voice, in the way a person holds his hands,
in how he sits, for example.

"Now, most gestalt therapists do this sort of work with each
group member individually, one at a time, as Perls did. The rest
of the group enters in only infrequently, mainly in exercises in
which everybody participates. Of course, people identify with and
are stimulated by each other, but there is not much interaction
among group members.

"This type of individual work is purely a historical accident
arising from Fritz Perls' personal style, just as the psychoanalytic
couch was a historical accident arising from Freud's distaste for
facing his patients. The principles of Gestalt Therapy are *not at*

all bound up with Perls' style, and the sooner we break away from being junior Fritzes, the better."

Interactive Groups

From the time John began working with Perls in 1963, he started incorporating Gestalt methods into his practice with interactive groups. "It often happens," he told us, "that a person will talk in a generalized, distant way about what people do and how they feel. That's to avoid activating the tension he would experience if he spoke directly to another person in the group. In a case like this, I try to direct his style of talking in order to put him in better touch. It might go something like this:

P: When someone does that to you, you certainly feel put down.
T: Try saying "I" instead of "you."
P: Well, when someone does that to me, I . . .
T: Who did that to you?
P: Last week, Carol did it twice.
T: Tell Carol.
P: Carol, I felt put down when you ignored me last week.

"In that way," John continued, "I control style but not content. He is still talking about the subject matter he brought up, but he's involving himself and Carol in an interaction in which his wider self is more likely to come to awareness.

"Another device a person might use in a group to avoid contact with his wider self is to talk a lot about his problems. Usually such a person will have practiced the statement of the problem to himself (or to others) so many times that the statement becomes a kind of preconceived and stereotyped self-image, leaving out a lot of data that might come up in a more spontaneous presentation. In gestalt terms, he has rearranged the figure-ground relationship so that some facets of his personality are brought into the foreground and others are pushed into the background. In such a case, I interrupt the way he wants to talk about himself and get him to talk about himself in a new and unrehearsed way. When he can do that, he shows himself much more freely and fully; it's as though the truth comes blurting out every time he opens his mouth.

"Often I will deflect his attention from the *content* of the problem entirely by directing his attention to the present act of stating the problem to me or to the group. For example, after he has put on a sober face and presented his problem, I may say, 'Okay, look around the group and estimate the impact on everybody of what you have just said.' That way, I haven't ignored him, but I've switched to a different frame of reference—one more in the Here and Now. If he says that he believes people are feeling sorry for him, I ask him if that's what he wanted. Did he succeed in what he was trying to do? At that point we are off and running with what he's doing right now, with his personal style, and we never get to the content of the problem."

Do other group therapists do this? "Most competent nondirective group therapists focus on present feelings, but they don't actively push problems aside the way I do. They merely let them die on the vine."

"Asking questions," John continued, "is another mode of avoidance. In ordinary social discourse, asking good, well-timed questions is an excellent way of keeping things going with an absolute minimum of energy and personal involvement. Every question is a disguised statement. That's one of the basic principles of Gestalt Therapy. So when someone asks a question of me, I may say 'Try that as a statement.' If people in the group are asking questions of each other, and I feel there's a lot of energy and emotion in the interactions, I'll say, 'Wait a minute; I want to hear what you have to say; please make it a statement. Maybe what he just said triggered off a memory; give us the memory. Your question grows out of a personal concern; let's know that concern.' Frequently, changing a question into a statement will uncover an underlying demand upon the other person. Fritz once said, 'The question mark is the hook of the demand.' Very dependent people often ask questions continually; this allows them to feed on verbal goodies from the other people without doing any work themselves. When a question is turned into a statement, it usually becomes apparent that the question was an attempt to manipulate, or that the answer was already known, or that it was disguised advice.

"After people have tried converting questions into statements for an hour or two, most will catch on to the difference. They can feel inside how much harder and riskier it is to make a statement, but how much more revealing and exciting the interchange becomes. Perhaps half the people in my groups will comment spontaneously on this difference.

Three Levels

"All the techniques I've mentioned so far can be seen as ways of mobilizing excitement and developing a clear focus to facilitate awareness. As I see it now, there are three levels to Gestalt Therapy, three types of things a Gestalt therapist does. They are: (1) mobilizing excitement; (2) developing focus, and (3) placing responsibility.

"Without excitement, there's nothing. If everyone is simply sitting, slumped into a favorite posture and scarcely breathing, nothing is going to happen. We can talk for an hour—as happens often in traditional therapies—and get nowhere, because there's no excitement. So if the level of excitement is very low, I will do something to mobilize it. Sometimes I will use a simple physical interaction exercise—it hardly matters what—just to get the pulse up and the adrenalin flowing, to get people keyed up and living in the present time.

"Then, when there's excitement, the next step is to focus it. Someone might say, "I feel kind of scared,' and I'll say, 'Look around the room. Is there someone here you can focus the frightened feeling on? Whom here are you most scared of?' The goal there is to help him focus.

"There are countless techniques for focussing. Many gestalt techniques both mobilize excitement and develop focus. For example, if a person complains that he has an inferiority complex, I'll say, 'Look around the room and pick two or three people you feel inferior to.' That person's level of excitement will rise immediately and at the same time he will begin to focus.

"Responsibility comes last. If someone says, 'Joe insulted me,' he's excited and focussed, but he has cast the event outside himself. I may then direct him to say, 'I feel insulted' to help him realize that the feelings are his, to help him take responsibility for those feelings as something that *he* is doing rather than something Joe is doing.

"So excitement, focus, and realization of responsibility happen in that order, though sometimes very rapidly. There cannot be focus without excitement, and there cannot be responsibility without focus, because there's nothing to be responsible about. I think all that a gestalt therapist does can be viewed as ways of developing excitement, focus, and responsibility—often two or even all three at once.

"With a very withdrawn person I might spend a lot of time at the level of mobilizing excitement. With most of my groups, however, enough excitement will be present, and I work mainly at the level of focussing. That's where gestalt techniques are at their best, I believe."

Verbal Behavior

John told us that he now works predominantly with verbal rather than nonverbal behavior. "I'm a very verbal person myself," he explained, "and I think my forte is picking up the fundamental value assumptions concealed in language. When a person is talking, I'm usually very sensitive to the style of life implied by his choice of words and phrases. For example, the other day one of the men in my group came out with 'I like him, but I don't agree with him.' So I asked him to stop a moment to consider what that 'but' means, to try several sentences rephrasing the idea slightly so that the full implications become clear. The rephrasing became 'I like him; *therefore*, I should agree with him,' and I asked him, 'Is that one of your assumptions about life—that you should agree with people you like?'

"That's a very simple example. More important is the repetitive use of language that places the source of action outside the speaker. For example, 'It occurred to me,' 'Doubts come creeping in,' and so on. My usual response is to ask the speaker to rephrase the statement so as to make himself the source of the action—to say 'I thought' or 'I started doubting.' Or after three or four such statements, I might say, 'You live in a strange world; everything seems to start outside you. Where are you in all that? Give me a sentence that starts with "I." '

"One of my rationales for working with verbal behavior," John explained, "is that it's easier for people to become aware of what they are saying than of what they are doing nonverbally. If someone comes to a realization like 'Wow! That's right. I keep asking questions when I really mean to say something myself!,' he will begin noticing when he manipulates the kids at home with questions. So there's more likely to be some carry-over to life outside the group."

From time to time, John uses doubling as a group technique. "If I haven't done that in the group before," John explained, "I'll go over to someone and say, 'I'm going to say something now that I think may be going on in you, but if it isn't exactly right, stop me. You know what's in your head; I don't but I have a guess.'

"Or I might walk over to somebody and start feeding him incomplete sentences that are very close to what he's saying. If he says, 'I don't want to confront you,' I'll say, 'Instead of confront-you, I'd rather . . .' If somebody plays coy or is afraid to get into something, I'll say, 'Fine; try this sentence: "Right now I'd rather play safe than risk exposing myself" or "Right now I'd rather play safe than find out something about myself" or some other sentence that fits the situation. When someone can say that loud and clear, he usually can't live with it, and within a few moments he'll be back into whatever he was being coy about. Or if he doesn't, that's all right, too. I spend almost no effort urging people to take risks. I figure they'll take exactly as much risk as they're ready to, and as long as they're aware of the alternatives, they'll make the best possible choice for themselves. If somebody says he has a secret that he hasn't told anybody, I'll urge him not to tell until he feels completely comfortable. That way he won't get caught up in a game with the group saying 'Please tell us!' I see all this business of urging people to take a lot of risks as pure irresponsibility. They obviously are not going to do much more than they already did anyway, and if they take the risk at everyone else's urging, they go away with the feeling that somehow somebody else did it for them. Even if they learn a lot from it, it's less valuable than if they were clearly aware of doing it themselves."

The Contract

John believes that the contract set up between the leader and the group members is of crucial importance. A *growth contract*, he maintains, is much better than a *therapy contract*. "In the case of a therapy contract," he told us, "the people in the group consider themselves to be sick or somehow below par or abnormal. The job of the therapist, then, is to cure them, make them well. With a growth contract, however, the people consider themselves to be all right, normal. They want to become better.

"A disadvantage of the therapy contract is that people want a problem solved or a symptom removed and are consequently pre-occupied with a limited field of awareness. A person who says he wants to get rid of an obsession, for example, may resist my efforts to talk about his sex life. He wants to keep attention focussed on his symptom. An image I often use is that of a person who brings to a florist a plant with a withered leaf. If the florist starts poking around the roots, the person might complain, 'No, no, it's the leaf that's diseased.' Obviously, the whole plant has some-thing wrong with it, and maybe the place to work has nothing to do with the apparent problem. People coming in with a *symptom* resist looking at their whole life style, which is where the roots of the symptom are.

"Focussing on a symptom actually reduces the chance that it will disappear. When symptoms do disappear in the course of gestalt therapy it is as a pure side effect of other changes. Some-body may come to a group and say, 'I want to change this one symptom; that's all.' I tell him it's like suggesting you shift Mars to some place else in the solar system. It can't be done. The whole system has to change.

"Let me give you a classic example of symptom removal by gestalt methods. A woman in one of my groups remarked that she had hurt her foot, and I suggested that she have a conversation with her foot. While playing the role of her foot, she became very hostile towards herself, saying such things as 'God damn you! Why don't you take better care of me!' This hostile interchange went on for three or four minutes. Two of the people in the group were a little taken aback, but after it was over, everyone had a little laugh and that was it. The next week she came in looking stunned. 'I've got fingernails for the first time in my adult life,' she said, 'and I remember now that I stopped biting them after last week's session.' I did not lay out one word of theory about internal aggression being acted out. Somehow, this violent expres-sion of anger cleared some awareness barrier in her, and she didn't have to act out any more. She had never mentioned her problem of biting her fingernails.

"A more important disadvantage to the therapy contract is the implied—or even explicit—notion that somehow I am going to help the patient. But if I'm hooked on the necessity of helping someone, I can't succeed. As long as I need to help him, need to produce some effect in him, he has a manipulative hold on me.

"Many people with long-persisting symptoms and screwed-up life patterns seek out people who are trying to help them in order to frustrate those people. It's a fairly common pattern. Fritz called them beartrappers. Eric Berne called them 'Why don't you—Yes butters.' Every school of therapy has a name for people who seek out a helping relationship, seem to be cooperative, but somehow frustrate the helper. So if I'm committed to helping people, I'm absolutely trapped. On the other hand, if I feel free to do something other than trying to help him, there is some chance I *can* help him. The paradox here is very much like that of the Zen master who cannot and does not deliver directly what the Zen seeker wants. He can only help him get there by frustrating him.

"As long as people want help in some form they are familiar with, as long as they need me to give them something, they are so narrowly focussed on what they are getting from me that they can't do anything for themselves. Only when I frustrate their need to get something from me are they able to do anything for themselves. Sometimes when dealing with a persistent beartrapper who is playing good boy, being very spiteful, and frustrating every suggestion I make, the only thing I can do is fall back on simply reporting my own experiencing, my own sense of frustration and helplessness. He might say, 'But that's not helping me,' to which I'll respond, 'I can accept that.' If he really believes it's okay with me that I'm not helping him, he goes through some serious frustration. He can no longer play the game and must begin to deal with himself in a useful way—that is, unless he's so committed to a therapy contract that he leaves to find a new therapist who will play the game, till *he* fails too.

"The advantage of a growth contract was brought home to me vividly one weekend when I held a weekend experiential group for people who wanted to know more about family therapy. It was clearly a learning situation, with a growth contract. Unknown to me, eleven of my patients had registered, patients I worked with in groups based on a therapy contract. The first morning when I looked out over a roomful of seventy-five faces, there they were! I was momentarily stunned, but I got myself together and went on as planned. We formed simulated families, had one person play the role of therapist, and so on. Hour for hour, my patients got more from that weekend than from their therapy groups. And they were the *same* people, with the *same* leader, using basically the *same* techniques. Only the contract was different. Since they couldn't call themselves patients and cop out for that reason, and they were pulled along by others who were plunging in, they did much more than usual—took risks—just like everyone else. This was a vast improvement over their behavior in the therapy groups, where they tended to sit around acting like patients and complaining about their problems. For me that weekend was a crucial test of the influence of the contract. I had been moving toward the growth contract for some time, but from then on I began actively asking people to set aside their sickness and their problems while we did something else.

"I now distinguish at least three contracts under which I work: a custodial contract, a therapy contract and a growth contract. A custodial contract is one at a state hospital where patients may not even want to be in the group, much less want help from the therapist. If people come in under a custodial contract, I try to move them into a therapy contract, and if they are there under a therapy contract, I try to set up a growth contract.

"Groups that I run privately operate under a growth contract. When someone says he wants to join such a group, I usually don't discuss the contract with him at that time. If he says he has a problem, that's okay. I suggest he come and stay for about six sessions, whether what happens seems relevant to his problem or not. At the end of that time, I explain, it will be clear to both of us whether or not he can profit from the group. During those six sessions I will nudge him away from a problem-centered focus in the ways I discussed earlier. So at the end of this period he has had an experiential sample of the growth contract, and I never have to give him a verbal orientation."

John usually begins his weekend groups with a discussion of the contract. "You put out some bread for this," he tells them, "and I've given up a weekend for it, so I need to know what you want, and you need to know what kinds of things I can do. Do you want me to talk or do you want to talk first? Sometimes people have a lot of energy, and they want to talk," he told us. "But if everybody hangs back, I'll say, 'Okay, I'll talk myself for five minutes about what I want to do.'

"One thing I'll often do is ask each person to say just one sentence about where they're at. Just: 'What's your dominant experience right now?' So everybody will say one sentence, without any response from anyone else, and then I'll say, 'Okay, I've got some sense of where people are now. Let's break up into small groups. Pick out two or three people whose sentence you resonated with—that you thought, "Hey, I could have said that" or "Yeah, that's true"—and get together, and let's work in subgroups for a day.' It's awful hard to sit in a group of sixteen people and start cold. Breaking up into subgroups is almost inevitable.

"After they've formed subgroups and talked for a while, I might say, 'One member from each group introduce the others.' Up to this time, almost everybody has been talking without listening, so now they have to listen in order to do the introductions. And whoever does the introducing might make a mistake, and someone will complain. It builds up a lot of tension and energy. Later I may direct the subgroups to select other subgroups and in that way bring the whole group together again."

Groups

How much does John participate in the group? "Very much," he replied. "If there is a lull in a group of very passive people, I'm likely to start talking about myself. I'll take whatever theme seems to be hanging in the air and remember an incident from my past and start talking about that. I do this mainly with people who are psychotic or very withdrawn. Silence in such a group is devastating. Their anxiety will go inward instead of out. Healthier people will turn the anxiety outward, but withdrawn people need stimulation and structure from the outside.

"I try to be a role model of good communications style, the style I hope the group will learn. I avoid acting like a guru, because that encourages the group to adopt the same style. For instance, if I do an excellent job of analyzing a group member and drawing him out while remaining behind a screen myself, the rest of the group will have learned that style. If I walk out of the room and come back, I'll find them all psyching each other out. Consider the bizarreness of this situation, in which I must conclude that the group isn't doing very well because they are beginning to act like me! And the more brilliant my interpretations, the more likely it is that group members will learn my interpretive style. They will fail to take strong positions of their own, fail to express themselves, and continue to hide, speculate, and ask questions of each other."

How large are John's groups? "I prefer fairly large groups," John said, "of around sixteen people, because there's likely to be more action. Eight people meeting together regularly will tend to form an intuitive unverbalized mutual protective society. Often this is very hard for the leader to detect and break up. That's why I prefer a larger group with more variety—a stable core, perhaps, with new people joining frequently. That way, people must adapt to new kinds of challenges continually. Often, however, I will split a large group into subgroups—not only when I start a weekend, but also any time the large group polarizes on some issue. For example, if there is a split in feeling about whether to withdraw or come out into the open, I may say, 'Okay, those who want to withdraw go over to that corner, and those who want to be more active get together over there.' When they form subgroups, I spend part of my time with each. I want them to be without me part of the time because that's when they really get a chance to practice on their own. As long as I'm around, there's a tendency to lie back and wait for me. For the same reason I encourage my groups to meet on their own in between sessions with me."

Speaking on how people grow in his groups, John said: "What happens to prevent growth is that awareness barriers between parts of the person are set up. Parents define certain parts of the child as bad, or as not him, and he buys this definition. He buys it because it's expedient to do so in the face of a lot of pressure. So he leaves parts of himself out of awareness; he denies, for example, that his sexual feelings or aggressive feelings are a part of him. He puts a lot of energy into not allowing these figure-ground formations to emerge—not allowing the expression of sexuality, not allowing the expression of aggressiveness. So he forms a personality in which some parts are out of touch. But whereas the acceptable parts may be expressed through his words, the unacceptable parts will be expressed in his posture, his tone of voice, the way he is fiddling with his hands, or what he is doing with his eyes. Expansion of awareness happens when two or more of these parts—or ego states—are brought together and put in touch. Let's say a person is talking in a rather monotonous voice about some ambition he has and his eyes are staring rather fixedly at the floor. It turns out that when we ask him, he says he's looking at a tiny spot of dirt on the floor. So I might ask him to describe it. If, by his description, he shows that he was really caught up in it, I might suggest that he identify with it, describe himself as a little spot of dirt on the floor. And then perhaps he gets in touch with some rather strong feelings of being insignificant and dirty, no good, and so forth. Even though this feels bad to him at the time, when he gets that together with whatever he was talking about, there's a kind of release of energy—the energy that went into holding those two parts of him apart; let's say the ambitious part and the part that feels like a dirty, insignificant little piece of shit on the floor. When these are brought together, he suddenly feels, 'My God, they're both me!' The self-hatred, the pride, all the bound energy that was involved in keeping them apart are loosened up, and suddenly there's a burst of free energy. And he's free to do both things better. He can express his insignificance more fully, because after all, everyone feels insignificant in some way at some level. And he can express his ambition more fully.

"To give another example, a girl in one of my groups was noticeably leaning away from a woman while saying to her, 'Gee, I feel warm toward you.' Her words were accurate, but her body was saying, 'I'm frightened.' When I had her get in touch with her body and translate what it was saying, she became aware of her fear. It turned out that the woman reminded her of her mother, and when she could bring both her feelings of fear and attraction together, they took on a depth and richness. The resulting relationship was more subtle and complex than either aspect alone would have been, and it was a fuller one, expressing more of herself. Breaking the awareness barriers between parts of the person frees energy, allowing him to express more of himself in a coordinated way.

"Of course, Gestalt techniques can be misused. Uusually when Gestalt work is done badly it obsessively focuses on tiny things. After all, I'm doing a million things right now, but only two or three of them are really important to work with. It takes a hell of a lot of hard-won skill to really know what's going to go some place, to feel where the energy is. If people do Gestalt badly, they say things like, 'What's your left toe doing now?'—they lose the main thrust of a person's energy."

John doesn't urge people to change their life-styles, but he does help them become clear about what they're doing and express themselves fully. "Full expression of any affect," he said, "usually discharges it and leaves the person more fully finished and ready to go on to something else. Limited or covert expression leaves the person clogged up with a lot of unfinished business. Resentment, for instance, is unexpressed anger. For me and for a lot of people I run into, resentment is one of the major clogs, sitting around cluttering up my head and my thinking all the time. The more fully I can express the anger, the less resentment I have. And the more fully I can claim responsibility for what I've done, the less I need bother resenting anybody else. Full and open expression is valuable in that it finishes business and clears the figure-ground field so that the person is ready for new figures to form, new needs to be expressed, new behavior to occur. The whole process of living can go faster. It's as though there's only room for a limited amount of material in consciousness. The more I spill into overt expression, the more can bubble up from underneath, and the faster life goes—faster in the sense of more full experience from moment to moment.

"One sign of growth in a group member is a certain quality of feeling that goes with the moment of new awareness. It's often accompanied by an exclamation like 'Whew!' and a happy sense of having made a liberating discovery. There's always a sense of pleasure no matter how painful the new awareness is, the pleasure of welcoming another part of me that I have shut out. The feeling tone invariably is lightened and brightened. If that pleasurable feeling isn't there, I suspect that the awareness is incomplete, that something else is going on, probably some kind of unconscious manipulation.

"Another sign of growth is increasing courage and willingness to take risks, as demonstrated by the person who wouldn't say 'boo' at the beginning of the group and now says 'boo' loud and clear. Generally speaking, increased flexibility and fluidity of feeling are signs of growth, whether it is someone who habitually apologizes beginning to take a firm stand or someone who habitually stands firm beginning to apologize now and then.

"Sometimes growth is purely internal. A person will do exactly what he always has done but will feel okay about it. I'm pleased if a person walks out with the same problems he brought in, as long as he sees them in a different perspective—and can have some fun at the same time. I guess what I value most is increasing lightness of affect and more ability to have fun. It's very hard to be really sick and have fun—I mean to have fun in the deepest sense, to be lighthearted."

CHAPTER XII

CHICKEN SOUP IS POISON

ROBERT W. RESNICK

IN ORDER TO MAKE CHICKEN SOUP, you have to kill a chicken. Although not particularly leading to self-actualization for the chicken, this sacrifices the bird to a greater cause—being helpful. Combined with onions, greens, carrots, water and seasoning, the resulting elixir is ready for its role as a helper. The giving of chicken soup is an attempt to help the other—to do for him, to make him feel better. The chubby, sponge-like matzo ball, not unlike the unconscious, lies 90 percent below the surface of the soup. By the time the unaware gourmet has had enough of this brew, the soup around the submerged matzo ball has cooled, and, like a dead submarine, it spews forth its fatty oil slick. **CAUTION**: Chicken soup is likely to be as fatal to the recipient as it was to the contributing poultry. Now don't run around like a submarine with its head cut off—there is an antidote.

Many therapists see themselves as members of the *helping professions* engaged in the helping relationship. Beware! Such people are dangerous. If successful, they kill the humanness in their patients by preventing their growth. This insidious process is somehow worse realizing such therapists typically want the reverse. They want their patients to grow, to live, and to be, and they guarantee the antithesis with their help. The distinction between true support and help is clear: *To do for the other what he is capable of doing for himself insures his not becoming aware that he can stand on his own two feet.* The difficulty is in judging whether or not the person is potentially capable of doing or being himself. This depends on your own convictions about human beings and possibly your own need to be helpful. If you are convinced (sucked in) that the person is as helpless, as impotent, and as incompetent as he plays, then you are helpful.

142

Gestalt Therapy has as a basic goal the substituting of self-supports for environmental supports. Perls talks about the therapeutic impasse—what the Russians call the *sick point*. Typically people experience confusion, helplessness, and nothingness at such a point. Their usual attempts to manipulate their environment for support by playing deaf or dumb, by misunderstanding, by crying, by demanding, by playing crazy, by pleading, etc. are not working. If the therapist (or anyone else) walks into the manipulation by trying to be helpful, he successfully keeps the other an infant. In order to achieve integration and to potentiate growth, the patient must do his own dirty work. Perls, in a more poetic mood, states that the essence of Gestalt Therapy is allowing (by frustrating) the patient to discover that he can *wipe his own ass*. He illustrates this point by talking about the human embryo in utero. Here, the organism does nothing for himself. He is completely dependent on environmental supports. Sustenance, warmth, and oxygen are all provided by the mother. At birth, the child enters his first impasse; he can breathe for himself or he can die. Throughout development, the neonate becomes more and more able to crawl on his own four limbs. At birth he cannot stand by himself. Soon, if allowed, he stands autonomously. Carry a baby around all the time and he may never learn to walk. His muscles may atrophy and he may even lose the possibility of ever walking by himself. In western cultures mothers are helpful and their babies walk, on the average, almost a year later than children in other cultures where the child is allowed to experiment, to make mistakes, to grow, to be. Children who get others to satisfy their needs with baby talk never need to learn to speak. As long as they have someone helping them—taking responsibility for communicating their needs to the world—they never need speech. Without their helpers they are like a Robisperre without his Baby Snooks. Initially, they may scream and cry for others to support them. Eventually, they will learn to communicate directly themselves or die.

No one can be completely without some environmental supports nor is it easy for me to conceive of wanting to be in such a position. There is a great difference in getting from the environment that which I cannot do for myself and conning others into doing what I can do for myself. Most of us, to varying degrees, are under the illusion that *we can't*. Typically I have found that *I can't* really means,

I won't. I won't take the risks involved. To want the environment to help, to comfort, to support, even when I can rely solely on my own self-supports entails taking the risk of asking for such help. I take the responsibility of asking for help rather than manipulating the other into offering what he believes I am incapable of generating for myself. Even the manipulation can be self-supporting if I am aware that *is* what I am doing. Such awareness allows me the choice and freedom to do this or to do otherwise. I am then still me—not relinquishing my autonomy, my power, unless *I* want to do so.

People coming to therapy usually want something. Often they ask for help and what they want from therapy is a way to change the consequences of their behavior without changing their behavior themselves. They state that they eat spicy foods and get heartburn. "Can't you do something about my heartburn since I am sure I can't stop eating spicy foods. Stop the heartburn or at least help me to find out *why* my eating spicy foods gives me heartburn." (They are under the illusion that the only possible way for them to change *what* they are doing is to find out *why* they are doing it.) Their cop-outs vary. The unconscious, although diminishing in popularity, probably still gets the most blame. Parents are always popular as are wives, husbands, social systems, economic systems, world situations and the *soup-man* (or Superman, depending on how you see your therapist). As long as they attribute responsibility for *their* behavior to another person or concept, *they* remain powerless. More exactly, they are *giving* their power/autonomy/humanness to the other person or concept. Their implicit therapeutic request is: Let's you and he (or it) fight. The therapist, if he is unaware, willing, or both, is pitted against the free-floating unconscious or whatever via the patient's manipulation while the latter drools over the flow of chicken soup and is never sated. Slow down or, noodles forbid, stop the soup, and the patient tries that much harder to unclog his lifeline. When the help is not forthcoming and the patient has not yet discovered his own ability to give himself his own chicken soup, he then encounters his impasse. If the therapist successfully frustrates the patient's attempts to manipulate, the impasse is pregnant with growth. If the therapist is helpful, he assures the impotency of the patient and up comes the oil slick from the murky depths of the soup. Even when a person breaks through his own shackles, as often happens in encounter groups, sensitivity groups, nude groups, marathon groups, and drug groups, he typically has great difficulty in integrating his behavior and experience into his everyday life. I am convinced that his freedom was given to him by the situation, the group, the leader, fatigue or drugs. Chicken soup comes in many flavors.*

The most popular way patients avoid standing on their own two feet is by looking for reasons. Simkins calls this the *why merry-go-round*. (I'm sure you're all familiar with the tune.) The patient hops on the why merry-go-round and plays thirty-two bars of "why, why, why does this happen to me?" After finding the reason, he hops off the merry-go-round only to find that nothing has changed. He crawls back on his outside horse looking for the brass-ringed *why* —spends more time, effort and money so that this time his new reason is elevated to the status of an insight. Stumbling off his horse, brass ring in hand, he finds nothing has changed. Some people have been on this carousel of therapy for five, ten or twenty years. Many of those who got off the merry-go-round have changed their tunes. The first eight bars go something like: "So now I know all the reasons and I'm still miserable." Indeed, if you allow them, they'll delight in relating their insights interminably (Excedrin® headache No. 2002). It's as if the purpose of therapy is to find out why. I'm convinced the purpose of therapy is to change behavior, experience or both. Behavior *is* caused and knowing the whys has nothing to do with change.

The most popular way therapists help their patients to avoid standing on their own is to first deny that they have the blueprints and answers the patient is asking for. (Of course, the therapist doesn't believe this.) This done, the therapist "helps" the patient with the content of his problems (e.g. he manipulates the patient into discovering for himself what the therapist knew all the time). Even if I assume (and I do not) that the therapist is better equipped to make decisions than the patient himself, I am convinced that this leaves the patient no better off than when he started. If anything, he is a worse cripple. The lyrics of his problem change over the months

*With this statement I in no way wish to condemn encounter groups, etc. I feel they can play an extremely important role in potentiating human growth by allowing people to experience possibilities. This, however, is not enough. It is only a beginning. The work then is to find out how (not why) I prevent myself from enjoying my possibilities.

and years, but the melody lingers on and on and on. The process by which he stops himself from fuller functioning continues as long as he deals with the content of his problem to the exclusion of the process. Blaming his parents *for making him weak or insecure* is not his problem . . . *HIS BLAMING IS.* What he is doing is making his parents responsible for who he is now. How he is doing this is by playing victim and blaming them. Why he is doing this is irrelevant to changing and, if pursued, guarantees his staying stuck. Is it any wonder he remains weak and insecure. Only when he becomes aware of his blaming his parents for who he is now does he have a chance to grow. When he is in touch with his *response-ability*—his ability to respond—he enters a world of possibilities, choices and freedom. As long as he blames the other, he remains impotent.

The making of chicken soup is a fine, old art with many variations. However, one thing remains unchanged: In order to make chicken soup, you have to kill the chicken.

TECHNIQUES AND EXPERIENCE
IN GESTALT THERAPY

ERVING POLSTER

O NE OF THE BASIC DEVELOPMENTS in Gestalt Therapy is an increased concern with formal aspects of emotional experiences
in contrast with the more usual concern with the content of these
experiences. The concepts of Oedipus complex, castration-anxiety,
transference and many of the other psychoanalytically discovered
phenomena are used as background rather than in an explanatory
way. One basic formal direction is to bring the patient into contact
with his body resistances so that he may become open to those crucial
emotional experiences which have been unfinished in his history.
This is accomplished through expansion of the range of techniques
open to the therapist. In psychoanalytic theory and its application,
we find a narrow range of techniques such as free association, dreams
and interpretation. In non-directive therapy, reflection and clarification have been the major techniques. We hope in Gestalt Therapy
to free the therapist to create his techniques as he proceeds and to
fashion them according to the specific media through which the patient is most capable of working and according to the particular
theme development required.

By dint of loose empiricism, we have found the function of the
first stage in therapy to be the establishment of a loosening up process
enabling the individual to receive new experiences and tolerate them.
Some of the types of experimental approaches that have been discussed in this symposium may seem superficial; in the beginning they
are. In relation to requests for simple awareness of self, it is common
to encounter resistance. What's the use of this? This is silly! This is
not therapy! And so on! But these early experiences show areas of
possibilities to the patient that formerly were not evident to him.

Part of the loosening-up process is the discovery of the breathing structure of the individual. As Dick Wallen mentioned earlier in his theoretical presentation, the breathing process is considered the basic bodily contact with the environment, repeatedly receiving air, using it, and returning to the environment an altered chemical composition of air. It is this breathing process that is the most centrally involved function when difficult emotional experiences present themselves. For example, people hold their breath to keep from crying, or they tighten up to ward off blows, or they limit the intensity of sensations. The breathing process is viewed as an essential part of the individual's contact with the environment and its functions as an integrator of the person's capacity for assimilating excitement within himself.

The breathing process works two ways: 1) it responds to excitement by distributing it either through release by expression or through spreading the sensation of it throughout the body so as to be bearable; 2) it produces excitement through its own stimulating effects. Once the initial stages of therapy have been worked through, the individual becomes more brave about his own bodily functioning. Then it becomes possible to deal with more crucial and basic types of resistances that are closest to the potential emotional experience. One of the techniques is to use fantasy. The dream is one form of fantasy and has long been central in psychoanalytic therapies. In Gestalt Therapy, the waking fantasy produced on the spot, is a central therapeutic instrument. It turns that which might otherwise be merely talked about into fresh reality. One of the great barriers is the tendency to talk about things, thus to intellectualize away basic experiences. Here is an illustration of one type of waking fantasy, similar to dream work, but having the advantage for my patient as having been experienced as her own perception, a product of the present moment.

She had closed her eyes and I asked her whether she visualized anything. She paused for a few moments and said she saw a kind of art-object. She continued to be aware of the art-object and soon it turned into a wax dummy. To digress a moment, one of the techniques of Gestalt Therapy is the shuttling technique: ranging back and forth between various types of therapeutic approaches, one moment using fantasy, another moment attending to bodily experi-

ence, then focusing on a memory and perhaps returning to fantasy. Thus, for example, if the individual during the course of a fantasy alters his breathing, it would be apparent that something is going on which is important for the patient to come into contact with. The therapist may then bring the patient into this awareness and help him to extend it. There may develop a feeling of tingling, for example, as well as other possible sensations. With this new awareness as background, one may return to the original fantasy prepared to develop it but with a more whole background of self entering the engagement. Now, as to the particular patient mentioned above, on finding that the art-object had turned into a wax dummy, she began breathing more deeply. After some attention to this and also to a growing tingling sensation under her eyes, she returned to her fantasy and this time the figure had become a discus thrower. The discus thrower was seen as very large. She said that if she touched it, it would snarl. The patient's father was an athletic, vigorous, dominant, *All American* type of man who had little to do with little girls, and it was the patient's fate to have been able to make a little contact with him. It once would have been very tempting because of psychoanalytic tradition to interpret the meaning of the image as a reflection of father. However, such a technique may well have interrupted the genuine process of development and the genuine emotional experiences to which she ultimately came. So, resisting this temptation (since I formerly was oriented with psychoanalytic therapy), we went further into her experience and she began to realize that she couldn't get any response from the figure. Then, she began to have a deep feeling of aloneness as she tried to contact the image. She spoke of being alone, then she began to cry. It was a physical explosion to which she gave in and the accompanying muscular spasms supported and directed her release. Her body had been ready and some moments after she finished crying, she opened her eyes and looked at me. She noticed that her vision had become remarkably clear, that she felt real even in the face of aloneness, not that she felt good, but she felt whole, and she felt a newly experienced worthiness.

Thus, it becomes evident that psychosomatic unity is a central factor in Gestalt Therapy: It is more than a lipservice, paying homage to the one-time strange phenomenon of psychosomatic illness. It is a recognition of the characterological psychosomatic unity in every day expressiveness.

Another example concerns a sixteen-year-old boy. It is difficult for many adolescents to come into contact with themselves, to tolerate the self-awareness of psychotherapy. Insights and interpretations make them self-conscious and defensive. Actions and interaction which are relevant and lively prove to orient and stimulate, usually unbeknown even to themselves. Here is an example of an intense emotional undercurrent related to a fairly simple physical movement. I noticed that the boy had his legs crossed and was swinging one leg up and down. I asked him if he noticed what he was doing and he said he did. I then asked him to notice any effect which would accompany this. He told me some of the sensations that he felt, some pressures and the feelings of swinging. Then soon he switched legs and started to move the other one and he told me his specific experience of this. Soon he began to be aware of the unity of his sensations and movements, each affecting the other, and he began to feel some excitement. He had put his hand on his leg and I called this to his attention. He looked at his hand and saw a vein in his hand. He said that this was a nauseating thing to see. He began to feel nausea. The traditional temptation would be to interpret the meaning of this experience, anxiety about having an erection or such. The Gestalt view is that in the full perception of the vein, in the experience of nausea, and in the recovery from nausea, the boy's range of acceptable confrontations would be widened naturally, and through self-regulation, he would recover those possible confrontations for which the vein was a poetic agent. In this instance, he recovered from the nausea. He pulled out his wallet, took out some pennies and began to look at the pennies. He said, "You know, pennies are a nuisance. You have to save up so many of them before you can get a load." Then he looked back at the vein in his hand, rather serenely and acceptingly, a little quizzical but with a half smile, perhaps amused, perhaps more complete, perhaps renewed, perhaps. . . One does not know. The boy did make great advances in his life. There were vastly improved school grades and a new softness in his relationship with his father, perhaps because of his *experiences* in therapy.

CHAPTER XIV

TRENDS IN GESTALT THERAPY

ERVING POLSTER

Introduction

G ESTALT THERAPY is an historical extension of psychoanalytic theory and methodology. However, while assimilating the original psychoanalytic foundations, it takes contrasting stands on many crucial therapeutic issues. The theory and method were introduced by a German psychoanalyst, Frederick Perls, who had come into contact with the holistic thinking of the early Gestalt learning theories.

In this union, there were the beginnings of an integrative approach to psychotherapy, wherein diversity was energized into a unified methodology. The assimilation of many contemporary formulations and techniques was facilitated by the then new theoretical positions taken by Gestalt Therapy. As a result of these positions, one may see commonalities with existential psychotherapy, psychodrama, role playing, Rogerian and experiential psychotherapies, group dynamics, semantics and many of the psychoanalytic revisionists, including especially Rank, Reich, Jung, Adler, and Groddeck. For the valid formation of new psychotherapeutic integrations, we must take into account what this array of orientations reflects—namely, the needs of historical progression, meaningfulness to a particular society and the authenticity with which the actual practitioners can work. In harmony with this view are the following words of Otto Rank, one of the great psychoanalytic perspective makers.

"Human psychology is constantly being influenced by all the forces that are building and molding the particular civilization of which it is an outgrowth. Every system of psychology is just as much an expression of the existing social order—as it is an interpretation of the same. Psychology is not a science beyond or above the civilization it presumes to explain. On the contrary, these psychological theories themselves have to be explained as part of the whole social system and understood as an expression—representing one particular layer of it. This makes intelligible the different schools of psychology we find simultaneously within one and the same cultural strata. Each of these contradictory systems claims to present the absolute truth, whereas in reality they represent different types, groups, and classes, and register the shifting of human conditions along the lines of change. In that sense, theories of psychology change, one might almost say, like fashions, and are perforce compelled to change in order to express, as well as make intelligible, the existing type of man in his dynamic struggle for maintenance and perpetuation.

How, then, does Gestalt Therapy harmonize with contemporary diversity, and, in so doing, how does it contrast with the psychoanalytic doctrine from which it emerges? In answer to these questions I have chosen four cornerstone concepts in psychoanalytic therapy and will describe and illustrate the corresponding modifications which are also the cornerstones of Gestalt Therapy:

1. In psychoanalysis there is the concept of the unconscious; in Gestalt Therapy, it is figure-ground formation.

2. In psychoanalysis there is transference; in Gestalt Therapy, it is contactfulness.

3. In psychoanalysis, there is interpretation and insight; in Gestalt Therapy, there is awareness.

4. In psychoanalysis, there are free associations and dreams; in Gestalt Therapy, there is experiment.

Figure-Ground Formation

Let us move to the first of these issues, the unconscious process. The functions which the concept of unconscious describe seem incontrovertible; that is, there are dynamically powerful forces within the individual which are inaccessible to his awareness but which, nevertheless, seriously influence his style of life. However, the concept of unconscious—conscious invites a dichotomous, either-or, view of psychological function, weakening the holistic view of man. Psychoanalysts have, of course, always acknowledged the interplay between the unconscious and the conscious, even introducing the pre-conscious as an intermediate state of accessibility. Nevertheless, the ongoing and permanent effervescence of mind, the free flow between the accessible and inaccessible, is not given as much attention as in Gestalt Therapy, either in the conceptualization nor, as would logically follow, in the therapeutic methodology. The unconscious is a concept which views that which is beneath the surface as more therapeutically attractive and potent than that which is at the surface. This serves as a deflection from immediacy and invites an attitude once-removed from that which is overtly going on to that which is presumably *really* going on.

The figure-ground concept, on the other hand, supports the surface experience as providing greater therapeutic leverage. It may be defined as that process wherein the individual is constantly and spontaneously selecting from the ground of his total present experience that which is salient, allowing it to emerge as a significant figure, one which is always viewed in unity with the context from which it came.

This process can apply to very simple functions, such as seeing. One sees not merely another person, but rather another person who is sitting in a chair, a black, patterned chair in a white-walled room with specific pictures hung on the walls. This room is in a house which has a familiar atmosphere and it is a house where one is going to spend the weekend, and where one has already had some very fulfilling experiences with the person sitting in the chair. The inner sense is one of excitement, anticipatory, confident, and uncluttered. What a different experience from the person who sees another person, period! It is through such union of figure and ground that enrichment comes. Many of our patients are in the position of either seeing the person, period, or suffering the opposite flaw, mostly experiencing the background and minimally seeing the person. They are molded in either case into a rigid selectivity, keeping themselves dead set against certain feelings or awarenesses.

The concepts of figure-ground formation also encompasses the existential view that that which exists, exists only now. In the next moment it will change because of the native flux which characterizes present experience. Only psychological hanging on can maintain the experience of sameness. If one is in a room with another person, one may experience a series of figure formations, flowing perhaps from absorption with long successions of words and ideas, flitting also intermittently to a twitch in his facial musculature, to a glow in his face, to the strength in his jaw, to the play of colors in his eyes, etc.

Each figural development contributes its share in the total experience much as the single film negative contributes in the uninterrupted flow of a moving picture. If the machine breaks down the flow is immobilized. If single films are blank, the flow will have gaps, seriously disturbing the meaningfulness or interestingness of the film.

The patient, therefore, must learn the method of unfixed attentiveness, permitting successive awareness to emerge. Many people have either become so transfixed on a small aspect of life that they imprison themselves in preoccupations, obsessions, personal prejudices, phobias, and the like, or are so labile that the overly flexible figural arrangements never develop the unity, continuity, or meaningfulness that a good life requires. Thus, the pervasive theme of our therapy is to draw into the foreground the unintegrated or blocked material from the background so that these experiences may all contribute in the stream of free figure-ground interrelationship.

An illustration of how this concept works is the story of a thirty-five-year-old patient, long divorced, classically dissatisfied in spite of successes in her work and easy sociability. She always maintains her aloofness, though, and those feelings which need to come into the foreground, remain fixed in the background, leaving her in a vague state of longing and always feeling incompleted. She suddenly realized that she was afraid of falling in love if she got close to people. She was afraid that if the feeling were not returned in kind, she would purgatorially need the other person. This was the emergency of a new figure. As she spoke, I asked her to describe what she felt. She said there was a twinge of sensation, which she felt afraid of—another new figure. As she continued concentrating on the sensation, a technique for recovering present experience, she began to feel that if she really yielded to it, it would get so strong she would have to *do* something. I asked her to close her eyes and allow a fantasy of any situation to come to her. She fantasied the scene in my office. I asked her to visualize what she would like to do. She saw herself coming into my arms and crying. The color rushed to her face as though having experienced something most surprising and new. She never looked warmer. She said she felt the warmth and it made her feel whole and independent. She left, having let her need come forward and be completed. A new configuration formed.

Contactfulness

Let us now go on from figure-ground formation to discuss transference and its Gestalt counterpart, contact or contactfulness. Freud's concept of transference has many interpretive possibilities. One may see in it the bare, as-though quality which deflects all present inter-relationship into nothing but a disguise replacing a past concern, merely a regurgitation from the past having nothing to do with present sensibilities. Or one can see it as an ingenious device to bring past events right into the room so that one is no longer talking about a relationship which is distant and dull, but rather is living a new relationship with his analyst. One can actually go to Freud's work and find support for either point of view. For example, in his "Outline of Psychoanalysis," Freud makes two statements. In one place he says, in relation to erotic and dependent attachments to the therapist, that "the danger of these states of transference evidently consist in the possibility of the patient misunderstanding their nature and taking them for fresh experiences instead of reflections of the past." This would make the actual relationship with the therapist merely a red herring. In contrast Freud also says in the same reference, "Another advantage of transference is that in it the patient produces before us with plastic clarity an important part of his life history, of which he would otherwise have probably given us only an unsatisfactory account. It is as though he were acting it in front of us instead of reporting it to us." This statement supports the priority of the present fresh moment, in contrast to the finished historical event. It envisions the therapeutic scene as a symbolic, dramatic event, thereby having increased vitality. But, it does fail to acknowledge what Gestalt Therapy supports; good symbols come out of real experience.

We see the arts of our day using symbolic tricks so extensively that one is tempted to try to assimilate a play or a painting not for the experience itself, but only for what it means. This is putting the cart before the horse. An illustration of a novel that keeps the horse where it belongs is *Moby Dick*. It is an absorbing narrative and, if one so desires, one may appreciate it just that way. Yet, it is also symbolic because in its narrative, the events have implications which reach beyond its own microcosmic circumstances and tell us, therefore, how the whole universe works or even how our own individual lives are lived.

Similarly, in psychotherapy, the symbol is most powerful when the immediate experience is authentic in itself, yet also speaks beyond the import of the moment. For the patient to thwart the therapist or to bore him or to be afraid of him must be a real event of its own for the symbolic impact to be genuine and full. However, for the impact to be therapeutic, it also stretches beyond the office, as when the patient perceives his feelings and resolutions are pertinent and possible elsewhere.

It should be added that people in deep concentration together are likely to develop powerful feelings. This is the health to which one wishes to return. The therapeutic office has certain great advantages over many other life situations for the development of mutual concentration. Deep feelings do arise, not only because of neurosis but also because of the opportunities for a return to well-being. Continuity, understanding, openness, return to depth, and the bare simplicities of contact all become possible again. Accepting the surface means we can tackle the deep need for face-to-faceness. It also means we can be open and learn from the patient as well as teach him. When, for example, a homosexual patient called me a "damn Jewish mother, trying to get him married off," I wanted to know how I was doing that, and when he got through telling me, I had learned a lesson. He, too, but not the lesson I intended to teach! I did not like to face that aspect of myself, but there it was!

The first step, therefore, is for the therapist himself to meet the patient in a face-to-face encounter where authenticity of expression and communication are primary. The basic psychological function involved is for the individual to meet otherness through his senses and his actions, much as this function is reflected in Buber's writings about I-Thou interaction. Secondly, although for the therapist to be authentic is basic, it is hardly enough. The patient is really behaving in self-defeating ways, and the therapist must give specific attention to the characteristic ways barriers to contact are set up. We must see that certain patients look away when talking to us, ask questions when they mean to make statements, use lengthy introductions to simple observations, compulsively tell both sides of all stories, sit in statue-like position, use mannerisms and expressions which reflect disinterest, play for sympathy, use submissive words when their tones are hostile, etc., ad infinitum. In Gestalt Therapy, we approach these resistances frontally, believing that with resolution of resistances like these, good contact will naturally follow.

Awareness

At this point we have touched on the psychoanalytic view of the unconscious and described the Gestalt counterpart, figure-ground formation. We have also touched on transference and Gestalt counterpart, contactfulness. Now, let us move on to the Gestalt concept of awareness, our counterpart for the psychoanalytic concepts of interpretation and insight. Awareness refers to the experience and description of current ongoing conditions reflecting the person's sensation and perception plus the derivative experience of more complex emotions and attitudes. It is the means for keeping up-to-date with one's self.

Awareness differs from insight through its continuing nature as an ongoing process readily available, at all times, rather than the sporadic illuminations one experiences in special moments. Further, attention to self awareness emphasizes the what, how, and where, of experience, rather than the why attitudes which interpretations have fostered. Focusing on one's awareness keeps one absorbed in the present situation, thereby heightening the sensations of the therapy experience. With each succeeding awareness one moves toward completion of a theme, such as we may see in the following illustration. The therapy scene starts with the patient's simple awareness of a tight jaw, and moves through several intermediate steps to a loosening up of his speaking mechanism and then to the recovery of childhood memories. This patient, a minister, felt he could not pronounce words as he would like to. His words did have a metallic tone, and he spoke like a brittle machine. I was aware of an odd angle to his jaw and I asked him what he felt there. He said it felt quite tight. I asked him to exaggerate the movements of his mouth and jaw. He became aware that he felt quite inhibited about this and described some aspects of his awareness; embarrassment, then stubbornness. He then remembered that his parents used to nag him about speaking clearly and he would go out of his way not to. At this point he became aware of tightness in his throat. He was speaking from muscular strain rather than using the support of his breathing mechanism. I, therefore asked him to bring his air into the picture coordinating his speech with his breathing by using a little more air than usual and by trying to feel the air as the foundation of his words. His coordination was very faulty, so faulty as to border on stuttering. When I asked whether he had ever stuttered, he looked startled, became aware of his coordination trouble, and then remembered what, until then, he *had* forgotten; he had stuttered until six or seven. The he remembered a scene when he was three or four years old. His mother was calling on the phone from some distant place and asked him what he wanted. He tried to say ice cream. His mother thought he meant he was going to scream at his brother and became infuriated with him. Then he recalled another scene with his mother. He entered her bedroom. She was in the bathroom and he heard what at first he thought was her laughter. Then he was startled to suddenly realize it was not. She was crying hysterically and he remembers the horrible feeling about this incongruity. As he told the story his eyes were opened to the confusion that had been engendered to him. When he finished, he looked relieved and renewed, his speech became more open and it softened. His jaw temporarily lost the tight look.

Experiment

Now we come to our fourth psychotherapeutic issue. Traditional psychoanalytic methodology was centered around free association and dreams as a basis for interpretations and insight. In Gestalt Therapy, the corresponding technique is the experiment. To experiment is simply to try something out. It is here that a large variety of technique may be assimilated. All are aimed at focusing attention on specific themes in the patient's behavior. The themes are developed so as to reconstruct new modes of action in old problem-solving situations. Through this technique, experimentally safe emergencies are created. That is, the individual is placed into situations where the relevant anxieties are dealt with, but they are dealt with under circumstances which are more instructive and supportive than those found in everyday life.

Here is an example of what I mean:

A young college student, very talkative and very bright, bores people even though his ideas are very interesting. He sprays his words around rather than focusing them on the person to whom he is talking. His words don't feel like they have touched or met the other person. I tried several devices to impel him to make his words meet me. One was for him to look at me as he spoke. Another was for him to point at me as he spoke. A third was for him to use my name as he spoke. Everytime he actually experienced meeting me with his words, he beamed, and several times he burst into uproarious laughter, unable to contain himself, as though he had discovered the secret of the universe!

This example illustrates several characteristics of the experiment. The experiment attempts to establish learning by doing rather than only talking about it, as it faced the patient with making actual contact. It sets up a safe emergency by coming to grips with an anxiety provoking event under relatively safe circumstances, the event having been in this case, the meeting of another person, the therapist. It established small units of therapy which has certain theoretical and technical advantages (closure practices, tension cycle, theme setting, etc.). There was a problem, climax, and illumination all in an identifiable unit. Finally, the experiment extends the range of techniques available to therapy, having gone beyond verbalization. One is opened to a wide range of classes of experiments, including dramatization, fantasy, directed behavior, and other classes of experiments beyond what we can discuss now.

We must conclude, now, and perhaps it will be enough to say in summary that the four concepts presented here were figure-ground formation, contactfulness, awareness, and experiment. They emerge as an extension and modification of psychoanalysis. They form the basis for an integration of contemporary innovations in technique. And they assimilate the existentialist philosophy of being and authenticity.

CHAPTER XV

A REVIEW OF THE PRACTICE OF GESTALT THERAPY

GARY M. YONTEF

PSYCHOLOGICAL ORIENTATIONS are frequently dichotomized into those stressing behavioral variables and those stressing phenomenological variables. Although some psychologists have recognized the need for both, many are not aware that Frederick Perls has founded a type of psychotherapy that does integrate both. Perls' major works (1947; Perls, Hefferline and Goodman, 1951) stress his theory and not his psychotherapy practice. Although he and his co-workers have written papers stressing the practice of therapy, these have not been sufficiently available in popular professional journals (e.g. Enright [a]; Levitsky; Simkin). The practice of this type of therapy, Gestalt Therapy, is the focus of this paper. Gestalt Therapy as a type of existential philosophy (Enright [a]; Simkin; Van Dusen, 1960), as a theory of personality and research (Perls, 1947; Perls *et al.*, 1951) and the theoretical and historical origins of Gestalt Therapy (Enright [a]; Simkin) will not be directly considered within the confines of this review.

Two goals of Gestalt Therapy make a review of its practice particularly important. One is the goal of being exclusively orientated to Here-and-Now behavior without conditioning the patient and without excluding awareness variables. The other goal is to apply the existential attitude without being excessively global and abstract.

Models of Psychotherapy

To understand Gestalt Therapy, it must be located in relation to three schools of psychotherapy: the psychodynamic therapy movement, the behavior therapy movement, and the human potentials movement. This section will be devoted not to a theoretical comparison of theories of psychotherapy, but rather to the

161

sketching of a context or backdrop against which the discussion of Gestalt Therapy can meaningfully take place.

Psychodynamic psychotherapy is predicated on the assumption of a patient's having a disease or disability which the therapist will cure or eliminate. Because the patient has this disease, he is assumed to be irresponsible. The therapist discovers why the patient has become as he is (diagnosis), and the patient's cure results from discovering what the therapist has discovered (insight). This approach to psychotherapy emphasizes inferred underlying causes and relegates actual behavior to the secondary status as a symptom. Psychodynamic theorists deem changes in overt behavior as unimportant unless the real, i.e. hidden cause, is dealt with. By stressing their inferences (interpretations), dynamically oriented therapists neglect Here-and-Now behavior and stress the patient's cognition of the There and Then. Moreover, psychodynamic therapists seldom describe their methodology in sufficient detail to communicate exactly what behaviors take place in psychotherapy.

Behavioral therapists have replaced these mentalistic, inferential, and often unscientific characteristics of the psychodynamic movement with observations of actual behavior. New and clearly specified techniques have been offered by Wolpe, Skinner, Stampfl, Bandura and others. Derived from experimental learning laboratories, these have all stressed hard data and exact specification of procedures. Vague concepts and interpretations of behavior based on unsupported constructs were eliminated from the repertoire of behaviorally trained psychologists. Among the assumptions and concepts eliminated were the importance of the irresponsibility of patients, preoccupation with etiology and the importance of awareness (consciousness).

These two schools do have in common the assumption that the therapist is responsible for making the patient change. The therapist does the work of creating change; because of his expertise, he does something to the patient, or orders mediators to do something to the patient, that produces change. The psychologist manipulates the environment of the patient so that behavior compatible with some standard of adjustment is conditioned into the patient, and undesirable behavior is de-conditioned. The behavior therapist is in control of the subject, and the subject, consistent with basic

S-R theory, is seen as a passive recipient of stimuli.

A third force has arisen in psychology which rejects the stress on removing either negative behavior by conditioning or psychopathology by psychoanalytically oriented psychotherapy. The humanist rebellion sees psychotherapy as a means of increasing man's potential. A discussion of the methods of this third force movement will be undertaken after discussing Gestalt Therapy. Gestalt Therapy is a part of this third force movement in American psychology, attempting the non-manipulative observation of Here-and-Now *behavior* and stressing the importance of awareness. This combination of behavior and awareness in a humanistic matrix makes Gestalt Therapy an attractive model.

The Theory of Gestalt Therapy

Gestalt Therapy emphasizes two principles that need integrating if behavioral and experiential psychology are to be meaningfully combined into one system of psychotherapy: *"The absolute working in the here and now"*; and *"The full concern with the phenomenon of awareness"* (Perls, 1966, p. 2). The Gestalt Therapist claims neither to cure nor to condition—but perceives himself as an observer of on-going behavior and as a guide for the phenomenological learning of the patient. Although a full understanding of the theoretical support for this would entail a detailed examination of the Gestalt Therapy theory of psychology, personality and psychopathology, a short detour into this subject will be necessary.

Gestalt Therapy is based on gestalt theory (a discussion of which is beyond the scope of the present paper (see Perls, *et al.*, 1951; Wallen, 1957). Gestalt therapists regard motor behavior and the perceptual qualities of the individual's experience as organized by the most relevant organismic need (Perls *et al.*, 1951; Wallen, 1957). In the normal individual, a configuration is formed which has the qualities of a good gestalt, with the organizing figure being the dominant need (Perls, 1947; Perls *et al.*, 1951). The individual meets this need by contacting the environment with some sensorimotor behavior. The contact is organized by the figure of interest against the ground of the organism/environment field (Perls *et al.*, 1951). Note that in Gestalt Therapy, both sensing the environment and motor movement in the environment are active, contacting functions.

When a need is met, the gestalt it organized becomes complete, and it no longer exerts an influence—the organism is free to form new gestalten. When this gestalt formation and destruction are blocked or rigidified at any stage, when needs are not recognized and expressed, the flexible harmony and flow of the organism/ environment field is disturbed. Unmet needs form incomplete gestalten that clamor for attention and, therefore, interfere with the formation of new gestalten.

At the point where nourishment or toxicity (Greenwald, 1969) is possible, awareness develops. Awareness is always accompanied by gestalt formation (Perls *et al.*, 1951). With awareness the organism can mobilize its aggression so the environmental stimulus can be contacted (tasted) and rejected or chewed and assimilated. This contact-assimiliation process is operated by the natural biological force of aggression. When awareness does not develop (i.e. figure and ground do not form into a clear gestalt) in such a transaction, or when impulses are kept from expression, incomplete gestalten are formed and psychopathology develops (Enright [a]). This shifting figure-ground of awareness replaces the psychoanalytic concept of the unconscious; the unconscious is phenomena in the field which the organism does not contact because of a disturbance in the figure-ground formation or because it is in contact with other phenomena (Polster, 1967; Simkin).

The point at which this awareness is formed is the point of contact. "Contact, the work that results in assimilation and growth, is the forming of a figure of interest against a ground or context of the organism/environment" (Perls *et al.*, 1951, p. 231). Gestalt Therapy focuses on what and how, and not on content.

> By working on the unity and disunity of the structure of the experience here and now, it is possible to remake the dynamic relations of the figure and ground until the contact is heightened, the awareness brightened and the behavior energized, most important of all, the achievement of a strong gestalt is itself the cure, for the figure of contact is not a sign of, but is itself the creative integration of experience (Perls, *et al.*, 1951, p. 232).

Awareness is a gestalt property that is a creative integration of the problem. Only an aware gestalt (awareness) leads to change. Mere awareness of content without awareness of structure does not relate to an energized organism/environment contact.

Gestalt Therapy starts a process, like a catalyst. The exact reaction is determined by the patient and his environment. The cure is not a finished product, but a person who has learned how to develop the awareness he needs to solve his own problems (Perls, *et al.*, 1951). The criterion of success is not social acceptability or interpersonal relations but "the patient's own awareness of heightened vitality and more effective functioning" (Perls, *et al.*, 1951, p. 15). The therapist does not tell the patient what he has discovered about the patient, but teaches him how to learn.

Perls calls the system of responses or contacts of the organism with the environment at any moment the self (Perls, *et al.*, 1951). The ego is the system of identification and alienation of the organism. In neurosis the ego alienates some of the self processes, i.e. fails to identify with the self as it is. Rather than allow the self to proceed with the organization of responses into new gestalten, the self is crippled. The neurotic loses awareness of (alienates) the sense of "it is I who am thinking, feeling, doing this" (Perls, *et al.*, 1951, p. 235). The neurotic is divided, unaware and self-rejecting.

This division, unawareness and self-rejection can be maintained only by restricting the organism's experiencing. The naturally functioning organism experiences by feeling, sensing and thinking. When the person rejects one of his modes of experiencing, the formation of new gestalten becomes blocked by unmet needs that form incomplete gestalten and, therefore, demand attention. Without experiencing needs and impulses, organismic self-regulation is impaired, and reliance on moralistic external regulation is necessitated (Perls, 1948).

The rejection of modes of experiencing can be traced far back in Western culture. Since Aristotle, Western man has been taught that his rational faculties are acceptable but sensory and affective faculties unacceptable. The human organism has become split into the *I* and the *Me*. Western man identifies with his reigning sovereign (reason), and has alienated his sensory and affective modalities. However, without balanced organismic experiencing, man cannot be in full contact with nature or in support of himself and, therefore, is impaired in learning from his environmental transactions (Perls, 1966; Simkin). Western man has been alienated, split and out of harmony with nature (Perls, 1948; Simkin).

Learning takes place by discovery, by the formation of new gestalten, i.e. insight. As an organism interacts with the environment gestalten are completed, awareness develops, and learning takes place (Simkin). Perls found his patients suffering from alienation of ego functions and set out to find a therapy that would integrate the split personality so that new gestalten could be formed, the patient could learn, etc. (Perls, 1948). He noticed that patients showed their basically faulty figure-ground formation in their transactions with him. This was the clue for his founding of Gestalt Therapy. A fuller discussion of this can be found in the literature (Perls, 1947, 1948; Perls *et al.*, 1951; Simkin; Wallen, 1957).

The basic therapeutic dilemma as Perls sees it is that the patient has lost awareness of the processes by which he alienates (remains unaware of) parts of his self-functioning. He found (Perls *et al.*, 1951) that by using experiments with directed awareness, the patients could learn how he kept from being aware; in a sense, Perls taught patients how to learn.

The therapeutic change process in Gestalt Therapy involves helping the patient re-discover the mechanism which he uses to control his awareness. The directed awareness experiments, the Gestalt Therapy encounter, the group experiments which we shall discuss, all have as their goal making the patient aware of the habitual acts he engages in to control his awareness. Without this emphasis the patient might increase his awareness, but only in a limited and circumscribed way. When the patient re-experiences control of awareness control, his development can be self-directive and self-supportive.

> The ultimate goal of the treatment can be formulated thus: We have
> to achieve that amount of integration which facilitates its own de-
> velopment (Perls, 1948, p. 12).

The therapeutic tasks the Gestalt therapist gives the patient are all reports of the patient's awareness. In therapy the patient can gain something different than he gains from experiences outside of therapy, i.e. something other than an isolated piece of knowledge, a temporary relationship or catharsis. What therapy can create is a situation wherein the very core of a person's growth problem, restricted awareness, is the focus of attention.

For therapist and patient alike, Perl's prescription is "lose your mind and come to your senses." Perls stresses the use of the external senses as well as the internal proprioceptive system of self-awareness. By re-sensitizing the patient, the patient can become aware once again of the mechanism by which he (ego) rejects awareness and expression of impulses. When the organism once again controls the censor, it can fight the battles of survival with its own sensorimotor behavior, learn and become integrated, that is to say, self-accepting (Simkin).

When the neurotic—with his split in personality, under-use of affective and sensory modalities and lack of self-support—attempts to have the therapist solve his life problems, the Gestalt therapist refuses; the Gestalt therapist refuses to allow the patient to thrust the responsibility for his behavior onto him (Enright [a]). The therapist frustrates the attempt to operate manipulatively in core areas.

In Gestalt therapy the goal is not to solve The Problem (Enright [a]), for the patient will remain a cripple as long as he manipulates others into doing his problem-solving for him, i.e. as long as he does not use his full sensorimotor equipment. Gestalt Therapy is holistic and sees the human organism as potentially free of internal control hierarchies. The patient-therapist relationship in Gestalt Therapy is also relatively hierarchy-free.

The patient is an active and responsible participant who learns to experiment and observe so as to be able to discover and realize his own goals through his own efforts. The responsibility for the patient's behavior, change in behavior and the work to achieve such change is left to the patient.

Thus Gestalt Therapy rejects the notion that the therapist must or should assume the role of a conditioner or de-conditioner.

> Every patient barks up the wrong tree by expecting that he can achieve maturation through external sources . . . Maturation cannot be done for him, he has to go through the painful process of growing up by himself. We therapists can do *nothing* but provide him the opportunity, by being available as a catalyst and projection screen (Perls, 1966, p. 4).

The role of the Gestalt therapist is that of a participant-observer of Here-and-Now behavior and catalyst for the phenomenological experimentation of the patient. The patient learns by experimenting in the "*safe emergency* of the therapeutic situation" (Perls, 1966, p. 8). He continues to take the natural consequences of his behavior in and out of therapy.

> The basic assumption of this therapeutic approach is that people can deal adequately with their own life problems if they know what they are, and can bring all their abilities into action to solve them . . . Once in good touch with their real concerns and their real environment, they are on their own (Enright [a], p. 7).

Although the therapist in Gestalt Therapy does not focus on mentalistic concepts, or on the past, or on the future, no content is excluded in advance. Past or future material are considered acts in the present (memory, planning, etc.). Nor is Gestalt Therapy static. The focus is not on finding the *whys* of behavior or *mind* nor is it manipulation of stimulus consequences to bring about a change in behavior. "Contrary to the approaches of some schools which stress 'insight' or learning 'why' we do as we do, Gestalt Therapy stresses learning 'how' and 'what' we do" (Simkin, p. 4).

In Gestalt Therapy the therapist is not passive, as in older Rogerian therapy, but is quite active. Attending to behavior not mentalisms; to awareness not speculative questions, Here and Now and not There and Then, all necessitate action and assertiveness on the part of the therapist.

The goal in Gestalt Therapy is maturity. Perls defines maturity as "the transition from environmental support to self-support" (Perls, 1965; also see Simkin). Self-support implies contact with other people. Continuous contact (confluence) or absence of contact (withdrawal) are contrary to what is implied (Perls, 1947). Self-support refers to self-support in the organism/environment field. Confluence obviously is not self-support. Withdrawal still involves the essence of non-self-support. Critical here is continuous use of the sensorimotor equipment of the organism in transaction with the environment, with awareness (Enright [a]). Such is self-support, and leads to integration.

This process is achieved in the natural environment when there is struck "a viable balance of support and frustration." Gestalt therapists attempt to balance support and frustration. Excessive frustration, especially in individual therapy, will result in the patient's disowning the therapist. Excessive support encourages the patient to continue to manipulate the environment for that support which the patient erroneously believes he cannot provide for himself. While temporary improvement may result from such supportive treatment, the patient will not be aided in moving beyond the impasse point.

The impasse point is what the Russian literature calls the *sick point*. "The existential impasse is a situation in which no environmental support is forthcoming and the patient is, or believes himself to be, incapable of coping with life on his own" (Perls, 1966, p. 6). In order to achieve or maintain support from the environment the patient will engage in a number of maneuvers. Such manipulations or games are used by the patient to maintain the status quo, to keep control of his environment and to avoid coping with life on his own. When the neurotic patient avoids coping, he avoids the actual pains any organism avoids, and, in addition, "the neurotic avoids imaginery hurts, such as unpleasant emotions. He also avoids taking reasonable risks. Both interfere with any chance of maturation" (Perls, 1966, p. 7).

Therefore Gestalt Therapy calls the patient's attention to his avoidance of unpleasantness and his phobic behavior is worked through in the course of the therapy.

In summary, the therapist balances frustration and support while maintaining a relationship in the I and Thou; Here and Now tradition of Martin Buber. The patient at first works hard at avoiding his actual experience and the consequences of his actual behavior. Because the patient has long since learned and practiced the manipulating of his environment to obtain support and means of avoiding becoming aware of his actual experience, he is usually quite skilled at this.

> He does this by acting helpless and stupid; he wheedles, bribes, and flatters. He *is not* infantile, but plays an infantile and dependent role expecting to control the situation by submissive behavior (Perls, 1965, p. 5).

Gestalt Therapy Techniques

The literature of psychoanalysis is voluminous but does not describe the actual behavior that takes place in psychoanalysis with clarity sufficient to impart understanding to those who have not actually participated. The reader of *Gestalt Therapy* (Perls, *et al.*, 1951) will be aware that Perls' descriptions of Gestalt Therapy are not more successful at describing his procedures than the psychoanalysts were at describing theirs.

A clearer picture of Gestalt Therapy is available through numerous tape recordings, video tapes and movies. There are numerous papers by Perls and his co-workers that are available from the Esalen Institute, Big Sur, from the Gestalt Institute of Cleveland, and similar institutions. A detailed discussion of the background concepts of Gestalt Therapy, including the personality theory, the theory of psychopathology and the concept of the continuum of awareness are available in Perls' books. *Gestalt Therapy*, Perls' most complete work to date, has a series of eighteen experiments which the reader can try at home and which form the crux of the work that Perls does in his psychotherapy. The experiments skillfully bridge the gap between the experience of the reader and the words of the authors.

Gestalt Therapy is not written for rapid perusal. Perls has an unusual configuration of attitudes, techniques, language, and theories which need creative and persistent effort to assimilate. Communication may be particularly difficult with behaviorally-trained psychologists who are accustomed to an exact, precise specification of what is d ie. Moreover, the idiom of Gestalt Therapy and behavior therapy are different. When reading the work of a psychologist that fits in recognized categories and who uses familiar terms, the amount of time that went into acquiring essential assumptions and terminology is often forgotten. To understand even the basic terminology of Perls' theory requires time and a willingness to chew over new material beyond that which is customarily demanded when reading in one's own area of interest.

Gestalt Therapy is selectively and differentially practiced according to the personality and needs of the therapist, the patients and the setting. Perls does not recommend or approve of imitation of the way he as a person applies his theory. Each therapist has to find his own way.

Perls recognizes that a corollary to the unity of the organism/environment field is that a change anywhere in the field will affect the entire field. Thus it is possible to intervene at many points and from many angles and the immediate results may generalize to the rest of the field. Some changes necessitate environmental changes, e.g. in the level of environmental support. Intervention with the single organism can often achieve results even when approached from a unidimensional point of view—e.g. sensory awareness. However, Perls himself advocates a multiple variable approach as the only way of helping patients move beyond the impasse. The Gestalt Therapist uses many aspects of the Here-and-Now situation to create growth opportunities, encounter, experimentation, observation, sensory awareness, etc.

THE EXPERIMENTAL MODEL OF PSYCHOTHERAPY

Gestalt Therapy, by emphasizing the awareness continuum of oneself and the world, is a way (Tao) of living and enhancing one's experience. It is non-analytic. It attempts to integrate the fragmented, split personality through non-interpretive focusing in the here-and-now (Esalen Programs, Summer, 1968).

Virtually all activity in Gestalt Therapy consists of experiments in directed awareness (Simkin). Perls defines an experiment as:

. . . a trial or special observation made to confirm or disprove something doubtful, exp. one under conditions determined by the experimenter; an act or operation undertaken in order to discover some unknown principle or effect, or to test, establish, or illustrate some suggested or known truth; practical test; proof (Perls *et al.*, 1951, p. 14).

The aim is for the patient to discover the mechanism by which he alienates part of his self processes and thereby avoids awareness of himself and his environment. All rules and suggestions in Gestalt Therapy are designed to aid discovery and not to foster a particular attitude or behavior (Levitsky).

The prototypical experiment is to ask the subjects to make up a series of sentences beginning with the words "Here and now I am aware that . . ." (Enright [b]; Perls, 1948; Perls *et al.*, 1951). The therapist continually relates back to what the patient is aware of (experiencing). The therapist encourages a continuation of the experiment by asking: "Where are you now?" "What are you experiencing now?" Questions by the patient are translated into: "Now you are aware of wondering . . ." When the patient begins to avoid the instructions, this is also translated into awareness reports: "Now I am aware of wishing to stop."

The variations on this basic experiment are limitless (Levitsky). The experiments are arranged in a graduated series so that each step challenges the patient, but are within the patient's grasp. In each experiment the patient can try new behaviors which can be experimented with only with great difficulty in the natural environment (Polster, 1966).

Ordinarily we think of the control of the experiment and the observer of the data as the psychologist. In Gestalt Therapy the psychologist sets up the experiments, but shares the control and observation with the patient. External behavior is directly perceived by the psychologist and the patient; internal behavior is perceived by the patient alone through his enteroceptors and proprioceptors. The relation of the two in the whole gestalt is the focus of attention. One can regard Gestalt Therapy as a process of focusing on the consecutive unfolding of simultaneous internal and external behaviors. As in any experimentation, the results of the experiments indicate directions for new experiments. When the patient can experiment and experience without the therapist, the therapy is finished.

Three aspects of this Here-and-Now experimentation should be noted: the functional concept of *now*, the role of observation of the patient's total behavior, and the difference between introspection and directed awareness.

Now

Now is a functional concept referring to what the organism is doing. What the organism did five minutes ago is not part of now. An act of remembering a childhood event is now, i.e. the remembering is now. Perls states that the past exists as "precipitations of previous functions" (Perls, 1948, p. 575). The future exists as present processes, e.g. planning, hoping, fearing, etc. The exclusive orientation with any one tense (past, present or future), the isolation of the three from each other, or the confusion of the three are all signs of disorder (Shostrom, 1966b). Gestalt Therapy experiments operate Here and Now in this functional sense (Levitsky).

Observation and Body Language

Observation is at the heart of the Gestalt Therapy experimentation. The observation concentrates on the means of avoiding awareness of the alienated and inaccessible. When the patient shows incongruences, often attending to one aspect of his total communication and not another, this is reported to the patient. Often the verbal content is incongruent with the tone of voice and posture of the patient. This is not silently noted, but is brought to the attention of the patient.

It has been stated that:

> This tendency to limit the discourse to the present is feasible only because in Gestalt Therapy we are listening to the *total communication* rather than the strictly verbal. The relevant past *is* present here and now, if not in words, then in some bodily tension and attention that can be hopefully brought into awareness. It is impossible to overstress the importance of this point. For a purely verbal therapy to remain in the here and now would be irresponsible and disastrous. It is only the aggressive, systematic and constant effort to bring the patient's total communication into his awareness that permits a radical concentration upon the here and now (Enright [a], p. 15).

Listening to the total communication necessitates the active use and trust of the senses by the therapist (Perls, 1966). Gestalt Therapy is non-interpretative; in his activity the Gestalt therapist clearly separates his observations from his inferences and emphasizes the former. For example, Gestalt Therapy starts with and stresses the obvious (Perls, 1948; Simkin). The obvious is frequently overlooked by patients and therapists. The opening gambit of the patient, e.g. sight, smile, handshake, are obvious behaviors and are sometimes more laden with meaning than the ritual verbal greeting (Enright [a]).

Body language is an important part of the total observation. Physical symptoms are taken seriously and considered more accurate communications of a patient's real feelings than his verbal communications. Simkin calls such physical symptoms truth buttons. By experimenting with taking one side and then another of a conflict, the patient "will inevitably bring on the body language—the truth signal—when he takes sides with that aspect of the conflict which is anti-self" (Simkin, p. 3).

Asking the patient to exaggerate an unwitting movement or gesture may result in important discovery by the patient (Levitsky). As an example:

> A constricted, over-inhibited man is tapping his finger on the table while a woman in the group is talking on and on about something.

Asked if he has anything he would like to comment about what the woman is saying, he denies much concern with it, but continues the tapping. He is asked then to intensify the tapping, to tap louder and more vigorously and to continue this until he feels more fully what he is doing. His anger mounts very quickly and within a minute or so he is pounding the table and expressing vehemently his disagreement with the woman. He goes on to say that she is "just like my wife," but in addition to this historical perspective, he has had an experiential glimpse of his excessive control of strong assertive feelings and the possibility of more immediate and hence less violent expression of them (Enright [a], pp. 3-4).

Without sensitive observation the experimental approach in psychotherapy is impossible. Perls' unique contribution to psychotherapy methodology lies in replacing interpretation with behavioral observation and experimentation. The Gestalt therapist does not interpret—he observes, sets up experiments, is a living person in the therapeutic situation as well as in other contexts.

Awareness Experiments and Introspection

The Gestalt Therapy directed awareness experiments are not the same as introspection (Perls, *et al.*, 1951, p. 389; Enright [a], p. 11). In introspection the organism is split into an observing and an observed segment.

When you introspect, you *peer at yourself.* This form of retroflection is so universal in our culture that much of the psychological literature simply takes it for granted that any attempt to increase self-awareness must of necessity consist of introspection. While this, definitely, is not the case, it probably is true that anyone who does these experiments will *start* by introspecting. The observer is split off from the part observed, and not until this split is healed will a person fully realize that self-awareness which is not introspected can exist. We previously likened genuine awareness to the glow produced within a burning coal by its own combustion, and introspection to turning the beam of a flashlight on an object and peering at its surface by means of the reflected rays (Perls, *et al.*, 1951, pp. 157-158).

To observe yourself in action, and eventually to observe yourself as action, introspection is inadequate. Introspection is dualistic and static. Moreover, it down-plays the awareness of the body that is possible through internal sense receptors and is instead speculative. After all, there are available numerous sensory inputs from internal receptors which the organism can allow to enter into awareness or which can be kept from awareness. These form observational data available to the organism and not to the experimenter. The experimenter can only infer what he does not observe.

Perls' formulation offers an alternative to Titchnerian introspection, behavioristic mindlessness, and psychoanalytic speculation. Internal self-observations are valuable even though they are somewhat unreliable. The difficulty with the reliability and validity of external observation is difficult enough; the reliability and validity of inference about private events is obviously in even greater doubt.

Perls, being aware of this difficulty and of the ease with which even a trained observer can contaminate observation with inference, stresses the need to separate sensory observation and cognitive inference. He does not ask patients questions which lead to cognitive processes (inference and imagination) at the expense of sensory processes (observation, use of the senses).

In addition

> the general strategy of Gestalt Therapy does not depend on the patient's accuracy in self report. We simply tell him, in effect, to sit down and start living, then note where and how he fails (Enright, p. 6).

The therapist's observations while the patient is reporting his awareness can provide some data to check internal observation, for what exists internally in an organism is usually reflected in external behavior in some manner. Since the psychotherapist and patient are observing the same organism from different angles, the simultaneous use of both observations can be expected to shed some light on basic processes.

The Gestalt Therapy experiments return always to the primary sensory data of experience. For example, Gestalt Therapy does not ask why, but instead focuses on what and how. What and how are amenable to exact observation; why leads to speculation (Enright [a]; Simkin). This will be discussed further below. The obvious, the minute and concrete, and physiological processes are all stressed in Gestalt Therapy; they are often neglected in clinical psychology.

The separation of observation from inference with emphasis on the former is as applicable to internal as external processes. Gestalt therapists attempt to pin down exactly what experience is represented by a particular phenomenological report. The therapist asks about exact sensations, as in the following example:

T: What are you aware of now?

P: Now I am aware of talking to you. I see the others in the room. I'm aware of John squirming. I can feel the tension in my shoulders. I'm aware that I get anxious as I say this.

T: How do you experience the anxiety?

P: I hear my voice quiver. My mouth feels dry. I talk in a very halting way.

T: Are you aware of what your eyes are doing?

P: Well, now I realize that my eyes keep looking away.

T: Can you take responsibility for that?

P: ... that *I* keep looking away from you.

T: Can you *be* your eyes now? Write the dialogue for them.

P: I am Mary's eyes. I find it hard to gaze steadily. I keep jumping and darting about ... etc. (Levitsky, pp. 5-6).

The results of this kind of observation and experimentation have confirmed Perls' original observation of over-emphasis of reason. Simkin reports:

> In all cases that I have seen thus far, people seeking psychotherapy show an imbalance among their three primary modes of experiencing. Most patients that I see, and this seems to be also true of the bulk of the patients seen by my colleagues, are very dependent on and have overly stressed their development of the intellectual or the "thinking–about" mode of experience. Most of the time, these people are in touch with their thought processes and their experience is with a fantasy (memory) of the past or a fantasy (wish) (prediction) of the future. Infrequently are they able to make contact with their *feelings* and many are also *sensory* cripples—not seeing or hearing or tasting, etc. (Simkin, pp. 3-4).

The Existential Attitude

Most existential therapies place importance on the interpersonal existential encounter. Gestalt Therapy is no exception, and I and Thou; Here and Now has been called a capsule description of Gestalt Therapy (Simkin, p. 1; see also Polster, 1966, p. 5). In time-space Gestalt Therapy locates both the experiments in directed awareness and the encounter in the Here and Now. The therapeutic relationship is seen as an I-Thou relationship as discussed by Martin Buber.

Participants in an existential encounter function on the self-actualizing model (Enright; Greenwald; Shostrom, 1967; Simkin). According to this model, there is a continuum from manipulation (Shostrom) or deadness (Perls) to actualization (Shostrom) or aliveness (Perls). The actualizer treats each human being as an end (a Thou) and not a means (an It); the manipulator controls himself and others as things, or allows himself to be controlled as a thing. The actualizer expresses his feelings directly to people as they arise; the manipulator judges, withdraws, blackmails, gossips, lives exclusively in a single time dimension. The manipulator does not trust his natural organismic self-regulatory system, and therefore depends on the moralistic regulatory system of society, not on his own support.

The neurotic patient comes to the therapist with his characteristic pattern of manipulating support. He frequently wishes to give up his self-direction and self-support or manipulate the therapist into giving up his. By design or accident, some therapists accede to these manipulations. The Gestalt therapist may refuse the assent, dissent or other support the patient seeks. Selective reinforcement via approval cues of therapist approved behavior would be merely a form of conditioning, and therefore manipulative rather than actualizing. The patient looking to Perls for approval may find him intensely involved via eye contact and general attitude, but finds no clue to approval or disapproval. His unaverted gaze can be quite disconcerting to such patients. This is an example of the clinical use of frustration. The Gestalt therapist does not give support to a patient because he is too weak to support himself. The Gestalt therapist may indicate by his interest, behavior and words that he cares, understands and will listen. This true support is nourishing for many patients. Observers of Gestalt Therapy who have not had an intimate, diadic encounter with a Gestalt therapist sometimes miss the intensity and warmth of the true support offered by most Gestalt therapists while they are simultaneously coldly refusing to direct or be responsible for the patient.

Some existential theorists discount the importance of technique in psychotherapy (e.g. Carl Rogers, 1960, p. 88), emphasizing the encounter instead. Walter Kempler, an *experiential gestalt* therapist, is one spokesman for the therapist-as-person position:

> *Upon these two commandments hang all the law*—upon which experiential psychotherapy within families stands: attention to the

current interaction as the pivotal point for all awareness and interventions; involvement of the total therapist-person bringing overtly and richly his full personal impact on the families with whom he works (not merely a bag of tricks called therapeutic skills). While many therapists espouse such fundamentals, in actual practice there is a tendency to hedge on this bi-principled commitment (Kempler, 1968, p. 88).

Kempler gives several long, verbatim examples of his non-technique (1965, 1966, 1967, 1968; see Shostrom, 1967, pp. 204-205 for short illustrative examples). In the following example Kempler becomes angry at a patient who has been whimpering during the session to his wife and to Kempler.

P: What can I do? She stops me at every turn.

T: (Sarcastically to provoke him): You poor thing, overpowered by that terrible lady over there.

P: (Ducking): She means well.

T: You're whimpering at me and I can't stand to see a grown man whimpering.

P: (Firmer): I tell you I don't know what to do.

T: Like hell you don't (offering and at the same time pushing). You know as well as I that if you want her off your back, you just have to tell her to get the hell off your back and mean it. That's one thing you could do instead of that mealy-mouthed apology, "She means well."

P: (Looks quizzical; obviously he is not sure he wants to chance it with either of us but is reluctant to retreat to the whimpering child posture again): I'm not used to talking that way to people.

T: Then you'd better get used to it . . .

P: You sure paint a bad picture.

T: If I'm wrong, be man enough to disagree with me and don't wait to get outside of here to whimper to your wife about how you didn't know what to say here.

P: (Visibly bristling and speaking more forcefully): I don't know that you're wrong about what you're saying.

T: But how do you like what I'm saying?

P: I don't. Nor do I like the way you're going about it.

T: I don't like the way you're going about things either.

P: There must be a more friendly way than this.

T: Sure, you know, whimper.

. . .

P: (Finally in anger): I'll say what I damn please. You're not going to tell me how to talk . . . and how do you like that? (He socks his hand.)

T: I like it a helluva lot better than your whimpering. What is your hand saying?

P: I'd like to punch you right in the nose . . .
(Kempler, 1968, pp. 95-96).

Gestalt Therapy does not exclude either a purely personal or a purely technical therapist response if it expands the awareness of the patient (Enright [a]).

The Gestalt therapist retains his right to be independent in the I-Thou relationship. This independence can help remove the therapist's reinforcement of dysfunctional behavior, and allows the therapist to be self-supportive, self-directive and therefore model self-actualizing. This is possible only with the careful observation and awareness discussed in the last section.

Although in Gestalt Therapy the therapist is allowed to be spontaneously himself, the Gestalt therapist is self-committed to increasing the awareness of the patient, and uses the technique of experimentation. Perls goes so far as to state that he interrupts any "pure verbal encounters without any experimental substance . . ." (Perls, 1966, p. 9). Whatever Perls may believe philosophically about interpersonal relationship models, as a therapist, he advocates discovery by the patient using his own senses while maintaining for experimental purposes an I-Thou; Here and Now relationship. The aim of such an encounter is discovery, increased awareness; such an encounter is not designed for catharsis. If expression is honest, it is usually not interfered with; it may be fostered as a learning device—but is not encouraged simply as a safe discharge of aggression.

One can question whether the therapist, by not attending to his inner response and by concentrating on setting up experiments for the patient, is not at odds with the I-Thou model of relationship. The Gestalt Therapy position is that the therapist makes direct contact with the patient with his senses, attending to an agreed on task, expanding the awareness of the patient. A competent Gestalt therapist must be able to be aware of his inner feelings as he attends to them, and express them spontaneously when he wishes. There is no preconceived injunction against expressing his feelings to a patient. In general, the moral *(should)* is to be aware—the control or expression of a feeling is up to the individual. The Gestalt therapist's human reaction is also used for its diagnostic value (Enright [b]).

Related to the technical versus human response question is the question of influencing the patient's choice of values in his life. There is, in Gestalt Therapy, an attitude against taking a stand on moral issues of the patient. The Gestalt therapist may communicate a feeling Here and Now, or communicate something of his own values if this is in the interest of expanding the patient's awareness of alternatives. This is not accepted as a means of inculcating values. Contrast the following two views.

Bach states:
Concerning the therapist's communication to his patients of his own values by which he lives, my clinical experience shows this can be of great service, provided, however, that the patient is actively prevented from using such information to avoid finding his own identity by imitation . . . I stress that my ways of wrestling with value problems are to be taken only as a reference point to gain perspective, to compare, rather than to imitate. As a technical general rule, I reinforce and stress *self-differentiating* experiences in therapy . . . over identification processes. I consider growth through "identification with" a transitory process while self-actualization through "differentiation from" is a lifelong mode of self-assertive living (Bach, 1962, p. 22).

Simkin states:
In my opinion, the therapist, in taking a "personal stand," uses a defensive maneuver as a result of feeling threatened by the patient at this point. I feel it is a technical mistake if the therapist forces his own values on the patient under the guise of "education". Even though in a few instances I gave in to my own needs to voice an opinion, I consider this my own weakness. And my principle is that such statements should be generally avoided, and the patient should be left to find his own values (Simkin, 1962, pp. 21-22)

Simkin discusses two cases (Simkin, 1962, pp. 205-209) in which he makes the judgment to share or not share his values.

In one case, a seventeen-year-boy reports that he is going to use his observation of his father with a girl friend to blackmail the father. Simkin lets the patient know that to him blackmail was immature and repugnant. It was made clear to the patient that he had a right to make his own choice. Simkin's rationale was that the boy was living in a family where there was not an adequate amount of mature behavior to sample from and the therapist's attitude could serve as a source of information about possible behavior models.

In another case he reports that a twenty-two-year-old patient was discussing behavior which Simkin regarded as unacceptable for himself (and socially). The therapist did not communicate this to the patient. This judgment was made because: (1) The behavior provided good material for analysis; (2) The therapist's objection to the behavior was neurotically motivated; (3) The patient was not unduly at the mercy of his parents as in the previous case.

The primary function of the Gestalt therapist is to help the patient learn to discriminate, and for this, direct exposure to the therapist's values may be necessary. The therapist has the function of helping the patient to perceive his behavior and the consequences and implications of his behavior. Beyond that the value choice is an individual matter.

For the I-Thou relationship the responsibility question is most crucial. The actualizing model is not imposed on or recommended to the patient; the Gestalt therapist simply refuses to give up his freedom, or accept the patient's surrender of his. The Gestalt therapist takes responsibility for behaving according to his own values, but for the patient there is only the prescription, "Try this behavior in therapy as an experiment and see what you discover." If the patient likes the Gestalt Therapy model he *may* choose to adopt it. Diversity of values and behavior is highly regarded in Gestalt Therapy and the patient is left with responsibility for himself. If the patient finds the therapist's behavior a model which is satisfying, he may adopt any part of it he wishes. That is his choice and the Gestalt therapist wants it no other way. The Gestalt therapist has a deep commitment to the patient's behaving on the basis of knowledge (awareness), but has an equally abiding commitment to the value in diversity of behavior. The Gestalt therapist does not try to trick or manipulate the patient out of his behavior, only out of his state of unawareness.

The importance of this last point cannot be overstated. The Gestalt therapist does not manipulate the patient into accepting the self-actualizing model. One must pick and choose from Gestalt Therapy whatever is palatable for him and reject the rest (Enright [a]; Greenwald; Levitsky; Perls, 1947; Perls *et al.*, 1951; Simkin). Gestalt Therapy insists only on the value of discovering and regaining control over the mechanism of awareness. Perls' first book, *Ego, Hunger and Aggression*, 1947, makes clear that each person must treat psychological experience as we do food— we bite, chew, digest and reject food according to our own needs. Greenwald states: "Avoiding what is toxic or non-nourishing is the critical point in enabling the person to experience adequate emotional nourishment and growth" (Greenwald, 1969, p. 6). To Perls this takes mobilization of aggression (Perls 1947, 1953-54; Perls *et al.*, 1951).

The freedom of the therapist is not absolute. Even Kempler, who regards any decision of his to change from catalyst to active participant as related to his own needs and not to objectivity, nevertheless goes on to say:

> For such behavior by a therapist the word "spontaneous" may be applied. However, it is incumbent upon any therapist, existential or not, to clearly distinguish within himself the difference between spontaneous and impulsive behavior. Impulsive behavior is not a thorough representation of a person but rather a fractional escape of behavior in a constricted individual (Kempler, 1968, p. 95).

Gestalt Therapy believes strongly and without qualification in the need for professional clinical training and discipline in the psychotherapist. Gestalt Therapy also believes that therapists are responsible for separating reports of his emotional feelings from his hunches. The Gestalt therapist does not say, "I feel you are such and such." Hunches or inferences by a Gestalt therapist are clearly labeled "fantasy," "guess," or "hunch."

Experimental encounters have revealed that negative and positive feelings are frequently censored. Patients are encouraged to experiment with expressing any feelings that are authentic. Heated words do not necessarily mean that authentic feelings have been directly expressed (Shostrom, 1967, Chapter IV). Heat may be a means of avoiding other emotions. The exchange of heated words is frequently a circular and repetitious intellectual exercise in which each person case-builds, name calls, verbally attacks, tries to impose his *shoulds* (judgments) on the other, expresses blaming reactions, etc. Gestalt therapists have found that simple and direct statements of feelings are frequently absent from the repertoire of the beginning patient. The implications of this in terms of specific therapeutic maneuvers will be discussed below.

The encounter in Gestalt Therapy does not imply forcing change by confrontation of therapist or other patients. In Gestalt Therapy the therapist is open to, responds to, and expresses feelings genuinely felt. Availability, honesty and openness are the key concepts. The therapist is available and models honesty and openness—he creates an atmosphere where the patient is most likely to try out that behavior. The Gestalt Therapist does not push, but does aggressively stay in the I and Thou; Here and Now framework.

Gestalt Therapy Workshops

Gestalt Therapy can be illustrated by discussing the use of workshops and the specific maneuvers in Gestalt Therapy workshops.

In a paper delivered at the 1966 APA convention, Perls reported that he had eliminated all individual sessions except for emergencies. He has come to the view that all individual therapy is obsolete, and now integrates individual and group work into workshops. However, he cautions that: "This works with a group only if the therapist's encounter with an individual patient, within the group, is effective and impressive" (Perls, 1966, p 1). The advantage of workshop therapy is not a matter of economy (although that is also relevant) but therapeutic power.

> Now, in the group situation something happens that is not possible in the private interview. To the whole group it is *obvious* that the person in distress does not see the *obvious*, does not see the way out of the impasse, does not see (for instance) that his whole misery is a *purely imagined* one. In the face of this collective conviction he cannot use his usual phobic way of *disowning* the therapist when he cannot *manipulate* him. Somehow the trust in the collective seems to be greater than the trust in the therapist—in spite of all so-called transference confidence (Perls, 1966, p. 7).

Perls mentions another advantage of workshops. In workshops, the therapist can facilitate individual development by conducting collective experiments, e.g. talking gibberish together, doing withdrawal experiments, learning to understand the atmosphere, etc. The individual can experiment and learn how he obtains the effects he does from the group. The group learns the difference between helpfulness and true support. Moreover, watching the manipulation of others in the group helps the group members in self-recognition.

Perls summarizes his approach to groups by saying:

> In other words, in contrast to the usual type of group meetings, I carry the load of the session, by either doing individual therapy or conducting mass experiments. I often interfere if the group plays opinion and interpretation games or has similar pure verbal encounters *without any experimental substance*, but I will keep out of it as soon as anything genuine happens (Perls, 1966, p. 9).

Perls states clearly, and this seems to be the case from the writer's observation of him in groups, that he is available for individual work in the group—but he does not push. The rest of the group watch and are involved in silent self-therapy when the therapist-patient diad are at work. Perls is aggressive in his work with individuals in the group, but he does not push the individual to participate. More often the patient is seen trying to push Perls, although unaware of doing so. This is followed by one of Perl's therapeutic maneuvers.

An encounter with one or both of the parties manipulating can be used experimentally, but not for catharsis. Any genuine I-Thou encounter necessarily involves experimental substance, i.e. discovery. In a genuine encounter both parties are becoming, and neither knows the outcome.

To summarize: workshops consist of one-to-one therapy, group experiments and encounter—and all three are experimentally based.

Rules

In setting up the experimental encounter, Gestalt therapists impose several rules (Kempler, 1965, 1966, 1967, 1968; Levitsky; Simkin).

From a Person to a Person

Communication in an I-Thou relationship must involve direct sending and receiving. The Gestalt therapist will frequently ask:

"To whom are you saying this?" In other words, each message is made into a statement from a particular person to a particular person. Every general statement is translated into a specific encounter, as in the following example:

> An intellectualized male graduate student in group therapy announces blandly to no one in particular that "I have difficulty in relating to people." In the ensuing silence he glances briefly at the attractive nurse co-therapist.
> T: "Who *here* do you have trouble relating to?" He is able to name the nurse as the chief offender, and spend a fruitful five minutes exploring his mixed frustration, attraction and anger focused on this desirable but inaccessible woman (Enright [a], p. 3).

The counterpart of speaking directly to a person, is active listening as opposed to passive hearing. Listening as an act by a person and not a passive reception of stimulation is stressed in the Gestalt Therapy encounter. Each person is expected to take responsibility for his statements, for directing them to another person (I-Thou), and for active listening to others.

Gossiping

A specific rule against gossiping is often made. Gossiping is "talking about an individual when he is actually present and could just as well be addressed directly" (Levitsky, p. 7; see also Kempler, 1965, pp. 65ff). Although this sounds quite simple, the use of this technique has generally had a dramatic effect. The direct confrontation mobilizes affect and vividness of experience, in contrast to a pale dissipation through gossip (Enright [a]). When discussing an absent person, the Gestalt therapist will attempt to bring about direct experiential dialogue by having the patient imagine and enact a direct conversation with the person and attending to his continuum of awareness.

Questions

Although questions are ostensibly requests for information, careful listening and observation have revealed that they rarely do so. Questions most often are disguised statements, or demands for support from the other person. In Gestalt Therapy patients are asked to translate questions into statements starting with the word "I" (Enright [a]; Levitsky). This procedure is an extension of the I-Thou relationship in that communication is made directly, openly and honestly. It is actualizing in the sense that the patient is encouraged to be assertive and self-supporting.

Semantics

The rule against question-asking is one of several maneuvers designed to help the patient discover the effect his choice of language has on his thinking. Semantic clarification can be used as a vehicle for improving observation and for conveying new outlooks or attitudes. Word choice is frequently habitual and out of awareness of patients. By explaining the operations and consequences of different words, distinctions not previously attended to can come into the patient's field of focus. The Gestalt Therapy encounter necessitates semantic clarification, e.g. distinguishing affect and cognition. To discover the benefits of expressing their feelings, the patient must be able to distinguish feelings from various cognitive processes. *I feel* referring to the affective realm (I feel an emotion) is distinguished from *I feel* referring to the cognitive realm (I imagine, infer, think, believe, etc.).

Work on greater awareness of the language of the patient has been a focus of Gestalt Therapy since Perls' first book in which he mentioned two tools that were helpful in his quest for an improvement on traditional psychoanalysis: "holism" (field conception) and "semantics" (the meaning of meaning) (Perls, 1947, p. 7). Perls recognized that "we still try to do the impossible: to integrate personalities with the help of non-integrative language" (Perls, 1948, p. 567). Thus the patient is trained to discriminate and label in a way that makes concrete and clear the exact referents of any word. If a patient says "I can't," the Gestalt therapist may ask him to experiment with saying "I won't" (Levitsky, p. 5). Vague, global, dualistic concepts are made concrete, specific and unitary.

But is a good example of a word that builds a double message into a statement. In the statement "I love you but I am angry at you," the words after *but* negate the words before. *And* is a conjunction that may more accurately portray experiential reality. If the person simultaneously experiences two facts: love and anger, a more accurate communication would be: "I love you and I'm angry at you."

An especially important semantic transaction for Gestalt Therapy encounters is the translation of the *it* language into the I-Thou language. *It* is a depersonalized form of expression which obscures the activity of the doer and the object of the action.

This deals with the semantics of responsibility (Levitsky). Neurotics frequently project their initiative and responsibility and see themselves in a passive role: thoughts occur to them, or they are struck by a thought, etc. The patient is unwilling to identify with some of his activities; he has alienated some of his ego functions Perls, 1948, p. 583). "If his language is reorganized from an 'it' language to an 'I' language, considerable integration can be achieved with this single adjustment" (Perls, 1948, p. 583). "It is common for us to refer to our bodies and to our acts and behaviors in distantiated, third person, 'it' language."

> What do you feel in your eyes?
> It is blinking.
>
> What is your hand doing?
> It is trembling.
>
> What do you experience in your throat?
> It is choked.
>
> What do you hear in your voice?
> It is sobbing.
>
> Through the simple—the seemingly mechanical—expedient of changing "it" language into "I" language we learn to identify more closely with the particular behavior in question and to assume responsibility for it.
>
> Instead of "It is trembling," "I am trembling." Rather than "It is choked," "I am choked." Going one step further, rather than "I am choked," "I am choking myself" (Levitsky, p. 4).

Another important semantic transaction that Gestalt Therapy helps people discover is what Simkin calls the *why-merry-go-round* (Simkin, p. 3; see also Enright [a], p. 4). The word *why* like many questions, demands that the respondent justify himself. The respondent most frequently starts his defense (or counter-attack) with the word "because." Everything after the because is a rationalization, a reason thought up to justify himself. "I did it because you made me." "I did it because I couldn't help myself." This round of case-building is contrary to the spirit of encounter in that it avoids self-responsibility, is manipulative and involves speculation on historical antecedents and causal factors.

Many patients have an internal dialogue in which they engage in the why merry-go-round. When people become aware of an aspect of their self that does not fit their intellectually chosen ideal, they look for reasons for the behavior (Simkin, p. 3). When they have found the justification they continue behaving as before, now having a reason.

In therapy, asking why leads to case-building, speculation, historicity and emphasis on causality at the expense of functional analysis. This leads away from the processes now maintaining the behavior. This avoidance of the Here-and-Now is frequent with psychoanalytically-oriented psychotherapists and many patients and their families.

The Gestalt therapist labels *why, because, but, it,* and *can't* dirty words. Whenever they are used the therapist may call attention to them. Thus a behavior, use of certain words, which was out of awareness, is brought into awareness. This may be done through the therapist's whistling whenever these bad words are uttered (Simkin whistle). Note that no case is being made here for vocabulary change by itself apart from other procedures. Simply stated, calling attention to language is another experimental technique for patient discovery.

Gestalt Therapy Games

Principles and techniques can be made more concrete by discussing specific techniques or games used in Gestalt Therapy. These games are used in individual and group work with a goal of discovery and sensitizing. Gestalt Therapy does not advocate a cessation of game playing, but an awareness of games so that the individual can choose which games he shall play, and can choose companions who play games that mesh with his own (Levitsky, pp. 8-9). The following are a few Gestalt Therapy experimental games. This section relies heavily on Levitsky (pp. 9-15).

Games of Dialogue

When a split within a person is observed, the Gestalt therapist suggests that the patient experiment by taking each part of the conflict in turn and having a dialogue. This can be done with any split, e.g. aggressive versus passive, or with another person who is significant and absent. In the latter case, the patient pretends the person is present and carried on the dialogue. Frequently a dialogue develops between parts of the body, e.g. right and left hands.

An internal conflict frequently takes place between the individual as Top Dog (Perls, 1965; Shostrom, 1967; Simkin) and as Under Dog. The Top Dog is a bullying and moralizing authoritarian. Typical Top Dog statements are: "I (you) should." " I (you) ought to." "Why don't you (I)?" Most people identify with their Top Dogs. The Under Dog controls by passivity. The Under Dog gives nominal acquiescence, and excuses, and goes on preventing the Top Dog from being successful. Shostrom's (1967) therapeutic diagnostic scheme of types of manipulators is derived from Perls' original discovery of the Top Dog/Under Dog conflict.

In Gestalt Therapy, this conflict can turn into an open dialogue between the warring parts of the patient. This often begins with semantic analysis of words and phrases such as: "why-because," "yes, but . . .," "I can't," "I'll try . . ."

Making the Rounds

While doing individual work in the group, a theme often arises involving others in the group. The patient may be concerned with an imagination of what the others are thinking, or may have a feeling about others. The therapist may suggest that the patient make rounds, and suggests that the patient communicate the theme to each person in the group. Spontaneous and authentic encounters developing during rounds are treated as any other encounter.

Unfinished Business

Any incomplete gestalt is unfinished business demanding resolution. Usually this takes the form of unresolved and incompletely expressed feelings. Patients are encouraged to experiment with finishing business which heretofore was unfinished. When the business is unexpressed feelings toward a member of the group, the patient is asked to express them directly. Gestalt therapists have found that resentments are the most frequent and meaningful unexpressed feeling, and often deal with this with a game in which communication is limited to statements beginning with the words "I resent . . ."

The "I take responsibility" Game

Gestalt Therapy considers all overt behavior, sensing, feeling and thinking acts by the person. Patients frequently disown or alienate these acts by using the *it language*, passive voice, etc. One technique is to ask the patient to add after each statement ". . . and I take responsibility for it."

Projection Games

When the patient imagines another person has a certain feeling or trait, he is asked to see whether it is a projection by experimenting with experiencing himself with that feeling or trait. Often the patient discovers that he does indeed have the same feeling he imagines he sees in others and that he has and rejects the same trait he rejects in others. Another game is playing projection. A patient who makes a statement characterizing another is asked to play the role of a person so characterized.

The Game of Reversals

When the therapist thinks the patient's behavior may be a reversal of a latent impulse, he may ask the patient to play the role opposite that which he has been playing. An overly sweet patient might be asked to act spiteful and uncooperative.

The Rhythm of Contact and Withdrawal

Withdrawal from Here and Now contact is treated experimentally; the patient is not admonished not to withdraw, but to be aware of when he withdraws and when he stays in contact. A patient or group of patients is sometimes asked to close his (their) eyes and withdraw. Staying with the continuum of awareness, the patient(s) reports his (their) experience. The work continues as the patient comes back to Here-and-Now having met his need to withdraw, and attention having been drawn to the process of attention itself.

The Rehearsal Games

The reaction of a patient to the group is itself a valuable source of therapeutic material. The patient that is afraid of exposing his feelings to the group is encouraged to report his imagination and feelings about revealing his feelings. One frequent phenomenon is internally rehearsing for a forthcoming social role. Stage fright is a fear that the role will not be conducted well. Awareness of the rehearsing for one's own role, failure to listen while another has the stage, and the interference with spontaneity can be heightened by group games of reporting awareness of rehearsing and sharing the rehearsals. Related phenomena, such as censoring, are similarly handled (Enright [b], for example).

The Exaggeration Game

Small movements and gestures may substitute for and block awareness of affective processes. The Gestalt therapists observe bodily movements and report them. One game or experiment is to ask the patient to repeat and exaggerate a movement. This heightens the perception of an important means of blocking awareness (see Enright [b], p. 6; Levitsky, p. 13). An example of this was cited above (the inhibited man tapping his finger).

The "May I Feed You a Sentence Game"

When the therapist infers an unstated or unclear message, he may phrase it into a sentence and ask the patient to say the sentence aloud, repeat it, in short, to try it on for size.

"Of Course" and "It Is Obvious That" Games

Patients frequently fail to use and trust their senses. As a result they miss the obvious and search for support for their communications. The former is often dealt with by having the patient make up sentences starting with "It is obvious that . . ." The search for support for statements can be experimentally dealt with by having the patient add after each sentence ". . ., of course."

"Can You Stay With This Feeling?"

In reporting awareness, patients quickly flee from dysphoric frustrating feelings. The Gestalt therapist often asks the patient to stay with the feeling, to stay with his continuum of awareness. The endurance of this psychic pain is a necessity to pass through the impasse (Perls, 1966, p. 7; 1965, p. 4).

Dream Work

Gestalt Therapy has its own method of working with dreams. In Gestalt Therapy dreams are used to integrate; they are not interpreted. Perls considers a dream as an existential message, and not wish fulfillment. It is a message telling what a person's life is and how to come to one's senses—to awaken and take one's place in life. Perls does not regard the therapist as knowing more than the patient about what his dreams mean (Perls, 1965, p. 7; see also Enright [a], p. 14).

Perls lets the person act out the dream. Since he regards each part of the dream as a projection, each fragment of the dream—person, prop or mood—are considered alienated parts of the individual. The person takes each part—and an encounter ensues between the divided parts of the self. Such an encounter frequently leads to integration.

> A restless, domineering, manipulative woman dreams of walking down a crooked path in a forest of tall, straight trees. As she *becomes* one of these trees, she feels more serene and deeply rooted. Taking these feelings back into her current life, she then experiences both the lack of them and the possibilities of achieving them. *Becoming* the crooked path, her eyes fill with tears as she experiences more intensely the devious crookedness of her own life, and again, the possibilities of straightening out a little if she chooses.

Couples

Gestalt Therapy is most effective in family and marital therapy (Enright [a]; Levitsky; Kempler, 1965, 1966, 1967, 1968). The family as a whole, as well as the individual members of the family, come to therapy with unfinished business, incomplete awareness, unexpressed resentment, etc. The same techniques apply to families as to other Gestalt Therapy groups. Workshops with couples have been quite successful. Marital partners frequently discover that they do not relate to their spouse as is, but to an idealized concept of the spouse.

Marital therapy games are an extension of the games already discussed. As an example, the partners may be asked to face each other and take turns making up sentences beginning with "I resent you for . . ." This may be followed with "What I appreciate in you is. . ." Other possibilities are: "I spite you by. . ." "I am compliant by. . ." Discovery can be emphasized by making sentences beginning with "I see. . ." The emphasis is Here and Now; I and Thou, and discovering the means of avoiding immediate experience. Gestalt Therapy couples work emphasizes discovery of blocks to the awareness of the nature of the current marital encounter.

Walter Kempler, discussed above, achieves dramatic results working with the entire family, and stressing the therapist's communication of his own feelings as the chief therapeutic tool.

Discussion

The behavioral therapy literature tends to narrow the alternative models to behavior modification on the one hand and the medical model on the other. Gestalt Therapy is certainly a third alternative and the first existential school to work out a model of psychotherapy that avoids the faults inherent in the medical model upon which the practice of psychodynamically oriented psychotherapy is based. Moreover, it is one of the few experiential psychotherapy models emphasizing behavioral observation and experimentation.

Gestalt Therapy and behavioral therapy have what the average clinician lacks, emphasis on observable behavior in the Here and Now. Both approaches reject the concepts of the unconscious and inferred etiological causality notions and replace them with observation of behavior. Gestalt Therapy shares with the logical positivists and the radical behaviorists a preference for functional over causal analysis. Although both emphasize experimentation and verification of inferences with behavioral observations, Gestalt Therapy does not stress quantification. Both approaches also point out the undesirable consequences resulting from finding causes for an assumed inability of the patient to be responsible for his own behavior, i.e. the notion that the patient has a disease.

However, Gestalt Therapy shares with most clinicians the concern with awareness, although preferring the existential-phenomenological model of awareness to the psycho-dynamic model of the unconscious. Gestalt Therapy's concern with awareness does not sacrifice the psychologist's role as observer of behavior. The phenomenological articulations of the patient are in accord with his sensory information, while the psychologist adheres to his sensory information with his observation and experimentation. The experiments in directed awareness are an alternative to both the curing and the conditioning process. The individual discovers how to be responsible for choosing his behavior for himself, i.e. to fully use his faculties of awareness.

Both behavior therapy and Gestalt Therapy are based on behavioral science. The differences can be seen by looking at how they would apply themselves in a hypothetical but not atypical example. When a behavior therapist sees a mother who has a child that has temper tantrums, he is likely to prescribe a behavior regime to de-condition the mother-child interaction supporting the tantrums. A Gestalt therapist would focus on the mother's awareness of what the child does, what she feels, how she *shoulds* herself into passively allowing the child to manipulate her, etc. The psychologist would be aware of the results of experimentation in experimental psychology bearing on the problem. The Gestalt therapist would thus help the mother to grow into a fuller and more competent person. She is likely to remove the behaviors she has been engaged in that have been supporting the tantrums and simultaneously gain a perspective that can generalize the rest of the mother's life (and indirectly the child's).

History

Ego, Hunger and Aggression, Perls' first published work, was written in 1941-42. Subtitled *A Revision of Freud's Theory and Method,* it represents the bridge from his earlier practice of orthodox psychoanalysis and his later systematic practice of Gestalt Therapy (Perls, 1947, Introduction to the 1966 edition). Although there were changes in later works, many of Perls' basic attitudes can be seen in this early work.

When this work was written, many revisions of Freud's theory were abroad, including the ideas of Horney, Fromm and Sullivan. However, these revisions were still within the psychodynamic, medical model tradition. Experimental psychologists were then ignoring, rejecting or translating psychoanalysis, but still had offered no general clinical alternative. Behaviorism, gestaltism, phenomenology, existentialism, ideographic psychology had not yet developed a concrete clinical alternative to psychoanalysis.

Although Perls borrowed widely from psychoanalysis, phenomenology-existentialism and operationalism-behaviorism, he used an expanded version of Gestalt psychology for his framework. Perls used the holistic-semantic approach. By semantics (meaning of meaning) Perls seemed to mean the specification of the concrete behavioral referents for all terminology. He called for:

> A ruthless purge of all merely hypothetical ideas; especially of those hypotheses which have become rigid, static convictions and which, in the minds of some, have become reality rather than elastic theories ... (Perls, 1947, 1966 edition, Preface).

By holism (field conception) Perls referred to the whole being greater than a sum of the parts, to the unity of the human organism, and to the unity of the entire organism/environment field. He regarded Gestalt Therapy as correcting psychoanalysis' error in treating psychological events as isolated facts apart from the organism and in basing its theory on associationism rather than on holism. This is also a difference between Gestalt Therapy and most behavioristic theories.

Perls regarded his theory of psychotherapy as theoretically simple, although difficult in practice (1947, p. 185). Through social learning people lost the *feel of yourselves* and could learn through psychotherapy to regain this. The relearning was not an intellectual process but could be likened to Yoga, although Perls noted that Yoga had as its aim the deadening of the organism and Gestalt Therapy aimed to "waken the organism to a fuller life" (Perls, 1947, p. 186). He included in the book a section of exercises, later expanded into his system of Gestalt Therapy (Perls, *et al.*, 1951).

It is ironic that many ideas now in vogue were first articulated and/or operationalized by Perls, and yet he is seldom credited in the literature. He is chronologically a pioneer of the modern existential-phenomenological model of psychotherapy (Preface to 1966 edition of *Ego, Hunger and Aggression*), and Gestalt Therapy is still the only model combining this with orientation exclusively toward concrete, Here-and-Now behavioral realities. Many of his concepts and approaches have become popular in the last ten to fifteen years under various terminologies, and showing varying degrees of direct influence by Perls. In contrast to the lack of literary recognition, Perls has had great influence where he or his students have demonstrated Gestalt Therapy.

Although *Gestalt Therapy* (1951) remains Perls' most complete work, there have been developments since then. Earlier in this paper, some of these recent developments were discussed without identifying their recent origin. In a 1966 introduction to *Ego, Hunger and Aggression* (1947), Perls discusses some of these recent developments, e.g. "breaking through the impasse, the point of status quo at which the average therapy seems to get caught," and the view that, except for emergency cases, individual therapy is out-moded and workshop therapy a more efficacious modality.

In this same introduction Perls gauged the extent to which the ideas he had discussed have been generally accepted in the mental health field. He stated that the awareness theory, e.g. under the names sensitivity training and t-groups, has been widely accepted. The importance of spontaneous, non-verbal expression has also been increasingly recognized. And "in the therapeutic setting the emphasis begins to shift from the phobic (so-called objective) couch situation to the encounter of a human therapist with, not a case, but another human being." He also offers the opinion that there is growing acceptance of the concepts of Here-and-Now reality, organism-as-a-whole, the dominance of the most urgent need, and the treatment of psychological events in relation to the whole organism rather than as isolated facts apart from the organism.

Other ideas of Perls' have received less attention. He states that,

> . . . the significance of aggression as a biological force, the relation of aggression to assimilation, the symbolic nature of the Ego, the phobic attitude in neurosis, the organism-environment unity is far from being understood (Perls, 1947, Introduction to 1966 edition).

He notes also that while there is a growth toward increased use of groups and workshops, these are generally regarded as more economic rather than more efficacious. In actual clinical practice the importance of the balance of support and frustration seems not to be sufficiently emphasized.

Comparison of Models

The theoretical distinction between Gestalt Therapy, behavior modification and psychoanalysis is clear. In behavior modification, the patient's behavior is directly changed by the therapist's manipulation of environmental stimuli. In psychoanalytic theory, behavior is caused by unconscious motivation, which becomes manifest in the transference relationship. By analyzing the transference the repression is lifted, and the unconscious becomes conscious. In Gestalt Therapy, the patient learns to fully use his internal and external sense so he can be self-responsible and self-supportive. Gestalt Therapy helps the patient regain the key to this state, the awareness of the process of awareness. Behavior modification conditions using stimulus control, psychoanalysis cures by talking about and discovering the cause of the mental illness (The Problem), and Gestalt Therapy brings self-realization through Here-and-Now experiments in directed awareness.

Other models of psychotherapy are also alternatives to behavior modification and psychoanalysis. In the last decade there has been a growth of third force alternatives. New models of psychotherapy have been offered by Rogers (post-1960), Bach, Berne, Schutz, Satir, Frankl, Glasser, Ellis and others. Careful analysis is needed to separate true from semantic differences between these schools and psychodynamic psychotherapy and behavior modification. Careful analysis is needed also to separate the similarities and differences between Gestalt Therapy and the other third force schools.

The third force generally sees the therapeutic relationship as a direct relationship between human beings, i.e. an I-Thou relationship is preferred over a doctor-patient or manipulator-manipulated relationship. All claim to be holistic, interactional, and existential. In all the therapist is more active than in psychodynamically oriented psychotherapy. All use group modalities, e.g. encounter groups, family groups, sensitivity training, sensory awareness, etc. All are optimistic and stress the achievement of the potential of man.

The difference between psychodynamic and the third force therapies may be illusory. In psychodynamic psychotherapy and in most third force therapies, change is postulated to result from talking about the patient's life with a view of increasing understanding. In both the patient comes to greater self-acceptance as his understanding increases. The chief differences seem to be therapist activity, optimistic versus pessimistic attitude and the preference for discussion of current life circumstances to discussion of the childhood.

Gestalt Therapy is nominally a third force psychotherapy. When viewing the actual behavior of therapists and patients in psychotherapy, the third force therapies seem alike and quite different than either psychoanalysis or behavior modification. Shostrom (1967) discusses *actualizing therapies* in a way emphasizing similarities. The present review will present the ways in which Gestalt Therapy is unique from other third force therapies. Gestalt Therapy's uniqueness is in the direction of increased distinctiveness from psychodynamically-oriented psychotherapy.

1. Holism and Multidimensionality

Although many psychotherapists claim to be holistic, many are in fact really unidimensional (Perls, 1948, p. 579). Perls claims that only a comprehensive psychotherapy can be integrative and only a therapist with a comprehensive view can spot and tackle core difficulties. Therapists frequently have blind spots, areas which they will not see. They will avoid assimilating insights from schools emphasizing such areas. Patients who are ambivalent about change often seek therapists whose blind spot is in their area of difficulty. The more comprehensive the biopsychosocial outlook, the more likely is it that any difficulty is spotted in training a therapist or helping a patient. Gestalt Therapy views the entire biopsychosocial field, including organism/environment, as important. Gestalt Therapy actively uses physiological, sociological, cognitive, motivational variables. No relevant dimension is excluded in the basic theory.

2. *"Now" and the Mechanism of Change*

The modern notion of emphasizing the current life circumstances of the patient is in one sense now, in contrast to the Freudian notion of then. However, in Gestalt Therapy now is a functional concept referring to acts done *right now*. When recounting what one did last night, now one is recounting, last night was then. In discussing an encounter of five minutes ago, the encounter was then. Here-and-Now experience of immediate feelings and behavior is slighted at the expense of remembering the past. This emphasis on immediacy, on raw experience, has led to an explanation of the change process different than most other psychotherapeutic models.

Most therapists believe that change takes place as a function of increased knowledge, insight or awareness. They differ on how they define knowledge and what kind of knowledge is needed. In Gestalt Therapy knowledge is not equivalent to what is verbalized, orally or to oneself. Psychodynamic writers discuss this distinction in terms of real insight and intellectual insight. The kind of knowledge that Gestalt Therapy teaches is knowledge of how one takes attention away from the immediate raw sensory data of experience. The mechanism by which the subject substitutes for the active Here and Now on a matter of emotional concern is a particular object of Gestalt Therapy experimentation. It is by the return to awareness of this mechanism, previously out of awareness, that the Gestalt Therapy patient can analyze the processes by which he supports unsatisfactory behavior and acquires the tools to independently increase awareness in the future.

In therapy by Rogers, Bach, Berne, Glasser, Ellis, and Satir, the content, The Problem, the analysis of social interaction and the discussion of life circumstances is stressed. This is different than the Gestalt Therapy stress on *Now*. In Gestalt Therapy talking-about as done in some third force therapies, is taboo. In its place Gestalt Therapy uses experimentation.

3. Psychotherapy as Experimentation

Gestalt Therapy is experimental in the true sense of the term; it is experiencing oneself, or trying a behavior on for size—"the actual living through an event or events" (Perls, *et al.*, 1951, p. 15). This emphasis can be seen by looking at the existential encounter. Gestalt Therapy shares with other existential psychotherapies the belief in an I-Thou; Here and Now therapeutic relationship.

But this encounter is used in Gestalt Therapy to experiment with life and to discover. Roles are played in Gestalt Therapy not to practice new behavior, but for the patient to learn to discriminate which behavior meets his needs. The relationship is not curative in Gestalt Therapy; learning to discover is curative. Experimentation is more than a Gestalt Therapy technique—it is an attitude inherent in all Gestalt Therapy. Gestalt Therapy could be called a process of idiographic experimentation with awareness directed to the continuum of awareness.

This experimental focus is unique to Gestalt Therapy. It is influenced by oriental religions, e.g. Taoism and Zen Buddhism, and by phenomenological experiments. Without this emphasis and the techniques derived therefrom, the attitudes discussed under point number four (infra) could not be maintained. The alternative to Here-and-Now experimentation is re-conditioning—either openly and systematically as in behavior modification or covertly as in most psychotherapy. Although Gestalt Therapy frequently discovers the same patient processes as other third force therapies, in Gestalt Therapy the process of discovery is the end point, not the discovery itself.

What leads to change in Gestalt Therapy is not as much increased awareness in general as increased ability to be aware. Exercises used by Schutz and at the Western Behavior Research Institute at La Jolla appear to increase awareness, but frequently without focusing on the mechanism by which people habitually avoid awareness of unpleasant experience.

Virginia Satir (1964) helps each member of a family identify feelings and identify the imaginations about self, e.g. others and what others think about self that underlies the feelings. Lines of communication are traced back to the beginning of the marriage. However, the process by which the patient now focuses on the past instead of his current concerns, the process by which the patient avoids awareness of his own feelings and attends instead to the expectation of others is not emphasized.

Rogers believes that the encounter between a therapist with unconditional regard and the patient will result in change. This encounter and talk-about results in different psychotherapy techniques than Gestalt Therapy, although there are philosophic kinships between the two systems. Both use encounter and both aim for positive growth. Gestalt Therapy does not talk about; Gestalt Therapy experiments to discover how right now one is manipulating and keeping from being aware of the manipulation.

4. The Place of the Therapist's Value System

The only *should* (moral) accepted by the Gestalt Therapist is that the patient should be aware. Each person must contact novel elements in the environment, and decide for himself which is nourishing and to be assimilated, and which toxic and to be avoided. This discrimination changes with the constant change of dominant need. Gestalt Therapy does not have a vision of what behavior is more desirable for any particular person or at any particular time. Bach (1962) indicates more of a willingness to inculcate some values.

Where the patient has a choice of behaviors, Gestalt Therapy works on increasing the patient's awareness of antecedents, organismic reaction, consequences of behavior, etc. Myths and fears can be experienced in the safe therapeutic situation so that the patient can decide for himself what is nourishing and what is toxic. Contrary to Ellis' approach, the patient and not the therapist decides what is irrational for him. As an example, many patients have the myth that verbally reporting negative feelings is dangerous. By experimenting with direct verbal expression of negative emotions, the patient may discover that there are situations in which such behavior is quite rewarding. Further, he may become aware of the price he pays by not expressing such feelings.

In Gestalt Therapy morality is based on organismic need (Perls, 1953-1954). In contrast, adjustment to the group, commitment to group harmony, and cooperation are shoulds implicit and/or explicit in many third force psychotherapies, e.g. sensitivity training groups. Pressure by therapist or group is not used to achieve this in Gestalt Therapy as aggression is regarded as a natural biological force. When the patient is aware of ways he can express or restrain his aggression, the difference between aggression and annihilation, the consequences of his behavior, the Gestalt Therapist believes the patient can make his own choice.

Perls is explicit in regarding people as capable of self support, and not fragile or needing protection from inner or outer reality. Nor does he regard people as needing him as a dictator who forces change. Eliminating force he also eliminates a great deal of the need to protect patients from the therapeutic process. The patient already possesses what for him are the best mechanisms for avoiding unassimilatable information and the patient can best judge for himself what information is of use to him. When maximum use of group pressure is used, protection of some patients may be a necessary part of the therapist's activities. It is consistent that those who insist that people need pressure-type social confrontation also assume that people need the therapist's protection. Many of those using confrontation techniques tend to assume that therapy progress must await a carefully nurtured relationship. On the other hand, in Gestalt Therapy the patient can learn from the first experimental encounter.

This contrasts with the approaches of Bach, Berne, Satir, and Schutz. Satir regards maintenance of the system, e.g. the family system, as paramount. Both Bach and Schutz have definite norms they seek. Bach sets out rules for marital fighting; there are good and bad ways of cutting across individual differences. Both Bach and Schutz unqualifiedly exhort patients to share secrets with the group and/or with their spouses in marital therapy.

By contrast, Gestalt Therapy has a different game or technique to deal with secrets: " The 'I have a secret' game" (Levitsky, p. 11). The patient is asked to think of a well-guarded secret: "He is instructed *not* to share the secret itself but imagine (project) how he thinks others would react to it" (Levitsky, p. 11). The technique can be extended by having each brag about his terrible secret, thus working on the unaware attachment to a secret as an achievement. Knowledge of the guilt and shame and feelings and mechanisms for avoiding awareness of them yields different dividends than Schutz's and Bach's general advice to share secrets. A similar example is Berne's goal of the elimination of game playing. In Gestalt Therapy the goal is awareness so the patient can choose.

5. *Violence and Annihilation*

Schutz allows and encourages actual violence where people have such impulses. Although Gestalt Therapy encourages aggression, violence is seen as an attempt at annihilation. Gestalt Therapy workshops in contrast to Schutzian workshops are non-violent. Behavior which attempts to annihilate and hurt others, avoids experiencing one's own dysphoric feelings. Acting out one's anger in violence is antithetical to increased experience, direct expression of feelings and the I-Thou relationship. Gestalt Therapy accepts aggression and conflict as natural biopsychosocial forces and encourages experimentation with staying with negative feelings and directly expressing them in verbal reports (Enright [a]; Perls, 1947, 1948, 1953-4; Perls *et al.*, 1951; Simkin).

6. *Clinical Training*

Although Gestalt Therapy has suggestions for modification of the training of clinical psychologists (Enright [b]), suggestions similar to those advanced by Rogers (1956), Gestalt Therapy does not advocate abandonment of professional clinical training. The clinically-trained psychologist becomes aware of the range of psychopathology and of human limits. Although psychologists without clinical training have contributions of great value to clinical psychology, they are not qualified to practice psychotherapy. Some new psychotherapies are advocated and practiced by psychologists without clinical training. Gestalt Therapy deplores this development. Innovative psychotherapies have received a great deal of publicity, and there are reports of maladaptive social and psychological reactions to some workshops. The writer believes this results from the lack of professional clinical training of some human potentials therapists and the consequent lack of awareness of human limitations. Of course, professional training includes many disciplines, e.g. psychology, nursing, social work, etc. The use of non-professional assistants is a separate question entirely.

7. Range of Applicability

The Gestalt Therapy literature has not clarified the exact range of pathology to which it is applicable, and what modifications or additional techniques are necessary with psychotics, psychopaths, children, etc. But Gestalt Therapy is a clinical theory, and has been developed by clinical psychologists for a wide range of patients. The details are still being worked out. This contrasts with sensitivity training, which has been developed by non-clinical psychologists for use with already functioning businessmen. The need for further work on this point is discussed below.

8. Techniques per se

In passing it should be noted that Gestalt Therapy has many unique techniques, some discussed above. These techniques can be used within different frameworks, although with changed meaning. Similarly, techniques from various schools can be used within the Gestalt Therapy framework. The present writer, for example, has found that when working with hospitalized psychotics, psychodrama techniques in a Gestalt Therapy framework are more effective than the dialogue techniques usually used in Gestalt Therapy.

Criticisms

There are need areas in Gestalt Therapy which will be discussed in this section. In general, these areas point to potential in Gestalt Therapy that is unexploited. Since this article has not directly reviewed Gestalt Therapy personality and learning theory or views about basic research, criticisms in these areas will not be discussed here.

While we are not discussing the implication of Gestalt Therapy for basic research, the area of precision of definitions and validating research is germane.

Eric Berne takes the position that operational definitions are not possible in this area (Berne, 1964). In view of the extensive research by Rogers and his co-workers, this is difficult to sustain. In Perls' writings there is no case made against more exact forms of validation; he has just chosen not to spend his time doing this type of research.

Perls offers no quantified, statistical evidence that Gestalt Therapy works. He discusses this issue:

> "Where is your proof?" Our standard answer will be that we present nothing that you cannot *verify for yourself in terms of your own behavior*, but if your psychological make-up is that of the experimentalist as we have portrayed him, this will not satisfy you and you will clamor for "objective evidence" of a verbal sort, *prior* to trying out a single non-verbal step of the procedure (Perls, *et al.*, 1951, p. 7).

Perls has provided a series of graded experiments with instructions which one can use to verify the utility of Gestalt Therapy, and he includes a representative sample of the comments of experimental subjects who have taken these experiments. The experiments are clear and can be replicated by any interested reader.

While there are gaps in the system (Levitsky, p. 9; Polster, 1966, p. 6), there is a stress on separating knowledge from ignorance. Gestalt Therapy presents ideas within a molar framework, but with a concern for molecular details. Although he does not provide objective measures of his terms, his discussions stress concrete observation and concrete experience in preference to inference and speculation. In this sense, Gestalt Therapy is an empirical theory.

Although Perls also makes available live demonstrations and reproductions (films, tape recordings, video tapes, and several case examples are presented in the Gestalt Therapy literature: Kempler, 1965, 1966, 1967, 1968; Perls, 1948; Laura Perls, 1956; Polster, 1957; Simkin, 1962)), there are an insufficient number of systematic, detailed case histories. The most detailed are by Laura Perls (1956).

If quantified and objective research and validation techniques are demanded in an area at the outset of investigation, one may be limited to a narrow and sterile subject matter. Limiting the subject matter of a science is of doubtful validity. The subject matter of Gestalt Therapy appears to be important. Gestalt Therapy covers new areas, explores new assumptions, but has sacrificed exact verification for the value in ideographic experimental psychotherapy. Perls does not make the mistake of assuming he has the answers, but rather readily admits the state of ignorance of the field (Perls, 1948). Moreover, Gestalt Therapy does not claim that it has the only valid approach (Enright [b]). The burden of proof is heavier on those who define psychology so as to exclude differing approaches from the field.

Perls has presented a gold mine of insights and procedures which could be exploited in psychotherapy and by experimentally minded psychologists. But few Gestalt therapists have done much to carry out the research possibilities of Gestalt Therapy. (For an exception, see Shostrom 1966a, 1966b, 1967). It would be helpful if the literature were reviewed and experimental predictions and clinical expectations that could be made from Gestalt Therapy were made explicit even if the research is not immediately forthcoming.

A great deal is left to the discretion of the individual clinician in Gestalt Therapy. There is provision made for the style and personality of the therapist, within the bounds of professional responsibility (Polster, 1966, pp. 4-5). Even the question of the modifications in techniques and theory that need to be made for different patient diagnostic groups has not been formulated in the Gestalt Therapy literature. The writer knows from informal discussions and personal experience that Gestalt Therapy has been used with different patient groups, but the results are not reported in the literature. There is a particular need for a delineation of the limits of the application of Gestalt Therapy.

Similarly, a great deal of responsibility is left with the patient. The basic work of psychotherapy is done by the patient with the Gestalt therapist being a guide and catalyst. The therapist's job is to present experiments and observations that dramatically and clearly portray the perceptual field being studied. Failure to do this can be a cause of clinical failure attributable to the therapist (Perls, 1948). However, the basic work of discovery and utilizing the discovery is the patient's responsibility.

Perls' validation in terms of each reader's own experience is unique. It is quite different from the demand of psychoanalysis that a critic be analyzed, and from behavior modification's strict adherence to experimental measurement criteria. The psychoanalytic argument is an *ad hominem* argument which accepts validation only within the system. The length and expense needed for analysis renders this argument unacceptable. Gestalt Therapy experimentation can be tried from *Gestalt Therapy* (Perls, *et al.*,

1951) or from week-end workshops. This outlay of time is comparable to that required to experience any approach different than the person is accustomed to. An open and critical attitude is required, but faith in the system is not required to test Gestalt Therapy. It is the writer's observation that Gestalt Therapy is often experienced and appreciated only after a personal encounter with a Gestalt therapist; a single encounter often makes available to a participant a perspective not available to a non-participating observer.

There is also involved here a value question that is not answerable by laboratory experiments. Objective proof of technical success cannot answer the value question—Is it desirable for the clinician to control the patient's behavior? And ultimately, this question is decided by each individual. Recognizing this, Gestalt therapists offer Gestalt Therapy and leave to the individual the choice of whether it is useful *for him*.

Perls has provided a therapy that is exclusively oriented to Here-and-Now behavior without excluding awareness variables and without conditioning that behavior. It does apply existential attitudes with a unique system of psychotherapy, and validates the system in a unique way. The writer accepted Perls' offer and challenge to verify Gestalt Therapy for himself and found the system personally and professionally exciting, creative and useful. To each is left the burden of deciding if the potential from Gestalt Therapy for himself warrants personal experimentation, psychotherapeutic application or its use with basic research.

REFERENCES

Bach, G.: Comments. In Buhler, C. (Ed.): *Values in Psychotherapy*. New York, Free Press, 1962.

Berne, E.: *Games People Play*. New York, Grove Press, 1964.

Buhler, C.: *Values in Psychotherapy*. New York, Free Press, 1962.

Ellis, A.: *Reason and Emotion in Psychotherapy*. New York, Lyle Stuart, 1962.

Enright, J.: *An Introduction to Gestalt Therapy*. Unpublished, Esalen Institute. (a)

Enright, J.: *Awareness Training in the Mental Health Professions*. Unpublished, Esalen Institute. (b)

Glasser, W.: *Reality Therapy*. New York, Harper & Row, 1965.

Greenwald, J.: The art of emotional nourishment. *Voices*. 1969.

Greenwald, J.: *The Art of Emotional Nourishment: Self-induced Nourishment and Toxicity.* Unpublished.

Jourard, S.: *Psychotherapy in the Age of Automation* (from the way of a technician to the way of *guru*). Paper presented to the Gestalt Institute of Cleveland, May 19, 1967.

Kempler, W.: Experiential family therapy. *Int J Group Psychother, 15:* 57-71, 1965.

Kempler, W.: The moving finger writes. *Voices,* 2:73-74, 1966.

Kempler, W.: The experiential therapeutic encounter. *Psychotherapy: Theory, Research and Practice,* 4:166-172, 1967.

Kempler, W.: Experiential psychotherapy with families. *Family Process,* 7:88-89, 1968.

Levitsky, A.: *The Rules and Games of Gestalt Therapy.* Unpublished.

Nevis, E.: *Beyond Mental Health.* Unpublished, Gestalt Institute of Cleveland.

Perls, F.: *Ego, Hunger and Aggression.* Woking, Great Britain, Unwin Bros., 1947; San Francisco, Orbit Graphic Arts, 1966.

Perls, F.: Theory and technique of personality integration. *Am J Psychother,* 2:565-586, 1948.

Perls, F.: The anthropology of neurosis. *Complex,* No. 2, 19-27, 1950.

Perls, F.: Morality, ego boundary, and aggression. *Complex,* No. 9, 42-52, 1953-1954.

Perls, F.: Gestalt Therapy and Human Potentialities. In Otto, Herbert (Ed.): *Explorations of Human Potentialities,* in press. Unpublished manuscript, Esalen Institute, 1965.

Perls, F.: *Workshop versus Individual Therapy.* Paper presented at the American Psychological Association, New York City, September, 1966.

Perls, F., Hefferline, R., and Goodman, P.: *Gestalt Therapy: Excitement and Growth in the Human Personality.* New York, Julian Press, 1951; New York, Dell, 1965.

Perls, L.: The psychoanalyst and the critic. *Complex,* No. 2, 41-47, 1950.

Perls, L.: Notes on the psychology of give and take. *Complex,* No. 9, 24-30, 1953-1954.

Perls, L.: Two instances of Gestalt Therapy. *Case Reports in Clinical Psychology,* 3:139-146, 1956.

Perls, L.: The Gestalt Approach. *Annals of Psychotherapy,* 1961 *1* and *2.* (Ed.) Barron, J. and Harper, R.

Polster, E.: *Technique and Experience in Gestalt Therapy.* Paper presented at Ohio Psychological Association Symposium, 1957.

Polster, E.: A contemporary psychotherapy. *Psychotherapy,* 3:1-6, 1966.

Polster, E.: *Trends in Gestalt Therapy.* Paper presented at Ohio Psychological Association, February 22, 1967.

Rogers, C.: Training Individuals to Engage in Therapeutic Process. In Strother, C. (Ed.): *Psychology and Mental Health,* Washington, D.C., American Psychological Association, 1956.

Rogers, C.: Two Divergent Trends. In May, R. (Ed.): *Existential Psychology*, New York, Random House, 1960.

Satir, V.: *Conjoint Family Therapy: A Guide to Theory and Technique.* Palo Alto, Science and Behavior Books, 1964.

Schutz, W.: *Joy: Expanding Human Awareness.* New York, Grove Pr, 1967.

Shostrom, E.: *Manual for the Caring Relationship Inventory.* San Diego, Educational and Industrial Testing Service, 1966(a).

Shostrom, E.: *Manual for the Personal Orientation Inventory.* San Diego, Educational and Industrial Testing Service, 1966(b).

Shostrom, E.: *Man the Manipulator.* Nashville, Abingdon Pr, 1967.

Shostrom, E.: Group therapy: let the buyer beware. *Psychology Today,* 2:36-40, No. 12, 1969.

Simkin, J.: Contributions. In Buhler, C.: *Values in Psychotherapy.* New York, Free Pr, 1962.

Simkin, J.: *Introduction to Gestalt Therapy.* Unpublished manuscript, Esalen Institute.

Van Dusen, W.: Existential Analytic Psychotherapy. *Am J Psychoanalysis,* 20:35-40, 1960.

Wallen, R.: *Gestalt Psychology and Gestalt Therapy.* Paper presented at Ohio Psychological Association, Symposium, 1957.

Whitaker, C.: *The Psychotherapy of Marital Couples.* Lecture presented to Cleveland Institute of Gestalt Therapy, 1965.

Zinker, J.: Notes on the phenomenology of the loving encounter. *Explorations, 10*:3-7, 1966.

Zinker, J., and Fink, S.: The possibility of growth in a dying person. *J Gen Psychol,* 74:185-199, 1966.

Index